The WRAP ACCOUNT INVESTMENT ADVISOR

How to Profit from Wall Street's Most Innovative Investment

Daniel R. Bott   Larry Chambers

PROBUS PUBLISHING COMPANY
Chicago, Illinois
Cambridge, England

ISBN 1-55738-497-5

Printed in the United States of America

BB

1 2 3 4 5 6 7 8 9 0

TAQ/BJS

To my older brother, Gerald F. Bott,
who introduced me to this investment profession and has
been responsible for many of my professional goals.
To my 10-year-old son, D.R. Bott II.

Daniel R. Bott

To my children Logan and Christin Chambers.
To Nick Bapis for first introducing me to
the wrap program.

Larry Chambers

TABLE OF CONTENTS

Table of Contents

Table of Contents

Since the mid-1980s, all-inclusive, fee-based money management has seen meteoric growth. With that growth has come confusion and questions such as: What is it? Where do I get it? Who's the best? Is it too expensive? Do I need it? Who is qualified to provide it? Where's the best value?

The media has certainly covered the subject. However, not all of the articles are accurate or relevant. Some talk about costs, but not value. Others talk about performance, but without explaining risk.

Until the publication of *The Wrap Account Investment Advisor*, there has been no definitive source on the subject of wrap accounts or all-inclusive investment management. This book has it all: the history of the wrap fee business; the main providers; and how leading consulting and brokerage firms find and deliver the best of the best. It goes into detail on how to write investment policies, how to find the right manager(s), and how to analyze performance. This is *the* authoritative source on the subject.

You must read this book and use it if you are in any way involved in making investment decisions. Whether you are a pension plan sponsor, a high-net-worth individual, a broker, a consultant, an attorney, or CPA, you must possess the knowledge in this book to be fully equipped to make the most informed investment decisions on fee-based money management.

ACKNOWLEDGMENTS

The first person that deserves more than just an acknowledgement, but a true feeling of gratitude, is my wife, Judith Marie Bott, for her support, encouragement and understanding over the past twenty years.

I would also like to acknowledge the following individuals for having made an impact on or contribution to my career as a securities professional and, ultimately, as an investment management consultant.

James D. Awad, Edward W. Anderson, Dennis Ardis, Gerald F. Bott, Paul R. Black, Charles H. Brandes, John P. Calamos, F. Patrick Cavallero, Thomas Clark, Bryson C. Cook, Brian P. Cunningham, Derick L. Driemeyer, Grace Keeney Fey, Tolman F. Geffs, Bruce Genthner, Robert Gentry, John R. Gepfert, Frank B. Gibb III, Steven Goddard, Joseph C. Godsey, Alan Goldstein, John D. Gottfrucht, Carl Hulick, Anthony J. Iarocci, Jr., Dan Jamieson, Marty Jensen, James M. Johnson, Sydney LeBlanc, John R. Lohr, Anthony F. Lotruglio, Thomas M. Mahan, James Mann, Gilbert Meem, William G. Mullen, Chet J. Needelman, Robert L. Padgette, Roger B. Palley, L. Roy Papp, Jack C. Polley, James A. Pupillo, Leonard Reinhardt, Beth Schelling-Robinson, Jay H. Schmallen,

Acknowledgements

John E. Severson, Richard Schilffarth, Steven L. Shirley,
James Suellentrop, Timothy J. Tigges, Ephraim Ulmer,
Drew E. Washburn, Lee A. Weiss, Kurt R. Winrich,
W. Roberts Wood.

Daniel R. Bott

INTRODUCTION
by Richard Schilffarth

The stock transaction business that we had in the 1980s is gone. That's yesterday's business. Seventy percent of the trades of the New York Stock Exchange are now done by professional investment advisors—men and women who have multiple degrees, who work full time managing money. These are people who have enough revenue both in hard dollars and soft dollars to buy the best research from all sources. They are ardent traders who are going to make sure that they get the best execution they can. They present the dominant competition to the investor who "plays the market" and thinks he can win in the transaction business. It soon becomes entertainment—a game. It's his fun! He doesn't even keep score on how much money he makes at the end of the year. He just keeps score on how many times he wins versus how many times he loses.

On the investment account side rests the managed asset business and its extension, the wrap account. It is a portfolio machine, a unit structure where each security has its own place in the scheme of things. It is not the "three hot stocks of the week." The stocks in this asset machine are there to get us diversification so that we can control risk.

The essential thing about a portfolio machine is that, like all machines, it must have a blueprint, it must have output, it must have an operator, and it must have quality control.

There must be a blueprint that specifies just how the machine is going to be built. The machine is designed to generate a specific and predictable output. Since it is only a machine, it must have someone to operate or to run it. And finally, to complete the cycle, there must be a quality control step established to measure performance.

In our business, we call the blueprint the investment plan or policy. It is the essential ingredient that initiates the program. There is nothing more important in the investment process than the investment policy used to establish the guidelines and constraints and define the investment objectives.

It is from that blueprint—the investment plan—that we justify the criteria for the selection of the investment advisors. All advisors who are presented to an investor should have past performance records which comply with the investor's own investment objectives and his investment plan. When it comes to the operator—the portfolio manager—it is important that there be at least two. We would not want to recommend a single manager, but would rather present several managers. This gives the investor a choice of personally selecting his manager from a list of qualified managers who meet his needs, based on how they manage money. We have found that success in this business comes from staying with the right manager for an extended period of time. As in any marriage, divorce is expensive and painful.

The objective is to identify those qualifications that allow the investor to select a compatible manager based on his money management philosophy, and not on a raw hunch, a gut feeling, or an astrological chart. Wrap account programs find investment managers who will have a comprehendible risk output that stays within an investor's risk parameters, rather than collecting performance data on a manager based upon his best record to date, and then hiring him.

Buying yesterday's best performance to obtain short-term rewards doesn't work well in the investment business. History does not always repeat itself.

These are the four elements that make up a wrap account. When we talk about a "wrap account," we should not confuse it with "wrap fees." A wrap fee is merely a pricing vehicle. It was developed in June of 1975. Prior to May 1, 1975—"May Day"—a wrap fee did not even exist. On that day, all listed stocks were sold using a fixed commission schedule. We couldn't charge a wrap fee because we operated under a program that mandated that we charge a commission on transactions.

After May Day and the elimination of the fixed commission schedule, we were allowed to give the investor 100 percent transaction-based discounts and create an asset-based commission.

The brokerage industry provides custody of the investor's funds. They clear the investor's trades and produce his statements. They collect dividends and interest. They pay out distributions. They open the investor's accounts and they review the client's situation on an ongoing basis as it changes. They service the investor and execute trades.

In the transaction business, it makes sense to load all of those items on the cost of the transaction. The base cost of an execution might be something like $8.25 on a ticket and one cent per share. The commission a client pays includes the cost of all of those charges added to the execution cost.

In the transaction business that makes good sense. But in the investment account business, it doesn't make sense at all. We are not in the transaction business, we are in the managed asset business.

Introduction

So it only makes sense to take all of those costs, including the costs of execution, and charge them as a percent of assets to develop an asset-based commission.

In 1975, I went back and took a close look at the commissions we had developed in our E.F. Hutton Suggests program during the period from 1973-74. This was in a market that started at 1000 in early 1973 and spent the next 18 months tailing off to 580, a market where manager turnover was simply a matter of liquidating stock and going into cash rather than going into securities. Discovering that the average commission in our accounts ran 1.9 percent, I added that to a 1 percent management fee and came up with 2.9 percent as our cost of managing an account. I said to myself, "Well, why don't we make it 3 percent of the first $500,000, 2.5 percent on the next $500,000 and 2 percent for anything above a million dollars?" Basically, that's where we are today. Turnover (the percent of a portfolio traded each year) in 1973 and 1974 was 35 percent. Today turnover runs 55 percent. This is a product that uses all of the services mentioned earlier. The actual costs of brokerage services in the wrap fee program, like retail commissions, have risen approximately 35 percent since 1975.

You will read articles that state that the wrap fee is too high. I don't believe that there is a single company in the marketplace today that has a wrap account of $100,000 that is even covering its costs. It is only logical to discuss an increase in the fee for the wrap account going from 3 percent to 4 percent for assets under $250,000.

Those are all the normal brokerage services that are combined in the wrap fee. But we are here to address the four services we have put together in a wrap account. Not all wrap accounts charge a wrap fee. Some wrap accounts charge a transaction commission rather than a wrap fee.

Smith Barney Shearson's Select Program is an extension of E.F. Hutton's Suggests program that we started in 1973. We had a wrap fee program starting in 1975. Ninety percent of all managed asset accounts that come into the consulting services department of Shearson today are under a fee.

The old E.F. Hutton's Suggests Part One, based on transaction commissions, is declining, withering and not attracting many new accounts.

The broker has become the customer. The investor has welcomed the fact that all costs are now placed right in front of him. If there is a problem with the wrap fee, it is not that it is too high, it's that its fees are too visible. There is not a single bank in this country today that can operate with anything less than a 3.5 percent mark-up between the cost of its money—what it gets—and what it lends out. No savings & loan can operate with less than 4 percent, and no insurance company can get by with less than 6 percent. Physically, you can't see these costs, but they are there, buried.

So when we talk about our costs today, we are talking about the wrap fee as used by the greater percentage of all managed assets, the program packaging the four elements of the portfolio machine I would like to call "Wrap Accounts."

A wrap account integrates the specialized professional talents of the trained broker to service the account with the professional portfolio manager to manage the assets. It includes the specialization of trading, done not through the broker himself, but rather through a central network and servicing firms that provide custody of the assets, tied together by a sophisticated administrative system. At its nerve center is one of the high-tech computer programs that you will hear more about later.

A wrap account has a single contract. The sponsor of the wrap account is the investment advisor, while the money managers are his subcontractors. It is the investment advisor who contracts with the investor. It is the ideal product for today's market.

In the late 1970s and 1980s, we could build an investment management firm by going out and picking up $30 million pieces of large companies' defined benefit plans. But the defined benefit plan market is declining. We lost 30,000 defined benefit plans just in the last year. The people in that market have already made their contacts. The tax-free (qualified plans) market is over $4 trillion dollars in size—$2-3 trillion in corporate employee benefit plans, $650 billion to $1 trillion in public employee retirement systems, over $250 billion in Taft-Hartley plans, and $100 billion plus in foundations and endowments.

The market we have today is the taxable account market, your investment and mine. At the end of 1990, the market was $11 trillion according to the Federal Reserve. At the end of 1991, it was $13.5 trillion. Investment managers are just now looking at this viable market. If the managers are going after the tax-free account market, their average size account could be $30 million. Their average fee would be over $75,000. They can market it, they can service it, and they can run it themselves as investment advisors. But if they are going after accounts with an average account size of $300,000 and not $30 million, structurally they don't have the ability in their firms to market and service that money. So we build this new triumvirate, if you will, of the broker, the portfolio, and the administrative system which allows us to bring to the retail investor with $100,000 or more the same type of sophisticated management that had been presented for over twenty years to the tax-free marketplace.

Eighty-five percent of this taxable money is in banks today—85 percent of the tax-free money was in the banks back in 1972. Today, banks have less than one-third of the tax-free funds. Nearly 80 percent of the money in this area is owned by people who are over 55 years of age. They are past their prime earning years. Their focus is now on their retirement. They tend to be conservative and they want to get their money back. But in the early 1990s they are suffering from the shock of having the bank rollover their 8 percent CDs at 4.75 percent or less, and looking at their accounts and realizing that the interest rate they are getting is 2.75 percent. They face a tremendous challenge trying to live off their reduced income. How do they make up the money they lost now that interest rates have fallen to one-third of what they were when they started their investment program? Today the investor has two choices; he can dip into the principal, or plan a way to get higher returns.

This is a dynamic marketplace that needs help. It is a marketplace that the wrap account program is aiming for. It is a marketplace in which the investor finds himself in the bank for one reason only: because it is safe.

The investor uses a bank not because it has the best graphs and charts, but because he believes it can get his money back. These people are "risk adverse." Most bank trust departments end up as very passive investment managers because they don't think that: 1) Risk is allowing for any volitility, or 2) being in the top quartile of managers is important, or 3) having the managers' performance in the northwest quadrant of the scattergram (low risk/high return) is important.

Let's say you inherited $1 million from some long-forgotten aunt. You gave it to a money manager who just got back in touch with you the day before to report on the second quarter. In a rather soft voice he announced, "The second quarter wasn't our best work. Our management style was slightly out of favor with what the market did. Your $1 million is now worth $680,000. We lost $320,000 of your money." What are you going to do?

Introduction

I'll give you four choices: 1) Shoot him, 2) sue him, 3) fire him, or 4) give him 11 more quarters so you can calculate the standard of deviation.

Risk is loss of value. It is measured continuously. The fact is that 95 percent of investors want less risk and less involvement, not more. That's our marketplace in this program.

In this return concept, time becomes a critical factor. T-bills mature in 90 days, therefore their investment cycle is 90 days. They provide zero return on a real basis (return above inflation and they have zero risk).

At the other end of the spectrum, are small-capital-growth stocks. They return 10-12 percent above inflation. The risk is a 15-20 percent loss of value within any four-quarter period. Their times at the bottom of the market were May of '62, November of '74, and March of '84. This breaks down to an 8-10 year cycle, so time becomes critical. Money managers are in the investment account business, not the entertainment business. They never want to place their bets on where they are in the investment cycle. They want to come back and know what they are doing so that they can be assured that the investors' timeframe will encompass the entire cycle that the manager has to work with.

This is the business that is the basis for wrap accounts. Today, 19 percent of that $13.5 trillion is in equities. Historically, the taxable investor has put 41 percent in equities.

There is a $6.8 trillion generational transfer coming up. Money is coming from the pre-baby boomer generation to the baby boomers and the post-boomers. This money is coming from life insurance, defined benefit plans, and savings accounts. The next generation is not going to have the kind of retirement benefits that our current 60-and-older group has. With their defined benefit programs, the pre-boomers had a much better retirement program than the boomers have with their 401(k) programs. These are people who are

45 or younger. They tend to be less conservative, and give more direction to equity.

If we move from 19 percent in equity to 41 percent in equity, we have a move of $3 trillion! If we take just the growth of the taxable market, we could move about $1.5 trillion a year into equities. If we just invest that growth into equity, in two years we would have more assets than we have in our entire equity markets today. It is a dynamic, powerful marketplace as long as we convince the investor that equities are not like betting on stocks.

We have got to convince investors that stocks, like bonds, do work. We have got to convince them that we have better returns when we have a longer duration within which to work.

We need wrap programs if new investors are to survive in retirement. If the boomers and post-boomers are going to have retirement income, they are going to have to get to a spot where their earnings are greater than can be achieved in the CD marketplace.

That's the background we have for the wrap account program. We know where we've been and we know where we're going. It is a $3 trillion market potential.

As I mentioned earlier, banks were 85 percent of the tax-free market in 1972; they were 30 percent of the tax-free market in 1992. They were 85 percent in the taxable market in 1992, and by the year 2012—30 percent? That market is immense! And it is not a product of the brokerage industry, but rather a new process, a program that will replace the way the brokerage industry has done business. As this new investment profession evolves, wrap accounts will be first to evolve with it.

PART I

BASICS

WHAT IS A WRAP ACCOUNT?

A wrap fee is just what it suggests—a single, all-encompassing fee based on a percentage of assets under management. This fee covers all charges, including advisor costs, commissions and other transaction charges, and reporting. It includes identification and help in the selection of appropriate money managers, account monitoring, analyzing and reporting on a manager's performance, custodianship of securities, execution of transactions, and consulting.

Investors benefit from this arrangement by getting the same execution and discounts as larger institutional investors while being viewed as valued customers by their financial consultants.

The investor pays only a stipulated annual percentage fee based on the value of the portfolio under management. The total cost should run between 2.5% and 3% of portfolio value, which is negotiable depending on the size and type of services provided. From that single fee, all individual charges, brokerage commissions, fees for investment management and custodianship, and performance evaluations are paid.

During flat trading periods, a customer might be better off investing on a commission basis. However, in periods of heavy trading activity, the investor should save money using

We would like to thank James Pupillo, a CIMC in Scottsdale, Arizona, for his contribution to this chapter.

a wrap fee arrangement. Because no one knows when such periods will occur, it might be wise to look past the economics and judge wrap fee programs on more compelling issues like trust, integrity, and your fund's individual needs. The customer needn't fear that his wrap fee broker will do any excessive trades, since all trading is paid for in advance.

Wrap fee programs have the best chance for success when delivered by firms who have made a serious committment to this service because of economies of scale. To deliver a cost-effective program to the consumer, profit margins will have to be thin. For example, larger institutional accounts get all the advantages of economies of scale which tends to drive down the costs for a wrap program.

Many of the top money managers have minimum account sizes of $1 million or more. But under the wrap programs, they will accept lower minimums, primarily because they have no marketing costs and only have to be concerned about their main function, which is to "manage the money."

For the $100,000 to $800,000 investment range the wrap account makes the most sense because these smaller investors would not otherwise have access to managers with higher minimums.

Even the $1–$5 million accounts can still be money ahead in the wrap account. Other types of accounts might be diversified by having several managers whose minimum outside the wrap programs might be more than the entire retirement fund. It still comes down to a question of operating overhead.

Some critics assert that the wrap fee costs are too high, pointing out that at 3%, the fee is roughly double the "expense ratio" of most no-load mutual funds. But what they fail to mention is that the expense ratio of mutual funds doesn't include trading commissions. Or that wrap sponsors will discount their fee as assets increase in size.

Through the wrap programs an investor gets unbiased due diligence, report monitoring, assistance in writing his investment policy statement, and a manager search, all for a single fee. When you factor in these services and cost them out separately, you are dollars ahead with a wrap fee account.

As an example of the savings in a wrap fee account, consider that there are many pension plans being charged $10,000-$20,000 for the same type of independent manager search. Performance monitoring can easily run from $2,500-$5,000 annually. When you add these independent costs together you are money ahead in a wrap fee program.

In addition, the wrap fee approach shifts the basis of payment away from activity and minimizes the potential of churning and soft-dollar misuse. In this way, transaction activity no longer determines the broker's income. Brokers normally receive income when trades are made in their customer accounts. Under a wrap fee program, the broker benefits by generating a more predictable, continuous stream of income without the concern for generating commissions from the volume of trades only. His reward is not tied to mere activity, but profitability for his client. This eliminates unnecessary trading which is not rewarding to the client.

A manager's performance has a direct impact on his revenues. His fee revenues rise only if the account grows. If performance lags, fee revenues may fall and the pension fund investor may fire the manager. Commissions increase costs and decrease profits, so it is in the best interest of managers and funds to minimize such costs. With the wrap fee approach, the investor need not question motives. It's a fair and equitable arrangement for all parties concerned.

A wrap fee program marketed like any other product, with little personal attention, is doomed to fail in the marketplace. Priced and delivered correctly, a wrap fee is a valuable service to any serious investor.

Chapter 1

IS A WRAP ACCOUNT A GOOD INVESTMENT?

Most of the negative articles on wrap accounts have one thing in common—they strongly object to the 3% fee and react to it as being too expensive.

The point these articles fail to make is that any investment product must produce a profit to the business provider or it will be out of business. No one writes about the spread between the money a bank lends to its customers and what it offers to its CD holders. Banks need to make a 3.5% spread. It's not general knowledge that insurance companies need to make 4.5% on their products just to break even. The main difference between a wrap account and banks and insurance companies is that in the wrap account—the fees are not hidden.

These articles focus only on the costs. What they fail to understand is expense components that are built into the fee; transaction costs, consulting costs, and fixed costs.

The truth is that the fee is a fair and equitable arrangement for all parties concerned. With the wrap account approach, the investor need not wonder about the broker's trading motives. The wrap account has removed the conflict of interest that existed between the broker and the customer. This is good.

This way, transaction activity no longer determines the broker's income. The investors pay a stipulated annual percentage fee based on the value of the portfolio under management. The total cost for accounts under $500,000 generally runs between 2.5% and 3% of portfolio value, and this amount can be negotiable depending on the size and types of services provided. It is from that single fee that all individual charges, brokerage commissions, fees for investment management and custodianship, and performance evaluations are paid.

What Is a Wrap Account?

We should acknowledge that in some cases, retail stock-brokers (not specializing in managed accounts) merely mass-market the firm's neatly packaged managed money product. They provide no added value. However, there are exceptions to this stereotype.

A comparison of no-load mutual fund investing to privately managed portfolio investing is an "apples to oranges" exercise. Investing in shares of a no-load fund represents the purchase of a product. Investing through a privately managed portfolio program is only a part of a complete process.

There are investment management consultants who specialize and take the business seriously. Qualified consultants, seasoned by participating in educational courses, conferences and continuing education who offer the full range of consulting services do provide added value typically for reasonable costs less than the 3% wrap fee.

Our observation is that the average domestic equity-based mutual fund had a total expense ratio of 1.29% before sales charges. Additionally, this total expense ratio was before brokerage commissions. We think if you research you'll find brokerage commissions can conservatively average .75–1.25% (or more) annualized over a full market cycle.

In *Forbes* magazine's 9/4/89 article, "Hidden Costs," the author indicated average trading costs in mutual funds of 1.8%. This would bring the total costs to approximately 2.25–2.5%.

There are many investment managers who work for 1% and consultants who provide their services for 1.25–1.50% or less depending upon the size and securities makeup of the investor's accounts.

Therefore, the cost of buying even a no-load mutual fund or hiring a private portfolio manager through a consultant are relatively equal. However, let's examine the added-value provided through a qualified, accredited investment management consultant who provides access to private portfolio management. This will also illustrate the consulting process and services which are not available when purchasing a mutual fund product.

A qualified, accredited, or certified investment management consultant can analyze the investor's personal needs and circumstances. This analysis leads to the writing of a personalized investment policy statement which documents the investor's goals/objectives and establishes optimal asset allocation, investment guidelines, and risk tolerance parameters suited for the investor.

Then the portfolio manager receives the policy statement. He or she is to operate and tailor the portfolio under the guidelines established in this written document. Furthermore, this document serves as the foundation for future progress and objective evaluation reports on the manager provided to the investor by the consultant.

Once the written investment policy has been established, the next step in the consulting process is to properly match the investor to an appropriate manager, one who's style and discipline of managing money is suitable to meeting the investor's return expectations, cash flow/income needs and who is compatible with the investor's risk tolerance levels.

In addition, a qualified investment management consultant provides an objective mechanism of accountability. Behind the scenes there is continuous manager due diligence being conducted.

Finally, the consultant provides the investor ongoing performance monitoring and manager evaluation reporting. This gives the investor objective information so he or she can make intelligent decisions and/or adjustments to his or her portfolio under the professional advice of their investment management consultant and/or private portfolio manager.

What Is a Wrap Account?

We are not trying to say that mutual funds are not good. They definitely have their place and function. They are excellent tools for people with smaller pools of money who can't access private portfolio management. This is why they were created. Mutual funds allow the smaller pools of funds (less than $100,000) to participate in the financial markets with proper diversification. But investors today are demanding more.

HISTORY OF THE WRAP ACCOUNT PROGRAMS

Prior to 1985, wrap fee accounts were found only at E.F. Hutton and Company. They offered access to professional money managers using the structure of a wrap fee arrangement.

Professional money managers, going back over the years, have traditionally worked with large accounts. There were some managers who would work with accounts only in excess of $150,000. In the 1970s, ma and pa operations and one-man shops, began picking up the small accounts. That original handful of firms grew from a base of $100 million to over $1 billion in just a few short years. However, many of them turned out to be administrative time bombs.

A large number of these small firms grew too fast to manage the back office administration that went with the work load. Consequently, their initial level of enthusiasm, interest, and client cooperation soon changed—and not for the better.

For consultants, it was a constant flow of finding new managers over and over again. These managers built a comfortable base of business with small accounts and grew rapidly. By increasing their average account size, they were quickly forced to shut off the small investors.

The heat was back on to find managers who would take on small accounts. This left the broker consultant and the brokerage firm high and dry looking for the quality of manager with whom they had been used to working. As a result, they were constantly searching for new candidates.

Wall Street finally determined that instead of looking for money management advisory firms to do all of the administrative paperwork, they would attempt to identify brokerage firms that could do the job of recordkeeping, account separation, billing, printing of brochures, and conducting client meetings. All the investor had to do was walk in the brokerage firm's office and turn it over to them.

With Wall Street assuming the burden of account recordkeeping and client communication, the money manager's role became limited to simply investing money. Economies of scale came into play because now the advisor could manage the client's money and not worry about maintaining the relationship. The advisor now found it easy and attractive to offer his services at half the regular fee, since he was managing $100,000 instead of $10 million.

A number of the money management firms working with E.F. Hutton saw the possibilities and quickly jumped on the bandwagon. Some of the earlier E.F. Hutton money managers were Dreman, Gardner Preston & Moss, and Provident Capital.

These changes occurred in the summer of 1987. Prior to that, in '85 and '86, most other firms were only looking at establishing a money management consulting business.

Merrill Lynch got out of the consulting business in 1985 all together because they saw they were losing control of the broker and the accounts. However, they soon realized that they had made a big mistake in doing so. Two years later they returned to the consulting business, primarily with this packaged approach, similar to the program E.F. Hutton was promoting.

Dean Witter, along with several other firms, also recognized the opportunity of this approach to money management. *Registered Representative* magazine played a role in this process back in 1982-84 when most of their articles about big producers (successful brokers) bore one thing in common—they all used money managers.

There were individuals like John Vann, Tom Clark, Bert Meem and Tom Sakai who became million-dollar producers using money managers to handle their clients' assets. These brokers worked with a handful of managers, but it was really only the beginning stages of investment management consulting.

For most of us in the brokerage industry, investment consulting began in the mid-1970s. By 1980, those of us who had stuck with investment consulting realized that money management was a much easier way to conduct business and retain our client books. Still other brokers opted for the big commission tickets such as tax-sheltered investments and unit trusts. And we all know how they ended up.

Consulting was harder work and not as personally satisfying as hitting great stocks that increased dramatically. Usually, it took a broker a few years in business to recognize it. If you were going to be in the brokerage business long-term, say for twenty years or more, you learned that to be a survivor you had to make money for your clients.

When the mid-1980s rolled around, the tax-shelter business began to dry up—especially oil, gas and, a little later, real estate. The brokers who were doing big business in the early 1980s were the tax-shelter guys. The ones who were left doing big business in the mid-1980s were those doing managed money.

The brokerage firms, such as Drexel Burnham, PaineWebber, Dean Witter, Kidder-Peabody, and others quickly saw this as a way to recapture market share and to compensate for reverses experienced in other product areas. They also began to appreciate the consistency that went with a repetitive type business. In 1985, Dean Witter was actually coaxed

13

into it by some of its own brokers. Kidder was just a handful of people at the time. And Shearson had little interest in developing such a program internally prior to the merger with E.F. Hutton.

Then, when Shearson-Lehman Brothers acquired the firm of E.F. Hutton in 1988, they overnight became the biggest and the best. Not because of Shearson's infinite wisdom, but because of E.F. Hutton's initial development.

Early pioneers like Richard Schilffarth and John Ellis planted the seed. But it was the Shearson influence that changed the character of the Hutton program—being there to service the broker/consultant who wanted to do "real" consulting. Shearson took the product and made it available to all of its brokers. That was the philosophical change that took place. Even though it was a brilliant business decision at Hutton to launch the program, it was Shearson's hunger to market the program that made it the success it is today.

At last count, Shearson's "Suggest" program had 800-plus advisors and had reviewed at least 3,000 others. Over 300 advisors are on their "National Visit" list. No other firm on Wall Street has duplicated their efforts to those proportions. However serious competitors are making bigger commitments in their effort to provide a valuable service.

The Shearson "Select" program was really a derivative of the E.F. Hutton "Suggest" program. The Select program, however, differs in the sense that the contractual agreement is between the advisor and Shearson. Thus, the investor is actually hiring Shearson. Shearson in turn hires the investment advisor as a subadvisor. Most wrap account programs on Wall Street are structured in a similar fashion.

In the Suggest program, when an advisor is hired, the agreement is between the advisor and the investor, and the advisor communicates directly with the investor. In Shearson's Select program, Shearson uses about twenty-seven managers with whom the firm already has a strong working relationship. Relying on these managers to provide the best service to their investors, Shearson placed computers on site with each investment advisor. Every morning the advisor is informed of new accounts and new investable cash. All the advisor has to do is call in to the Shearson trading desk and place the orders. Shearson takes care of everything from there. Now Smith-Barney is the beneficiary of this well-structured program, as the merger of Shearson with Smith-Barney brings with it the Shearson Consulting Group and its consulting services division.

A lot of people thought this was just marketing hype, but it wasn't that at all. It was a way to satisfy the complaints of their advisors, who were saying, "Look, you brokerage firms have been helping us build our businesses, but now you are going to destroy them by feeding us all of these small accounts. All of this back office administration will crush us."

Shearson responded, "Okay, we can help you control your costs and your administrative overhead by creating a workable administrative highway."

But the advisors couldn't provide the same level of hands-on, account-by-account service and many of the initial firms failed.

One such program was Lexington Capital Management. Their accounts were overseen by administrative assistants behind computer terminal operators. They literally went out and hired computer terminal operators to replicate model portfolios. Then they sent eight marketing people running around the country trying to sell to the different brokerage firms. They were out-hitting all of the brokers, bringing in the accounts and helping to close them. These accounts were emulated, then matched up to a larger model portfolio that a larger firm was managing. This was a typical marketing hype approach. They had an extremely difficult time replicating the performance of a larger firm.

This was just one example of the investment advisor trying to corner the small account market ($100,000-$500,000). Predictably, it didn't work.

Many advisory firms did not want to take small accounts because they were not cost effective. The overhead of running and overseeing this type of program was very cost prohibitive. So the Wall Street brokerage firms came in and solved the problem for them. They accomplished this by putting a lid on costs, absorbing all of the exponential increases in operating these separate smaller accounts.

The larger firms agreed to do the recordkeeping, print the marketing brochures, make the client contacts, and all of those things that advisors thought were too burdensome. Now the advisor was free to go ahead and do what he could do best—manage the assets.

The brokerage firms then sent their own marketing people around to call on their own in-house brokers. That move proved to be the best value for their dollar that the brokerage firms were to make.

Unfortunately, certain sections of the financial media found it fashionable to attack the wrap fee concept, standing on the premise that it is too costly and the investor should pass it up and just invest in mutual funds. They give no credit to the fact that many investors actually want separate account management and not mutual funds. Not everyone wants to commingle his or her money.

The wrap fee account of today is quite different than it was a few years ago. In today's wrap fee account programs, the investor is not the customer of the advisory firm—the brokerage firm is.

In other words, the advisor is not hired by the investor, but by the brokerage firm. The brokerage firm is in the business of warehousing the money, handling the transactions, doing the recordkeeping, and producing the marketing brochures. When you select an advisor, in most situations, the brokerage firm actually hires the advisor and pays him a much smaller fee than he would ordinarily get. This has put a lid on the cost of all investment advisors. As brokerage firms bring in more and more wrap accounts, they are able to spread their costs over a larger base and their costs go down accordingly. It has to be a win-win situation for everyone concerned.

The brokerage firms have established their own trading desks for advisors. This also helps to keep their costs under control.

Most firms have a separate trading desk, an institutional desk or a designated desk that the firm uses to put its buy and sell orders through. But we are only discussing the mechanics of wrap, the real value comes from the brokerage firm's due-diligence efforts.

Most investors don't realize that they can negotiate wrap fees, and unfortunately, a large number of brokers won't tell the investors they can. Some brokers may disagree with this but it doesn't change the facts, since enlightening the investor on fee negotiations has a direct negative impact on the broker's income.

The roots of the wrap fee account programs began many years ago with the all-inclusive consultant services. These programs blended all the services that would normally be provided by an investment management consultant. At that time, they generally did not include the bundling of payments to the investment advisor. That came later.

In fact, it was the agreement between the advisor and the investor that worked so well. That agreement became the base for the wrap fee programs of today. The billing procedures in use at that time evolved into the standard method of payment. These earlier programs allowed widespread distribution of investment management services to the middle market investor.

By understanding the roots of these earlier programs you can arrive at a greater appreciation for their value. This is why we wanted to tell you the story of the man who started the wrap accounts.

It was snowing outside when a memo showed up on the desk of Richard Schilffarth. It said that Jim Lockwood of Investment Management Services, a division of Dean Witter, was going to hold an investment management seminar in Chicago. The seminar was to be held on February 12, 1972, at the Marriott hotel. Schilffarth thought it sounded interesting, so he decided to attend.

After trudging through six inches of snow, Schilffarth found himself in the lobby of the Marriott Hotel, and just in time for an elegantly prepared meal. After dinner, Jim Lockwood stood and said, "I am glad you are all here. We work in the managed assets area. I have with me Carl Zerfoss from the Supervised Investment Services of Kemper. He will tell you what an investment manager does." After Zerfoss gave a lengthy explanation of how money management works, Lockwood walked back to the front of the room, turned, and announced, "We work with accounts that are over $10 million in size."

Half the room promptly fell asleep. They had just discovered that they had showed up at the wrong ballpark. Undaunted, Lockwood continued, "Since these are rather large accounts and are subject to volume discounts, the commissions will run somewhere under one half of one percent." With that comment, those in attendance who were still awake, nodded off. All, that is, except for Richard Schilffarth.

When Schilffarth got back to Milwaukee he set up an appointment for March 14, 1972 with an insurance company that had $12 million in assets. He made arrangements for Jim Lockwood to come over and tell them how the program worked.

That Monday it snowed. Richard picked up his clients and brought them to the Milwaukee athletic club where he had rented a room for the presentation. When they arrived, Schilffarth had a telephone message waiting for him. When he picked up the receiver, it was Jim Lockwood on the other end, saying, "Sorry, Rich, but I'm snowed in at Saginaw!"

"Jim, I don't even know what it is we do," said Schilffarth.

"Well," Lockwood answered, "We evaluate managers and select them based on a set of investment objectives."

After Richard lay the receiver back in the cradle he repeated to his clients what Lockwood had told him. Impressed, they responded, "Well, what manager would you select?"

Schilffarth only knew one—Kemper's Supervised Investment Management. So the very next week, the insurance company put $12 million with Supervised Investment Services.

Schilffarth got excited, made a couple more calls, and on May 7 had a meeting set up with Milwaukee Mutual, which had $35 million to invest. Once again, Lockwood was invited to sit in on that meeting. This time he called back and said that he was in the hospital. He had just suffered his first heart attack.

Schilffarth told Jim that he didn't know if he could handle it himself, so Lockwood gave him the whole pitch again, over the telephone.

Schilffarth told Milwaukee Mutual exactly what Lockwood had said. "That sounds good, who would you recom-

19

mend?" they asked. "Supervised Investment Services," Richard said.

That next day Milwaukee Mutual gave them the account for $35 million.

In June, Richard called on National Insurance Company, who had $85 million to invest. He didn't even bother calling Lockwood this time. After the presentation they said, "Who would you recommend?"

So Schilffarth once again said, "Supervised Investment Services." They liked the idea and the very next week gave him the entire account to manage, $85 million.

That got Schilffarth in the consulting business.

In February of 1973, Jim Lockwood asked Schilffarth if he would leave Milwaukee and join his department. Schilffarth agreed, but said, "Sure, but I have a question for you."

"Fire away," Lockwood answered, smiling.

"Can we go below $10 million accounts?" Richard said. "When I had my company, we had a pension account for $500,000, and I have news for you, Jim, I needed management help more than the big accounts did. Why not set up some sort of program for smaller accounts." Surprisingly, Jim agreed.

The following week, they set up an investment management program called Dean Witter "Plus." They used two managers, Boston Company Advisors and S & P Capital, Joe Lamattas's company. Joe was very instrumental in helping them form the program.

It was March 23, 1973, when Jim presented the Dean Witter Plus program to the executive committee of Dean Witter. Bill Witter wasted little time in saying, "No, we're not interested. We don't want to raise money for outside people. We want to raise it for ourselves."

Jim Lockwood was very upset about Witter's answer. He had been the largest mutual fund salesman for Dempsey-

Tegler before they went out of business. He was not used to being turned down when he had a good idea.

At Dempsey-Tegler, Lockwood had worked for a fellow by the name of John Ellis. When Dempsey-Tegler went out of business, John Ellis took his office and put it with Dean Witter and brought Jim Lockwood and Tom Gorman along with him. So, when Lockwood called Schilffarth and said that he was not happy with Dean Witter's decision and asked him if he would like to join John Ellis, Tom Gorman, and him in finding a new home, Schilffarth said yes.

Ned Bailey of Capital Guardian suggested that they meet with E.F. Hutton. On Sunday, April 8, 1973, Jim Lockwood and John Ellis met with George Ball and Norm Epstien from E.F. Hutton. Lockwood told them what they wanted to do. George Ball, the president of E.F. Hutton, was taking notes. After a short period of time, he looked up and said, "Is this the kind of contract you guys are looking for? All of your expenses will be charged to the firm, and you will get a revenue of 7% of the commission. You will also get 40% of the profit after expenses, plus a bonus pool."

Lockwood picked up the paper, studied it, and politely said, "Yes, yes it is."

Later that week, the group was back in business. They signed with E.F. Hutton on April 24, and immediately set to work developing a program they called E.F. Hutton Suggests. Richard wanted to call the program E.F. Hutton Plus, but George Ball didn't like the name because there was a notorious massage parlor called "Relaxation Plus" on the corner of 53rd and Lexington in New York City. That made George nervous, so they agreed to change the name to Suggests.

Jim Lockwood handled the east coast, Schilffarth the midwest and Ellis the west coast.

Chapter 2

After Schilffarth opened a branch in Milwaukee, he decided that he would go help the brokers sell the program. His first stop was Denver where he met John Vann, a newly registered broker who had just been licensed in August of 1973. John Vann did everything Richard said.

The next day they called on his first account, a woman named Gulda Peck. She was 72 years old and lived with her son who was an insurance agent. She had $47,000 that she wanted managed. Of the two managers, the Boston company advisors would only take a $50,000 account, so she became the very first E.F. Hutton Suggests account.

Later in March 1974, Jim Lockwood wrote a letter to George Ball, saying, "The program is finally going, we have twenty accounts already in the program or in the pipeline." The truth was that the twenty accounts were made up of four with brokers, four that Richard had opened, three that Ellis had opened and one account that Gorman had opened. The other eight accounts never came in.

In spite of this, George Ball put Schilffarth in charge of the entire program.

Schilffarth immediately set about to rewrite the program, develop the training manual and set up coordinator training programs. They held their first training program in Washington, D.C., in early May 1974.

One year later, on May Day, 1975, Jim Lockwood, with his tremendous creativity, called Schilffarth on the phone and said, "What a great day, Dick!"

"Jim, you've been smoking something, this is not a great day. They drew up our first commission schedule on Friday and our commissions are going to go down the tubes."

"No, you don't understand; now we don't have to charge commission," announced Lockwood.

"What! Not charge commission! How am I going to get paid?" Schilffarth queried.

"Why not a fee?" said Lockwood.

"Jim, that's one hell of an idea," cried Schilffarth.

Later that week Richard Schilffarth worked out the first wrap fee program, taking all of the accounts that E.F. Hutton had in the program at that time. He computed the commissions on all of the Suggests Accounts which averaged 1.9%. He added 1% for the management fee, and rounded it to an even 3% on the assets under $500,000 and 2% on the assets over $500,000.

That's how wrap fees started. Schilffarth called it a "wrap fee" because he thought the clients wanted everything wrapped together, instead of separate items.

At the same time they created the wrap fee, they went to George Ball and suggested the direction in which they thought the company should go—to the employee benefits market. ERISA had just been passed in September of 1974 and all of the pension and profit-sharing plans had to be in place by the end of 1975 and had to be funded.

Schilffarth brought out the wrap fee in 1975 and Hutton Investment Management (HIM) in 1976. Hutton Capital Management came out in 1978 and Hutton Portfolio Management, where the broker has a full discretionary manager, in 1980.

They started this type of business so that Hutton could control its own destiny. This way, they cut down the tremendous costs of the broker and added the security of salaries to the brokerage business. This was Schilffarth's idea, a holdover from his years in the merchandising business.

The first in-house program Schilffarth suggested got off to a terrible start. The man who was in charge of the investment side of the program was the head of research, Dr. William Latterette. He had been trained by Douglas T. Johnson, a growth stock manager from one of the divisions of the Boston Company. He set the program up to have three facets, small cap growth, growth, and growth of income.

Hutton was about to come out with the program when Bill Latterette died of a heart attack. The program had to wait until December of 1975 to get started.

Charles McGullereck was the head portfolio manager at that time and he was not truly trained in the business. Then he, too, died of heart attack in March of 1976.

Finally, Allen Miller was hired as head of research and in April was given the job as head of the investment side of HIM.

Schilffarth believed that there was an inherent conflict of interest in being a broker and an investment manager where one has the authority to determine how often he trades and earns commissions on the trade. Wrap fee management solved that conflict.

By the end of 1974, the original two-manager universe had been expanded to a small universe of managers with various styles. In 1975, they added the quarterly performance monitor and the investment questionnaire.

The investment questionnaire was the input to the investment plan, the blueprint for the portfolio machine. From that blueprint was taken the criteria for the selection of one of these evaluated managers who became the operator of the machine.

By April 1, 1975, the four elements (the blueprint, the output, the operator, and the quality control) of the portfolio machine were in place. These four elements were later packaged into the "Wrap Account Program."

May 1, 1975, the Security Exchange Commission ended the fixed, transaction commission schedule. Before that time, a wrap fee would not have been possible. In May 1975 E.F. Hutton Suggests Part III was born. Part III because the client was offered a 3% wrap fee. This fee included the commission cost and the investment manager's fee (see Table 2–1). The Part III fee schedule was:

Table 2–1   The Part III Fee Schedule

Assets	Client	Manager	Commission
$0–500,000	3.0%	1%	2.0%
Next $500,000	2.5%	1%	1.5%
Over $1,000,000	2.0%	1%	1.0%

Although the wrap fee included the manager's fee and the commissions under a common fee structure, it had two client contracts. One contract to the client from the brokerage firm specifying the fee structure, and a second contract to the client from the investment manager stating his duties and authority. The account was controlled by the money manager, the broker and, in the case of outside custody, the custodian.

The wrap fee was unbundled in 1983 and divided into a manager fee plus a fee-in-lieu-of commission. There were three advantages to the brokerage firm in this unbundling. First, the fee structure didn't presuppose a manager's fee schedule. But the clients mistakenly felt that the entire wrap fee went to the broker. They had to show the client exactly what the brokerage firm was charging.

Many lawyers felt that including the manager in a wrap fee implied that he was a subcontractor of the brokerage firm, making the firm a fiduciary under ERISA. This turned out to be the second advantage.

The third advantage was to eliminate the contractor/subcontractor relationship that might be falsely perceived under the wrap fee program.

The firm's fee-in-lieu-of commission was truly a misnomer. It wasn't a fee that took place of commission. It was an asset-based commission rather than a transaction commission. The cost of executing the trade, clearing the trade, custody of the securities, collecting dividends and interest, paying out dividends and interest, serving the client all were present in the asset-based commission as they are in the transaction commission.

From the start of the Exchange, until May 1, 1975, the only commission allowed was a transaction commission. But then, the only business of the stock brokerage firm was transaction business. The E.F. Hutton Suggests Program was just getting a strong start when the fixed commission schedule was terminated. It was obvious that transaction commissions were less appropriate in the investment account business and that an asset-based commission was more acceptable.

In 1990, the term fee-in-lieu-of commission was relegated to the archives and the "asset-based commission" was initiated. It reflected correctly what it was, a commission not a fee.

Wrap account programs were developed in the last half of the 1980s. Unlike the wrap fee or the asset based commission, a wrap account has but one contract with the client. The contract is from the wrap account sponsor. In most cases, the investment advisor is a contracted sub-contractor to the wrap account sponsor. It is a mistake to use the terms wrap account and wrap fee interchangeably. A wrap account is a marketing program that encompasses the four elements needed by a portfolio machine (the blueprint, the output, the operator, and the quality control) into a single package. Although it uses a wrap fee, a wrap account program is a much more extensive concept designed to facilitate the delivery of the program to the client.

Wrap account programs will normally have at least four investment objectives so that they cover the needs of the greatest percentage of the managed asset marketplace. These programs will have at least two managers in each of the four objectives or a total of eight investment managers in a single wrap account program.

In joining a wrap account program, the investment manager reduces his minimum size of account, cuts his fees and adds a computer communication link.

Investment advisors will want a yearly asset flow of at least $5 million to $10 million per year to justify the cost of belonging to a wrap account program. With a minimum of eight managers in a program and each manager needing an asset flow of $10 million per year to cover his costs, wrap programs had to develop $80 million per year in new assets to keep the manager in the program. It takes a full-service brokerage firm of at least 800 brokers to develop $80 million per year in new assets, but there are fewer than 15 firms in that category.

Some of the programs existing at the time of this writing are: Merrill Lynch "Consults," Dean Witter "Access," Smith Barney Shearson "Selects," Prudential Securities "MACS," PaineWebber "Access," and Kidder-Peabody "Nova." In addition there are programs at A.G. Edwards, Wheat First Securities, Kemper, and a few other regional firms.

The second group that will sponsor wrap account programs are the major clearing houses for their fully disclosed brokerage clients. Since the clearing firms don't have product marketing forces and the brokers of their correspondents are not their employees, they will have to have a much greater number of brokers to generate sufficient assets. There most likely are no more than five clearing firms that are large enough to consider a wrap account program. The only operating clearing firms that are in wrap programs today are Pershing's "PEAK" program and Raymond James

Investment Management Services' IMS program run by Jerry Caswell.

The third source of wrap account programs will be mutual fund management companies. Wrap account programs have effectively capped mutual fund sales at $100,000 of assets and higher.

These management companies will be tempted to start wrap programs in which they are the only manager to fill in the gap between $100,000 (the top of their mutual fund sales) and $5,000,000 to $10,000,000 where for their separate account management starts. Like brokerage companies, only the larger funds will succeed. Of the top ten funds, it is doubtful that more than half will form their own wrap programs. These programs will be sold like mutual funds are today.

Independent sponsors will be the fourth provider of wrap account programs. These sponsors will have no connection to a brokerage company, a clearing firm, or a mutual fund. They will be the wholesalers of wrap account programs to the brokerage firms that don't have a sufficient sales force to generate required assets for a successful in-house program. Based on the cost of developing the program, the sales force required and the servicing network needed, it is hard to envision more than five independent sponsors of wrap account programs. There are two non-aligned programs today, PMC and Preferred Investment Management. That gives us a total of 27 sponsors of wrap account programs, but not all of them will survive.

CHAPTER 3

WRAP ACCOUNTS: FOR THE INDIVIDUAL

Wall Street's latest innovation is popularly known as the wrap account. Its name derives from the fact that individual investors are provided a variety of services, including money management, for an all-inclusive fee.

The concept has been lambasted in the press as another Wall Street product designed to take advantage of the individual investor, similar to the failed real estate limited partnerships of the past. Much of the criticism from the financial media centers around the comparison of wrap accounts to mutual funds and their different fee structures. This completely ignores the important consulting process integral to the wrap program.

THE ADVENT OF THE WRAP PROGRAM

There is no doubt that Wall Street has produced some questionable products over the years. However, the wrap account should not be viewed as a new product. It represents instead the culmination of a larger trend toward managed money that began in the seventies. When the Employee Retirement Income Security Act (ERISA) passed in 1974, modern portfo-

This chapter was contributed by John P. Calamos, President, Calamos Asset Management, Inc. Reprinted from *Personal Financial Planning* (New York: Warren Gorham Lamont). ©1993 with permission.

lio theory could be applied to pension fund management. The previously standard practice of buy-and-hold money management through bank trust departments gave way to active portfolio management and asset allocation techniques, which resulted in improved performance for pension fund assets.

The growth of pension fund assets created a demand for a group of professionals, called institutional consultants, who could counsel plan sponsors on the optimal combinations of asset classes for increased returns and reduced risk. The consultants also maintained database records of money manager performance and conducted manager searches for plan sponsors. In order to evaluate managers objectively, this process often included ongoing portfolio monitoring and the creation of performance benchmarks. The consultants incorporated the use of risk-adjusted returns for portfolio manager evaluation; it has since become a widespread practice.

In addition, the consultants provided investment guidelines and established the process by which asset classes could be added to a pension fund portfolio. They introduced the latest academic theories to the corporate boardrooms and promoted many innovative asset classes. This value-added service was instrumental in providing diversification of asset classes to both corporate and public pension funds. It also negated the then-prevalent ivory tower approach that contended that active money management did not add incremental value in an "efficient market."

Because the consultants were independent of the money manager, plan sponsors could rely on their advice, eliminating any conflict of interest in the selection process. Interestingly, many institutional consultants are now attempting to supplant the money manager's role by including money management as part of their business. This will only create new conflicts of interest.

Most would agree that the increasing influence of institutional consultants had a positive effect on the overall performance of pension funds. It also fostered the development of money management firms that specialize in unique investment styles, since the consultants frequently provided an objective basis by which these new styles could be properly evaluated.

THE INDIVIDUAL INVESTOR IN AN INSTITUTIONALLY DOMINATED MARKET

In large part due to the services of the consultants, institutional investors now dominate the market because of the large amount of assets they represent. Furthermore, the combined acceleration of the information age and advanced computer techniques has created an extremely fast-paced market. The individual investor, with much the same needs as the corporate plan sponsor although on a much smaller scale, is placed at a great disadvantage. However small the amount of funds, the investor wants it managed in a manner with the highest probability for success. But lacking the financial and consulting resources available to the institutional plan sponsors, many individual investors have found it increasingly difficult to manage their portfolios effectively.

The surge of the mutual fund industry over the past years points to the individual investor's mounting need for additional services. Mutual funds offer individual investors the opportunity to participate in a diversified portfolio managed by professionals. However, they do not provide the full spectrum of services available to the institutional investor.

The responsibility for the selection and monitoring of the funds for his or her particular portfolio rests with the individual investor. And as many mutual funds investors can attest, in a field where there are as many mutual funds as there are stocks on the New York Stock Exchange, the selection process alone is difficult. Simply relying on a third-party newsletter for mutual fund ranking is not equivalent to professional financial planning. Furthermore, monitoring the funds' performance is a complicated process. The media's constant—and unfortunate—emphasis on short-term performance leads many unseasoned investors to jump constantly in and out of the market, sometimes on an almost daily basis. This is not usually an effective way of producing satisfactory long-term performance results.

So, while mutual funds do provide diversification, many individual investors, like their institutional counterparts, feel the need for additional consulting services. It is this need that paved the way for the development of wrap accounts and that sets them apart from mutual funds.

WRAP ACCOUNTS: COMPREHENSIVE SERVICE VERSUS CONCRETE PRODUCT

Generally, besides actual money management, wrap accounts provide individualized consulting services (including both the selection of money managers and monitoring account performance) and custodial services (holding all assets). All transactions and trade executions are monitored by the financial consultant in charge of the account. And perhaps most importantly, the financial consultant works with the client to determine his or her investment objectives and risk tolerance, developing a long-term investment plan.

Often a questionnaire is used to facilitate this process as it is an extremely helpful tool for identifying the investor's risk tolerance level. After completing the questionnaire, an investor often finds that his or her current objectives and risk tolerance are at cross-purposes. The questionnaire also fosters discussion on the important tradeoffs of risk and return. Such discussions constitute an essential element of the professional consulting service.

Some attribute little value to ascertaining the client's investment posture, but those involved in professional investment management view this aspect of the program as probably the most important initial step of the investing process. Accomplished correctly, it sets the long-term investment plan in motion. Institutional plan sponsors periodically complete such plans, using fee-based professional services. The planning process, often cited as the single most important factor for investment success, is the underlying basis of most wrap programs.

Wrap accounts are not for everyone. Those individual investors who believe they have the necessary education, current information, skill, and time to manage their own portfolios probably will not want to take advantage of the services provided by the wrap program. Those who can use mutual funds effectively to structure their individual portfolios and do not feel the need for consulting advice will also probably not wish to invest in the wrap service. But there are investors who seek more than just money manager selection and who want a customized, professionally informed planning and consulting process; for those investors the wrap program provides a valuable service and is a wise investment.

Chapter 3

THE FINANCIAL CONSULTANT
AND THE WRAP PROGRAM

Obviously, the financial consultant plays a key role in the effectiveness of the wrap program. Paradoxically, as wrap accounts become more popular on Wall Street, selecting a consultant is made both more difficult and easier at the same time. Nearly every broker is capable of presenting the wrap program to clients. Many, however, are just beginning to understand the overall concept of the program themselves.

The essential role of the broker is that of a salesperson who deals with a product: securities. Coming from a transaction-oriented background, not all brokers understand the concept of money management consulting. Becoming a competent consultant requires a thorough understanding of investment management as well as a perception shift from product-oriented selling to process-oriented service.

The broker can attain the additional consulting knowledge needed to manage a wrap account through the brokerage firm's training resources or from formal programs like those offered by professional organizations such as the Institute for Investment Management Consultants (IIMC). These independent associations supplement the training programs of brokerage firms by providing a continuing education program. Several offer certification programs which designate the broker as having attained a specific level of competency in financial consulting. The level of professionalism, however, still remains in the hands of the individual financial consultant and a great deal depends on his or her tenacity at reaching a satisfactory level of competency.

THE QUESTION OF FEE

A common criticism leveled at the wrap program concerns the fee structure: it is too high, many claim, especially when compared to those of mutual funds. Confusion exists, however, because many people—both investors and journalists—do not understand that unlike most Wall Street programs, the wrap account is a comprehensive service and not a single product. Rather than contrasting it to mutual funds, then, a more accurate comparison would be to the professional fees charged by institutional consultants for their services.

Ongoing monitoring is extremely important. The financial consultant should communicate with the investor on a regular basis, and especially in difficult market periods. He or she should be able to explain why a down period for a money manager does not necessarily indicate that a switch is in order, placing the investment style in perspective. Investment styles and strategies have ebb and flow periods; making changes too often or too quickly can lead to poor longer-term results. However, should the manager's investment philosophy change abruptly or dramatically, or if the manager does not adhere to the firm's stated guidelines, the financial consultant should not hesitate to terminate the manager. Monitoring the manager is one of the value-added services the consultant provides.

THE INVESTOR'S RESPONSIBILITY IN THE WRAP PROGRAM

The investor, too, shares in the responsibility for the wrap account. He or she should gain a clearer understanding from the process of his or her own investment philosophy and risk tolerance. The investor should expect periodic reviews from the consultant and make a point of understanding the investment manager's philosophy and investment style. Simply relying on quarterly performance numbers often does not tell the complete story. The education process should continue as reports and reviews are conducted.

For many investors who require individual service, confidentiality, and the advantage of being able to discuss their investment objectives with both the financial consultant and money manager, the wrap account provides a valuable service. With the increasing volatility of the financial markets spurred by the computer and information age of the 1990s, securing valuable professional advice through programs like the wrap account may very well be the critical element for financial success of individual investors.

Furthermore, the consultant's fee is not the only cost involved; the institutional investor must also pay the money manager. Because the consulting costs are spread over a substantial asset base, they may seem small, especially when considered as a percentage of assets. However, unlike the case of the client in a wrap program who pays one fee for a comprehensive package of services, the consulting fees for the institutional investor are often unbundled, meaning that the various services are provided and billed separately. The institutional investor must also negotiate independently for the money manager's services. Plan sponsors therefore often require special departments responsible solely for coordinating the various activities and billing associated with the consulting services. This constitutes an additional source of cost that the individual investor in a wrap program is spared.

The individual investor's "wrap" fee represents not only the actual money management but also the customized services of the financial consultant as well as various services provided by the brokerage firm. Besides the various billing procedures involved in the account, the firm does considerable ongoing due diligence on the program's money managers and provides account performance comparison to industry benchmarks, in addition to other services.

When evaluating the cost of the wrap account fee, then, the value-added service of the account is what should be addressed. Whether the fee is fairly priced depends on the quality and level of the service provided by the brokerage firm and the financial consultant handling the account.

Because the financial consultant's role in the wrap program is considerable, a great deal of the quality of the service depends on his or her degree of knowledge, skill and professionalism. As has been discussed, not all brokers who call themselves financial consultants devote the time and energy necessary to reach the required professional level; for this type of broker, any wrap fee is too high. If little service is offered and the financial consultant has sold the wrap account as just another product, the fee is again probably too high. However, if the consultant provides the high level of service this comprehensive process requires, the fee of the wrap account is in line with those of other professional services.

The actual fee structure will vary depending on the amount of funds available to invest. Costs for the minimum-sized level may seem high, but the fee generally drops as the account reaches the $500,000 level.

WHAT TO EXPECT
FROM THE FINANCIAL CONSULTANT

What should the client expect from the financial consultant when investing in a wrap program? First of all, because the initial planning process is so important, the financial consultant should willingly spend time to review the questionnaire carefully with the investor. Be wary of the financial consultant who handles the consulting process superficially. This can signify that the consultant may not have the necessary knowledge to advise the investor.

Beware, too, of the financial consultant who emphasizes the highest return for the most recent time period when selecting a manager. Performance should be evaluated not on a short-term basis, but on the degree of risk assumed and considering appropriate investment cycles. Investment cycles typically last from three to five years; a rolling four-year performance often gives a good indication of what expectations can be met.

CHAPTER 4

WRAP ACCOUNTS VERSUS MUTUAL FUNDS

Historically, professional management was only available to the extremely wealthy. It is now available to those who have $100,000 or more to allocate to the capital markets. Mutual funds are still appropriate for smaller pools of funds to achieve adequate diversification.

An investor may be buying blindly into a mutual fund. Oftentimes, mutual fund investors are not aware of management changes (since 1985, 95% of all mutual fund managers have changed their post). An advantage of a wrap fee account is the ability to become familiar and comfortable with a particular manager and his style.

Talent in the money management industry gravitates out of the mutual funds toward the independent firms because of better compensation and the opportunity to become a partner and thereby build equity and net worth for themselves.

In a wrap fee account, qualified consultants can provide investors with the additional benefits of writing a tailored investment policy consistent with the investor's objectives, assist in the selection of top-performing managers appropriate for the investor's stated objectives, and produce ongoing performance monitoring. This keeps the investors more in-

We would like to thank Mark McIntire, Vice President, Savory Capital Management, for his contribution to this chapter.

39

formed regarding the results of their individual account. None of these value-added services are available through a mutual fund.

Management by Objectives—Wrap fee accounts can allow the customizing of the portfolio structure to the investor's written investment policy statement. Mutual funds do not manage or respond to an investor's written investment policy statement.

Most mutual funds remain fully invested with no sensitivity to investor's needs, or economic or market conditions. Individual management takes all these factors, and more, into asset allocation considerations.

Studies indicate asset allocation contributes up to 90% of a portfolio's return. With mutual funds, this decision is still the investor's responsibility. In a wrap fee managed portfolio, the experienced money manager can make these important decisions based on the investor's objectives.

Wrap fee providers are able to give the investor a much higher level of service than mutual funds, including the opportunity to speak and visit with the investor's personal portfolio manager.

Due Diligence—Many firms offering wrap accounts use a consultant for on-site due diligence visits to managers in their programs. The mutual fund industry lacks on-sight due diligence.

Performance Monitoring—Wrap fee providers offer individual account performance monitoring quarterly. Mutual funds offer no individual account performance monitoring for any period.

Net Redemption—In poor equity markets, mutual funds have thousands of redemptions, forcing managers to use cash for redemptions (thus missing buying opportunities) and/or liquidating equity positions at losses (losing the ability to recover with an equity up-tick). Wrap fee managed accounts have both the cash buying opportunity and the ability to recover during these market cycles.

Since professionally managed wrap fee accounts hold individual securities, the investor maintains complete ownership of his or her accounts. If the investor has the need to make a withdrawal, liquidate, or sell a portion of the portfolio, he can do this based on his specific needs.

In wrap fee managed accounts, investors are usually able to balance capital gains with tax loss selling. Mutual fund investors do not have that ability.

In a mutual fund, the investor might be buying other investors' gains. In a wrap fee managed account, your cost basis is established the day you begin the relationship. However, cost basis is inherited in a mutual fund; i.e., many times the investor must report gains in which he or she did not really participate during your holding period.

"Commingled no-load or low-load funds may not be as attractive an alternative for pension plan trustees or individual investors as they appear to be in the advertising sections of money magazines," says Kurt Winrich, president of Winrich Capital Management in Lake Forest, California.

"Fidelity's Magellan Fund manager, Peter Lynch, was forced to sell stock during the crash of 1987 to raise cash to pay out substantial liquidations. But what happened to the investors who bought into the fund during that summer and stuck with the fund after the crash?

"Say that a person invested $100 during the summer before the crash and his objectives were long term. October of 1987 comes along, and bang! The fund loses 30% of its value but the summertime investor decides not to liquidate and stays in the fund. Meanwhile the fund manager, Peter Lynch, sold stock during the October crash, deciding to take some of the unrealized gains that he'd built up in the fund before that summer. By year's end, the summertime investor's $100 is now worth $80. He figures, 'Okay, that kind of thing happens.' But then along comes January and our investor gets a notice from the Magellan Fund saying that he is going to have to pay capital gains tax on the unrealized gains the manager took in October of 1987, adding insult to injury. This could not have happened in an individually managed wrap account because an investor is not buying into a pre-existing fund. In an individually managed wrap account the only assets in that account are yours—they're not shared," says Winrich.

In an individual wrap account, the manager follows your individual objectives—not group objectives. The very nature of any mutual fund is based on what is best for the group as a whole, not what is best for you as an individual.

Fees—Wrap fee accounts versus most no-load funds are usually close or lower in overall costs.

In most wrap managed accounts, you can deduct all of the manager's fee and possibly some of the consulting fee (subject to 2% of A.G.I. rule). In a mutual fund, you can't separate out management fees to deduct them.

Fiduciary Liability—In a wrap fee managed account, the money manager agrees to become a co-fiduciary in the investment agreement. Currently, it is unclear as to whether a mutual fund can accept the same responsibility. Fiduciaries of retirement plans selecting mutual funds are selecting investments, and therefore take on that liability of doing so. Furthermore, the fiduciary must still make the asset allocation decisions among stocks, bonds, cash, etc. In a managed account, this responsibility may be delegated to the money manager.

CHAPTER 5

WRAP ACCOUNTS AND MISINFORMATION

Sometimes it becomes very confusing for the investor to determine the difference between a wrap program that is promoting a brokerage firm's internal money managers and a firm that is promoting outside money managers. That confusion starts at the broker level (see Figure 5–1).

Most unsophisticated stockbrokers will likely gravitate toward their own firm's internal investment managers because the sales brochures are handy, the information flow is better, and the firm has a department to support. This is especially true if the outside money manager program is relatively new to the firm.

When an investor goes into a stock brokerage office and talks to a broker, and says, "I have an interest in professional money management," the stockbroker will either have a high level of knowledge with all forms of wrap fee related accounts or have very little. If he has very little knowledge, he may just walk over to a file cabinet and pull out the first thing he sees. This scenario will vary from firm to firm. It will also vary from stockbroker to stockbroker within the firm.

An investor might go to a branch office and find only one or two stockbrokers who are fully aware of all of the different money managers available, and the other stockbrokers don't even care.

This chapter was contributed by Marty Jensen, CIMC.

Figure 5–1   An Organized Structure for Individual Investors

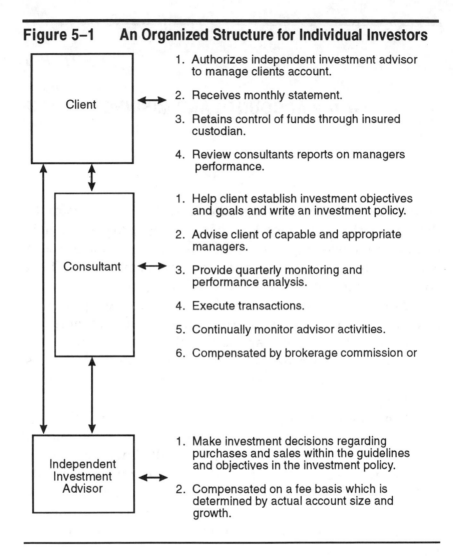

Client

1. Authorizes independent investment advisor to manage clients account.

2. Receives monthly statement.

3. Retains control of funds through insured custodian.

4. Review consultants reports on managers performance.

Consultant

1. Help client establish investment objectives and goals and write an investment policy.

2. Advise client of capable and appropriate managers.

3. Provide quarterly monitoring and performance analysis.

4. Execute transactions.

5. Continually monitor advisor activities.

6. Compensated by brokerage commission or

Independent Investment Advisor

1. Make investment decisions regarding purchases and sales within the guidelines and objectives in the investment policy.

2. Compensated on a fee basis which is determined by actual account size and growth.

There is often confusion from the investor who fails to realize that he doesn't necessarily need to pay the full 3% on a balanced account that is being managed in a very passive way versus an all-equity account that is being managed in a very aggressive way.

Wrap Accounts and Misinformation

There is also confusion on the brokerage side when a stockbroker sells the wrap account program and is unwilling to price it properly. This is the area the media picked up on and about which they printed a lot of misinformation. An example was an article printed in a major investment magazine which inferred that all wrap accounts are rip-offs and claimed that investors are being grossly overcharged.

The value a trained investment management consultant can provide is to help an investor understand these differences (see Figure 5–1). They can also help the investor write an investment policy and match money manager's styles with the investor's risk tolerances. In addition, the media has totally disregarded the value that brokerage firms have contributed in doing due diligence on investment advisors.

Still, a lot of investors hire an investment money manager on their own. The hidden danger in this approach is that the investor doesn't really know whether the money manager is appropriate for him, or whether the money manager's track record is real or perceived. All of these factors can account for misinformation.

Let's assume that an investor has a $100,000 stock account. It is an all-equity account and has twenty stock positions. The average cost is about $5,000 per stock position. In a typical $5,000 stock trade, the commission will run anywhere from $125 to $175—which is somewhere between 2 and 3%, on the buy side.

If the investor is fully invested he or she may have a 50% turnover on his or her portfolio during a one-year period. In essence, the investor turns over 50% of his or her portfolio selling, then another 50% buying new stocks and that translates into trades totalling 100% of portfolio value.

In the first year, the investor might have anywhere from 2 to 6% in commissions. In ongoing years, the investor could have anywhere from 1.5 to 3% in commissions on an ongoing basis, and that does not include the money manager's fee. If this were a balanced account with very little activity, the investor might be paying more than he would be paying on a retail brokerage basis. It will vary from account to account, manager to manager, and year to year.

The wrap relationship really begins by understanding the true cost of managing money. Investors sometimes misinterpret the role and the relationship of the investment consultant and their added value. The consultant can help identify these actual costs, help the investor identify what managers are appropriate and continue to maintain the ongoing analysis and dialogue as well as a performance analysis on the money manager.

Without a trained investment consultant it is like asking a stranger for directions. They may give you some of the directions and you may take off on your journey, but they didn't tell you all of the details, all of the potential road hazards, so you end up at the wrong location.

Many investors think, "Well gee, I got the directions now, I'm going to do it myself."

Unfortunately, they do not have all the correct details, yet this is what many discount commission houses provide—only some of the directions.

The wrap account relationship really exists between the investment consultant, the manager, and the investor.

Without guidance, an investor can make the assumption (or get hung up on the assumption) that finding a money manager is simply for the purpose of beating the stock market averages, instead of looking at a money manager to create a rate of return at the lowest possible level of risk.

The majority of the money being managed in this country today is being managed based upon the investor's investment objective. It is not being managed based on market averages or beating the market and producing a reasonable rate of return at the lowest possible level of risk, or even a controlled level of risk. That's what active portfolio management is all about. How it is done will be discussed in detail in later chapters.

How does one judge whether financial information advertised about wrap accounts is accurate?

The problem is that most investors have little time to spend on analyzing money managers so they can make smart investment choices, and not base them on what is being promoted by the financial press. Unfortunately, those wonderful returns advertised in the back of the financial magazines can't tell you how much risk the money managers took over a specific period of time.

For example: Let's say Barbara and Walter Jones are a retired couple. They decided to invest equal distributions of $200,000 from their retirement fund. They both invested $100,000 of their assets with different investment management firms which they had read about in a nationally known magazine. After five years, both of their investments had an annualized return of 15%. In effect, they had both doubled their money. But why is Walter pleased and Barbara upset about the results? A look behind the advertised returns of the managers reveals important risk-related information. Comparing year-by-year, the figures reveal certain important information about each investment firm (see Table 5–1).

Table 5–1   Value of $100,000 with 15% Annualized Return

Year	Firm A Gain/Loss	Firm A Portfolio Value	Firm B Gain/Loss	Firm B Portfolio Value
1	+34%	$134,000	+26%	$126,000
2	+27%	$170,000	+18%	$149,000
3	+19%	$202,000	+14%	$170,000
4	+31%	$288,000	+25%	$213,000
5	−30%	$200,000	− 6%	$200,000

Chapter 5

The fund which Barbara invested with (A) increased her money almost threefold over the first four years, yet lost nearly one-third of the gain in the fifth year.

Had Barbara invested in (A) at the end of their fourth year, she would have lost a significant portion of her capital.

The annualized return is a cumulative gain over a period of time restated as a compound annual rate of return.

Manager (B), the firm Walter invested with, took less risk to achieve the same rate of return as Barbara. Walter was spared the acute anxiety that Barbara went through in the fifth year.

Management firm (B) was more conservative, it had more consistent returns and preserved capital more carefully. So how can you avoid what Barbara went through? How do you find out how much risk an investment manager took and how do you get reliable information on the top money managers—the ones who consistently outperformed their peers as well as the stock market? Hire an investment management consultant who specializes in selecting an independent manager. An investment consultant acts like a marriage broker, helping the investor seek an investment partner who will be the right money manager for the investor's personal style.

These investment consultants are narrow in focus, with no interest in selling insurance products, individual stocks, leasing products, or oil and gas programs. They screen investment managers across the country and across the investment disciplines in order to recommend managers who will match the client's financial goals. They not only monitor the money managers on an ongoing basis, but they also help you verify the amount of risk the manager is taking and will notify you when inside changes occur. This keeps the investor out of the dark and allows the investor to make decisions based on accurate information, not advertised information.

CHAPTER 6

THE WRAP ADVANTAGE: PUTTING A LID ON COSTS— CLARIFYING METHODS OF PAYMENT

WRAP FEE

The wrap fee puts a lid on costs. Say that you hired a money manager who buys a lot of low-priced stocks. The stocks move very rapidly and there is a lot of turnover. Your portfolio turns over 75-100% in a single year. That could generate 3%, 4%, or even 5% a year in brokerage commissions, not including the management fee.

But under the wrap fee arrangement, by paying a flat annual 2.5-3% fee for smaller accounts and even less for accounts over $1 million, including the money manager's fee, you have a placed an effective ceiling on your costs. It doesn't matter how many times the manager buys or sells, the maximum that the investor will pay is the agreed upon flat fee.

The use of a wrap fee account or wrap (all inclusive) consulting account puts a lid on expenses if you are comparing services to the variable expense of a traditional brokerage account.

Also, investors need to understand the value of the consulting process when determining what they are getting for their money.

49

So, when we talk about putting a lid on brokerage (commissions) we need to look at all the unbundled services that go with a wrap account and what each service would cost on it own. These services are asset allocation studies, development of investment policy, multiple-manager selections, and performance monitoring. All of these services, if they were priced out separately, could be very expensive (see Figure 6–1).

Wrap accounts eliminate these variable expense aspects. One hidden benefit in controlling costs is the elimination of the conflict of interest. This is the unfortunate situation that arises when an individual stockbroker is recommending the services of a money manager and the compensation to the broker is based on the activity of the account (commissions generated by trading).

If a stockbroker/consultant's sole compensation is coming from brokerage commissions alone, the investor might wonder whether there is overactivity in the account, or whether a manager switch was not made for all of the right reasons. These are tough questions that need to be answered if you are going to control costs. They are also valid reasons for having a wrap fee account, because costs in a wrap fee account is not determined by transaction activity.

The real heroes of controlling costs in the wrap fee business are the men and women who are in the operational side of the business. They are on the front lines day in and day out. They are the "back office" organizational and technical people who service the investor on an ongoing basis. They are part of the team concept that has to be in place for any organization to be successful in this business. It is a system where all the processes are totally interrelated and incorporated into a smoothly running system. In fact, "back office" is a poor choice of words to describe them. It is not a back office operation anymore—these people are strictly

Figure 6-1   Projection of Wrap Account Expense

Size of Account	$150,000	$250,000	$500,000	$1,000,000
1. Cash $	$10,000	$5,000	$10,000	$20,000
2. Stock $	$140,000	$245,000	$490,000	$980,000
3. Number of stock positions	35	35	35	35
4. Size of each position	$4,000	$7,000	$14,000	$28,000
5. Number & price of shares per position	200/$20	200/$35	400/$35	700/$40
6. Full retail stock commission	$113.00	$161.00	$275.00	$459.00
7. At a 50% turnover of stock position				
Number of positions sold	18	18	18	18
Number of positions bought	17	17	17	17
8. Total x commission in line 6 equals	$3,955	$5,635	$9,625	$16,065
9. Total commission at no discount	$3,955	$5,635	$9,625	$16,065
10. Full commission % of equity	2.64%	2.25%	1.95%	1.61%
11. Stated percent of equity discount	10%	10%	20%	30%
12. Discount commission as % of assets	2.37%	2.0%	1.54%	1.10%
13. Management fee	1.0%	1.0%	1.0%	1.0%
14. Total management fee & disc. commission	3.37%	3.0%	2.54%	2.17%
15. Effective discount rate	25%	10%	20%	40%

Source: New York Stock Exchange Schedule and Consulting Firm Sources

front line. An investor needs the assurance that a workable system is in place within the organization to which he is trusting his assets.

What is needed by the firms offering wrap fee accounts is a capital commitment, and you should ask for that number.

Capital commitment at the brokerage firm level is critical in the wrap business, and it is a huge number. It increases exponentially as each firm adds more employees and as it accumulates the most important thing—the assets of the individual investors. If a firm has not made a significant commitment of its own money to the operational side of its wrap program, it would be best to find one that has.

To be successful and control all aspects of costs, you have got to know as much as possible about each firm offering these programs. Have them demonstrate to you, the investor, that these systems are in place and operating.

HOW TO EVALUATE
YOUR CURRENT INVESTMENT PLAN

If you have a managed account at a bank or with a brokerage firm how does it compare to a wrap account? The only way to go about uncovering the total cost associated with a wrap fee is to isolate each individual expense item by item. Sum them up and figure the total as a percent of assets. On the next page you will find a checklist of items that may or may not apply to your situation (see Table 6–1). Some of the items listed may be hidden within your statements supplied by the reporting custodian institution. Be sure not to overlook too many. Next to each item place the approximate total per item and total annual cost in dollars.

Table 6-1   List of Expenses

	Wrap Account	Trailing 12 Months or Annual Charge
Trustee Fee Typical trustee fees are quoted as a percent of total assets. Ex: Usually between 0.1% to 0.6% annually.	N/C	
Sometimes you may see them quoted as a dollar figure per thousand dollars. Ex: Usually between $1 and $6 per $1,000.	N/C	
Usually a minimum annual fee is attached.	N/C	
Custodian Fee Typical custodial fees are quoted as a percent of total assets. Ex: Usually between 0.1% and 0.75% annually.	N/C	
Sometimes quotes may be represented as a dollar figure per thousand dollars. Ex: Usually between $1 and $7.50 per $1,000.	N/C	
Usually a minimum fee is attached.	N/C	
— **Transaction Charges**—		
These charges usually have a per item expense attached.	N/C	
Receipts/Disbursements Ex: Between $5 and $15 per contribution or withdrawal to fund.	N/C	
Purchase/Sale Ex: Between $5-$30 per trade.	N/C	
Income/Dividend Ex: Between $5-$25 to receive in dividend and/or interest income per transaction, sometimes will be a percentage fee based on income received.	N/C	
Transfer of Securities or Funds Ex: Between $10-$25 per transaction. Sometimes charges vary depending on types of assets transferred into or out of the fund.	N/C	

	Wrap Account	Trailing 12 Months or Annual Charge
Beneficiary Payments Ex: Between $2-$10 per check.	**N/C**	
— **Miscellaneous Fees**—		
Investment Outside Management Charges for using outside investment management Ex: Usually quoted as a fixed annual fee per year.	N/C	
Multiple Managers Additional charges for using multiple managers Ex: Fixed annual fee between $100-$500 per additional manager.	N/C	
Mark to the Market Charges to value portfolio mark to market. Many institutions don't have this capability. The usual charge for those who do is between $1 and $5 per security holding.	N/C	
Acceptance Start-Up Fee One-time charge to set up the account initially ranging from $100 to $500.	N/C	
Termination Fee Usually quoted as a percent of assets ranging from 0.1% to 0.25% including some minimum fixed fee between $100 and $500.	N/C	
Fees for Extraordinary Services A reasonable fee for special services not expressly provided or included as a normal service to the consulting process.	N/C	
Consultant Fee Not offered through banks, the fee is usually negotiated. Some consultants charge straight hard-dollar fees. Ex: $5,500 per fund or some dollar amount based upon time involved for their services.	N/C	

	Wrap Account	Trailing 12 Months or Annual Charge
Soft-Dollar Conversion Other consultants offer commission dollar arrangements; must convert these back to hard dollars by some appropriate multiplier.	N/C	
Performance Evaluation Usually lumped together with one of the above. Most banks do not offer this service at all. If a bank must purchase this service from a vendor, the cost is usually passed on. Often consultants and/or investment managers will provide performance evaluation as part of their service.	N/C	
Investment Manager's Fee Usually represents between 0.25% and 1.25% of total assets per year.	N/C	
Total Fees		
Average Total Market Value of Assets		
Fees as Percentage of Assets (Divide total fees by average total market value of assets.)		
Total Average Commissions ($) (figured at approximately 1% of total average assets per year on a typical account from $500,000 to $1,500,000)		
TOTAL FEES PLUS AVERAGE COMMISSIONS ($) (Add Total Fees & Total Average Commissions.)		
$ TOTAL FEES PLUS COMMISSIONS AS A % OF ASSETS (Divide total fees plus average commissions by average total market value of assets.)		

PART II

INVESTMENT FUNDAMENTALS

CHAPTER 7

UNDERSTAND RISK—
AND HOW TO SUCCESSFULLY REDUCE IT

An investor can reduce his or her financial risk by diversifying into securities of different companies within different industries. In this way events affecting one company or industry will have only a small impact on the overall portfolio.

MARKET RISK

Market risk is the risk that the securities you own will fluctuate because of changes in price levels. Most people associate market risk with the stock market only. Stock prices can move up or down regardless of the health of the particular companies. But other securities are also subject to market risk. Bonds will fluctuate according to changes in interest rates. Even bonds which are issued by the United States government and are considered the safest investment from the point of view of financial risk, will show volatility as current interest rates change. When current interest rates go up, the prices of existing bonds go down and when interest rates go down, bond prices will go up. Although at maturity, the bond will be paid in full and the interest the bond pays doesn't change, the bond will fluctuate in value over the course of its life. This has proven out dramatically over the last ten years.

You can reduce market risk by investing in shorter term or fixed-principal securities, such as treasury bills, insured certificates of deposits, money market mutual funds or fixed annuities. But because of their low volatility, these securities tend to provide the lowest returns.

REINVESTMENT RISK

Reinvestment risk is the risk that the interest rate you receive today will not be available when your investment matures and has to be renewed. Most of you are familiar with renewing a bank's high interest rate certificate of deposit only to find that the interest rate at renewal is several percentage points less than you received initially.

As we have seen in the past, bank CDs made at higher rates have been reinvested at lower rates. This can come as a dramatic shock if your future retirement income is solely dependent on current short-term rates. Many investors make the mistake of seeking the comfort of stable, non- fluctuating, short-term investments, overlooking the fact that the interest rates of these investments tend to be the lowest of all rates over time.

Types of securities subject to reinvestment risk are short-term securities of all kinds (treasury bills, certificates of deposits, money market funds). You can reduce investment risk by making longer-term investments.

LIQUIDITY RISK

Liquidity risk occurs when you need your money and may not be able to receive it except after paying penalties or accepting a reduced market price. Liquidity is important if you need your money for retirement income or perhaps for an emergency. Examples of liquidity risk are the penalties that you will incur if you take money out of a certificate of deposit before maturity, or redeem an annuity or other investment which is subject to a back-out fee (some annuity back-out fees can be as high as 10%).

Liquidity risk is reduced by investing in mutual funds and publicly traded securities which have a large market. Mutual funds are required by law to redeem your shares at the current net asset value on the day the fund receives your redemption request. Consequently, they are considered liquid investments. However, some funds may have back-out fees if you have owned the fund for only a few years.

INFLATION

The risk of inflation might be the most important risk that an individual will face using a lump sum to provide him or herself with a retirement income.

Inflation has become an inherent trait of a progressive and dynamic American economy. In the early '90s inflation is running below 5% a year, and we tend to tolerate this as an acceptable level of modern growth. However, this level is far higher than it was during other periods of economic growth in our society. From 1952 to 1967 inflation averaged only 1.5% a year. Over that same time period, the purchasing power of the dollar declined by 63%. That's 5% per year. This is extremely important when you consider that your investment will have to provide you with income for many years during your retirement.

Today, people are retiring earlier and living longer. Life expectancies of people retiring in the '90s are still going up. It's not unlikely that your investments will have to provide you with income for 20 or more years after you retire. To stay even with a 5% annual inflation rate, your investments must increase by at least that amount every year. And they must increase by even more than that to provide you with growing real income.

To combat the risk of inflation, you must have an investment program which has the potential of providing you with growing income and capital in the future. Unless your investments can continue to grow in the future, you run the risk of receiving income with reduced purchasing power, requiring you to significantly alter your life-style in future years.

HOW TO REDUCE RISK

Regardless of your personal objectives, there are certain principles for investing large sums of money that have withstood the test of time and have served to reduce risk no matter what types of investments you select.

Wrap Accounts Can Reduce Risk

Our modern economy is subject to fast-moving changes, whether from foreign competition, interest rates, trade and budget deficits, or economic expansion and contraction. Successful investing is a full-time job and not suitable for part-time attention.

If you think back over just the past few years you can see the tremendous changes that have affected securities markets and investments. A company as stable as AT&T has been broken up into eight separate companies and is now subject to severe competition. IBM, one of the rocks of the computer industry, is now subject to competition from a host of companies that didn't even exist 10 years ago. Entire new industries have come into being; genetic engineering, personal computers, fast food, cable television, and waste management, to name just a few. The takeover phenomenon has restructured companies and has changed the face of American industry. The pace of change is rapid and requires investors to make first-move decisions based on complex and uncertain factors. It is for this reason that most investors seek professional management when they are investing their serious money.

Still there is no single wrap account program that is right for all people. Each person has his own needs for present or future income and his own concern about how much risk he can assume.

Diversification of Investments

Diversification is a way of reducing investment risk in your wrap fee account. By putting your money in a variety of investments, the overall performance should be less volatile than if you put all your money in one type of investment such as a single stock or bond.

Diversification offers this type of benefit because each kind of investment follows a cycle all its own. Each asset responds differently to changes in the economy or the investment marketplace. If you own a variety of assets, a short-term decline in one can be balanced by others which are stable or going up.

Chapter 7

For example, not all investments act the same. The stock markets may go up one year and down the next, but the bond market may remain unchanged. In this case, investors who owned both shares of a stock fund and shares of a bond fund would be better off than those who had limited themselves to just stocks.

Diversified versus Single Assets

The higher volatility of stocks and bonds compared with money market funds means higher risk. Suppose all your money was invested in stocks and you needed to sell some of your holdings for an emergency. If stocks were depressed when you needed to sell, you could be forced to take a loss on your investment. Owning other investments would give you more flexibility in raising the needed cash while allowing you to hold your stocks until prices improved.

While money market funds provide liquidity and low risk, their overall return is much less than the return from the diversified portfolio. That is a high price to pay for stability. The diversified portfolio provides both liquidity and comparative stability.

Over the long run, owning a wide variety of investments is the best strategy for the wrap fee investor, because most participants hope their investments will meet a number of different goals. Money market funds can provide a foundation of stability and liquidity that is ideal for cash reserve. Bonds are good for steady high income. Stocks have the greatest potential for superior long-term returns. Diversification can reduce but not totally eliminate risk.

There are two types of diversification; diversification among differnt companies and diversification among different types of securities.

1. Investing in a portfolio which contains securities of different companies in different industries will help an investor avoid the risks that are present in investing only in the securities of one or more company in a single industry. The economy and the financial markets are ever changing, and spreading your investment among different companies in more than one industry can significantly reduce the risk of unpleasant surprises.

2. The other type of diversification involves spreading one's investment over different types of securities, such as bonds, stocks, and short-term investments. Each of these securities bear different risks and will fluctuate diversely over time. Selecting different types of investments will help to reduce the risks that are present when a portfolio contains only one type of security (see Figure 7-1).

UNDERSTANDING RISK

The decisions you make before you place your assets with a wrap fee manager actually may have the greatest impact on the long-term performance of your portfolio. Looking more closely at time and its influence on your investment activities will help explain the importance of your early decisions.

Investments contain two broad categories of risk: investment risk and emotional risk. Together, these two types of risk are the driving force behind your investment decision-making process.

Investment Risk
The principles of financial risk are probably best understood by examining past market results of different types of assets.

Figure 7–1   Single Investment of $10,000 at 8% Return over 25 Years

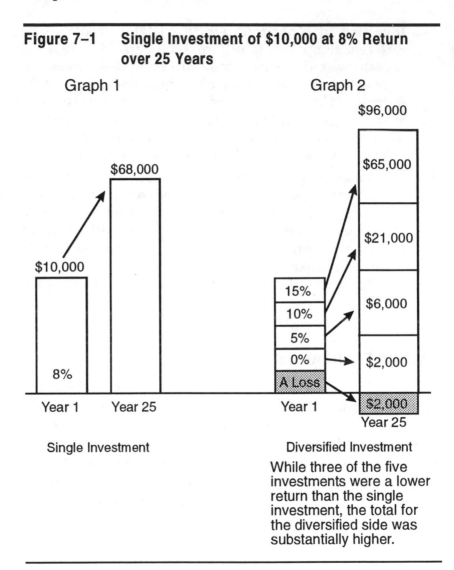

Graph 1

Graph 2

$96,000

$68,000

$65,000

$10,000

$21,000

15%

$6,000

10%

5%

0% $2,000

8%   A Loss

$2,000

Year 1   Year 25   Year 1   Year 25

Single Investment   Diversified Investment

While three of the five investments were a lower return than the single investment, the total for the diversified side was substantially higher.

Emotional Risk

Emotional risk is an intangible and sometimes costly form of risk. Investors who misjudge their ability to handle uncertainty often find themselves running out of patience with their investments at the worst possible times—at the top of bull markets and at the bottom of bear markets. For example, in bull markets the emotional element sometimes causes investors to increase their holdings in stocks by selling the "underperforming" fixed income portion of their portfolio, only to become overexposed in expensive stocks at market highs.

These same investors often do just the opposite in bear markets. They liquidate stocks which have declined in value precipitously and buy fixed income securities at market lows. Then, when the stock market recovers, they are no longer positioned to take advantage of it. How many people were selling stock as the market plunged during months leading up to the war in the Persian Gulf? Those who sold were acting on impulse, thinking that the stock market would continue to fall forever.

The ability to maintain your patience during difficult times requires more than just an understanding of the markets, it also requires an understanding of your own reactions to uncertainty. Only then can you arrive at a working balance between the desire to achieve the highest return and to preserve your capital.

ENSURE SUCCESS— LENGTHEN YOUR TIME HORIZONS

How do most investors define their investment objectives? The common response most investors give when asked to define their investment objectives is, "I want the highest possible return with the lowest possible risk." Well, it just may be easier than you think.

The following section looks at realistic time-conscious guidelines which will help an investor in the selection of a wrap fee investment manager.

The first stage involves taking an objective look at long-term goals, from both a financial and an emotional perspective. The investor's objective should be to balance the amount of risk he or she can afford in order to achieve the highest financial gain.

By adding the element of time to any investment plan, a new paradigm emerges. Study the charts in Figure 7–2 showing the correlation of risk over time and the effects on a portfolio over time.

Do you see a pattern developing? The secret to successful investing is the addition of time to your investment strategy.

Once you understand that lengthening your time horizons will ensure success, you are ready to step off the emotional roller coaster that most investors find themselves aboard.

UNDERSTANDING MODERN PORTFOLIO THEORY

By including assets that have low correlation with assets already in your portfolio, you will successfully diversify. As an example, real estate has a low or negative correlation with stocks and bonds. The stock market is affected negatively by rising interest rates. In the late 1970s when interest rates and real estate moved in locked steps, the stock market was flat.

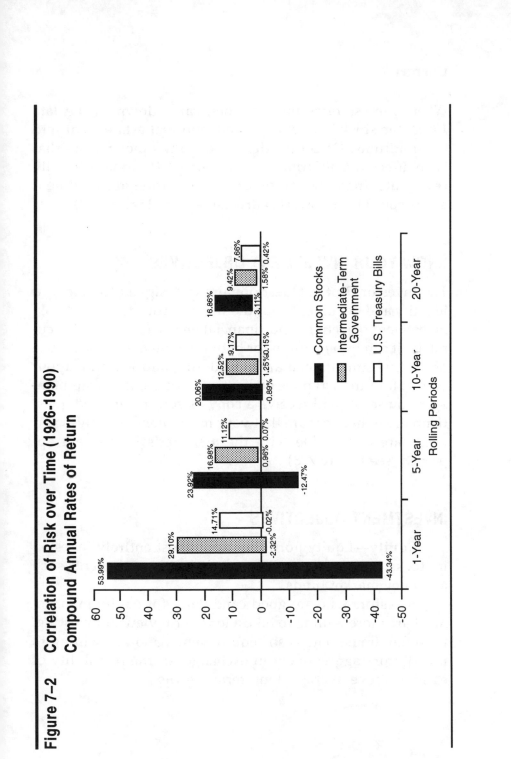

Figure 7-2   Correlation of Risk over Time (1926-1990)
Compound Annual Rates of Return

When interest rates peaked, then came down in the late 1980s, the stock market exploded, and real estate went into the doldrums. Of course there are many other factors that have affected California. But if your portfolio is primarily real estate, then owning other U.S. and foreign investment assets could be a powerful diversifier (see Figure 7–2).

KNOW YOUR INVESTMENT OBJECTIVES

The Investor Profile Questionnaire is designed to help you identify and document your distinctive attitude toward risk, investment objectives and financial needs. Completed accurately, it can be a medium for both learning about the nature of the investments you are considering and learning about yourself. In the wrap fee consulting process, the wrap manager you select will receive a copy of your completed questionnaire to help ensure that your investment objectives and needs are compatible with the manager's investment approach (see Figure 7–3).

INVESTMENT OBJECTIVES

Equity—Equity portfolios are almost entirely invested in stocks, with excess cash invested in cash-equivalents such as money market funds.

Investors who are good candidates for equity management are more willing to take a long-term view of investing, have few immediate cash requirements, and are willing to invest more aggressively in exchange for the possibility of earning above-average, long-term returns.

Figure 7–3   Investment Objective, Guideline and Restriction Questionnaire for Establishing a Written Investment Policy

INDIVIDUAL ASSETS
Including Personal Accounts, IRAs & Rollovers and Personal Trusts

The setting of investment objectives for individual pools of assets is extremely important. However, it has traditionally been greatly complicated by misunderstandings due to differences of definition and interpretation.

The answers to the following questions will assist in establishing mutually agreeable goals and, at the same time, establish a framework for communications and mutual understanding in a client/investment manager relationship.

ECONOMY

1. How do you feel about the short-term outlook for the U.S. economy (12-24 months)?

    a. __x__ I feel the outlook is good.
    b. _____ I'm neutral; there are opportunities and problems.
    c. _____ I'm quite concerned; the outlook is poor.

2. How do you feel about the inflation outlook over the long-term (5-10 years)?

    a. _____ It will be a problem for a long time and may get worse.
    b. __x__ The rate of inflation will probably remain at about current levels.
    c. _____ Inflation is only a temporary problem; the rate will back down.

3. How would you describe your outlook on the U.S. economy over the next five years?

    a. __x__ Positive
    b. _____ Negative
    c. _____ Undecided

ASSET ALLOCATION/DIVERSIFICATION

4. Do you think common stocks are a good inflation hedge?

    a. __x__ Yes
    b. _____ No

5. How do you feel about investing in common stocks in general?

    a. _____ I feel stocks are very attractive and should occupy a dominant role in a portfolio.
    b. __x__ Common stocks should have a place in an investment portfolio.
    c. _____ I have no opinion.
    d. _____ I feel stocks are relatively risky and their use should be limited.
    e. _____ I feel stocks should be used very sparingly, if at all.

INSTITUTE FOR INVESTMENT MANAGEMENT CONSULTANTS © 1989   (Individuals) 1

Figure 7-3 Investment Objective, Guideline and Restriction Questionnaire for Establishing a Written Investment Policy

6. Do you believe that a portfolio should include bonds if it is to be adequately diversified?

   a. __x__ Yes
   b. _____ No

7. Do you think that the stock market is currently offering enough potential over the next year to compensate for the increased risk versus the bond market?

   a. __x__ Yes
   b. _____ No

8. What is your attitude about owning stocks and bonds relative to cash at various points in a market cycle?

   a. _____ I believe stocks are always a good investment vehicle in any market phase.
   OR
   b. __x__ I believe the economic and market outlook should be evaluated first and the percentage in stocks should reflect that outlook.

   a. _____ I believe bonds are always a good investment regardless of the outlook for bond prices.
   OR
   b. __x__ I think the economic and market outlook should be considered in making bond investments and the percentage in bonds should vary with this outlook.

9. Do you have a predisposition regarding how a portfolio should be balanced among stocks, bonds, other fixed income items and cash in light of your ongoing objectives?

   a. __x__ I have no predetermined preferences regarding the proportions of stocks, bonds, other fixed income items and/or cash equivalents.
   b. _____ I have preferences for the mix of assets. However, these preferences need not be rigidly observed.
   c. _____ I have preferences for the mix of assets. These preferences are to be rigidly observed.

10. In a bull market, your preferred maximum equity exposure would be _80_ %, and your preferred minimum cash exposure would be _10_ %.

11. Do you require a portion of your assets to be in cash at all times?

   a. _____ Yes What percent? ____%
   b. __x__ No

INSTITUTE FOR INVESTMENT MANAGEMENT CONSULTANTS © 1989 (Individuals) 2

Figure 7–3   Investment Objective, Guideline and Restriction Questionnaire for Establishing a Written Investment Policy

12. What diversification pattern should your equity portfolio take?

   a. _____ The equity portion of the portfolio should have in excess of 30 positions.
   b. __x__ The equity portion of the portfolio should have 20-30 positions.
   c. _____ The equity portion of the portfolio should have 10-20 positions.

INVESTMENT PHILOSOPHY

13. For each group, indicate the attitude most closely resembling your own expectations regarding the policies of the investment counselor.

   a. _____ Invest in establish companies.
   OR
   b. _____ Invest in new companies which are considered to have good growth potential.
   OR
   c. __x__ Both a. and b.

   a. __x__ Generally sells individual stocks when the stock price is higher than the financial value when compared to other companies.
   OR
   b. _____ Exercises a high degree of timing judgement, selling stocks when technical market factors indicate (market timer).

14. How would you generally categorize your investment objectives? (choose one)

   a. __x__ **Growth** - maximum growth of capital with little or no income considerations.
   b. _____ **Growth with Income** - primary emphasis on capital growth with some focus on income.
   c. _____ **Balanced** - a balanced portfolio with equal emphasis on capital growth and income.
   d. _____ **Income Oriented** - income as a primary emphasis.
   e. _____ Other. Please describe.

15. Investment "risk" can be defined in different ways. Please indicate below (in order) the three items that best describe how you tend to view risk.

   a. __3__ The possibility of not achieving an established target rate of return.
   b. __1__ Long-term erosion of capital.
   c. __2__ High degree of fluctuation in the value of the portfolio over a full market cycle.
   d. _____ The chance of a great loss in the value of an individual security regardless of how well the overall portfolio might perform.
   e. _____ Other. Please specify.

Figure 7–3   Investment Objective, Guideline and Restriction Questionnaire for Establishing a Written Investment Policy

16. The investment process requires various trade-offs in the quest for superior results. Quantifying what trade-offs an investor is willing to accept in order to achieve a superior total return constitutes an ongoing challenge. In evaluating your own attitudes, please check one item for each where you feel **most uncomfortable**.

    a. _____ Holding large cash reserves during a strong market environment.
    OR
    b. __x__ Being fully-invested during a weak market environment.

    a. _____ Selling an investment and seeing it immediately rise.
    OR
    b. __x__ Buying an investment and watching it immediately decline.

    a. _____ Holding a relatively fully-invested portfolio throughout all market cycles.
    OR
    b. __x__ Attempting to anticipate and take advantage of market swings.

17. An increase in capital return is usually associated with an increase in the acceptable level of fluctuation of the portfolio value market cycle to market cycle. Would you be willing to accept a wider possible range of fluctuation in an attempt to achieve a higher return?

    a. __x__ Yes
    b. _____ No

18. While total investment return is a necessary consideration for most clients, the way in which results are achieved may also be important. In this regard, the degree of portfolio value fluctuation may be a consideration (fluctuation is the up/down movement of the values of the account). Portfolios constructed to achieve the greatest long-run results also possess the highest degree of fluctuation. Within the context of your objectives, what level of fluctuation could you tolerate during any given year?

    a. _____ Much greater fluctuation than the market.
    b. __x__ Slightly more fluctuation than the market.
    c. _____ Approximately the same fluctuation as the market.
    d. _____ Slightly less fluctuation than the market.
    e. _____ Much less fluctuation than the market.

Figure 7–3   Investment Objective, Guideline and Restriction Questionnaire for Establishing a Written Investment Policy

INCOME RETURN EXPECTATIONS

19. Total return on the entire portfolio is made up of income return (i.e., dividends and interest received) and capital appreciation. As a general rule, the higher the income expectation, the lower the capital return expectations. Do you have any absolute requirements for income returns?

    a. __x__ No
    b. _____ Yes. Please indicate the appropriate income yield range you expect the total portfolio to generate.
         _____ 8-12%
         _____ 4-8%
         _____ 2-4%
    c. _____ Other. Please specify annual dollar amount _____.

20. Do you see a need for growth in income within the next five years?

    a. _____ Yes
    b. __x__ No

21. One guide to the type of stock that might be applicable to the portfolio is the dividend yield. The higher the anticipated growth or capital appreciation, the higher the volatility and the smaller the yield. What total dividend yield do you feel is desired from the stocks in the portfolio?

    a. __x__ None. I feel capital appreciation is more desireable.
    b. _____ I would like all stocks to yield an average of 0-4%.
    c. _____ I would like all stocks to yield an average of 4-6%.
    d. _____ I would like all stocks to yield an average of 6-8%.
    e. _____ I would like all stocks to yield an average over 8%.

22. Bond interest rates generally vary inversely with the quality of the bond. What bond quality do you feel is appropriate for the portfolio?

    a. _____ All AAA rated - highest possible.
    b. _____ None lower than AA.
    c. __x__ None lower than A.
    d. _____ None lower than BAA.
    e. _____ Speculative bonds for high return and capital gains.

Chapter 7

Figure 7–3 Investment Objective, Guideline and Restriction Questionnaire for Establishing a Written Investment Policy

23. What average, annual target rate of return (as opposed to a "relative" return to a market index) do you consider to be the investment objective for the "total return" of the fund, on a long-term basis? In general, the higher the goal, the greater the risk the manager must take. The average total return for the past 50 years has been 9.2% for stocks and 4.1% for corporate bonds.

    Total
    - __x__ over 12% per year
    - _____ 10-12% per year
    - _____ 8-10% per year
    - _____ below 8% per year
    - _____ exceeds inflation (CPI) by ___%

MEASUREMENT

24. The primary emphasis in examining the investment performance for the account should be on:

    a. _____ "Absolute" comparison. That is, comparing the actual account returns to an absolute (target) rate of return.

    b. _____ "Relative" comparison. That is, comparing the actual account returns to various market indices

    c. _____ Comparing to a "real" return. i.e., exceeds the inflation factor by x%

    d. __x__ Using "target" and "relative" rate of return measurements

    e. _____ I have no real preferences

25. The time period used in evaluating an investment medium has a significant impact on the probability of realizing a stated return objective. The longer the period used, the better the chance that up and down market cycles will average out to some "normal" or "expected" return. What investment time horizon seems most appropriate for the account?

    a. _____ Ten years or more
    b. _____ Five years
    c. __x__ Three years
    d. _____ One year
    e. _____ A complete market cycle (3-5 years)
    f. _____ I do not know

26. Relative to popular stock market indices (S&P 500), rank your preference for equity performances 1 through 4:

    a. _____ Generally beat the market index in each UP market year
    b. _____ Generally beat the market index in each DOWN market year
    c. __x__ Surpass the market index, on average, over an extended period of time (without regard to each individual year)
    d. _____ Do as well as the market over an extended period of time
    e. _____ I consider performance relative to a market index to be irrelevant. I prefer to specify our objective in other way.

INSTITUTE FOR INVESTMENT MANAGEMENT CONSULTANTS © 1989   (Individuals) 6

Figure 7–3   Investment Objective, Guideline and Restriction Questionnaire for Establishing a Written Investment Policy

27. What time periods would be preferred for performance reporting and analysis of the investment advisor(s) and the portfolio?

Reports		**Evaluation Meetings**	
____	Annually	____	Annually
_x_	Semi-annually	_x_	Semi-annually
____	Quarterly	____	Quarterly
____	When deemed necessary	____	When deemed necessary

COMMUNICATION

28. What regularity of direct contact with your investment advisor is preferred?

Meetings		**Phone or Letter**	
_x_	Annually	____	Annually
____	Semi-annually	____	Semi-annually
____	Quarterly	____	Quarterly
____	When deemed necessary	_x_	When deemed necessary

Figure 7–3   (Continued)
Investment Objective, Guideline and Restriction Questionnaire
for Establishing a Written Investment Policy

Client Name _____ John Q. Public, Jr. _____

Address _____ 9999 E. Penney Lane   Cashmore, IL 60601 _____

Mailing Address _____
(if other than above)

Work Phone _ 312/555-4967 _____   Home Phone __ 312/555-2851 ____

Social Security No. ___ 123-00-9476 ____   Date of Birth ___ 12-23-41 ____

Employer's Name ___ Acme, Corporation _____

Years Employed _____ 19 _____   Years Until Retirement ___ 16 ____

Estimated Annual Income ___ $100,000 _____

Spouse's Name ___ Betty _____

Spouse's Soc. Security No. ___ 123-01-8572 ___   Spouse's Date of Birth _ 09-21-43 _

Spouse's Employer ___ housewife _____

Spouse's Estimated Annual Income ____ n/a _____

Bank Name and Address __ First National Bank - Chicago, IL ____

Tax Bracket ___ 28% _____

Est. Liquid Net Worth ___ $175,000 ___   Est. Total Net Worth ___ $500,000 ____

Current Portfolio Value ___ $100,000 _____

Do you currently have a retirement plan? ___ x __ No _____ Yes

If yes, please specify. _____

Do the assets to be placed under management constitute your entire portfolio?

___ x __ Yes _____ No _____ % of the portfolio

Comments

_____
_____
_____

This questionnaire was developed by the educational committee of the Institute for Investment Management Consultants for the specific use of its members and qualified consultants. Acknowledgements for contributions of material and/or time goes to:

Daniel R. Bott, CIMC
Gilbert S. Meem, Jr., CIMC
Ira E. Smolowitz, PhD.
Ephraim Ulmer, J.D.
W. Roberts Wood, CFA

John R. Gepfert, CIMC
James A. Pupillo, CIMC
Timothy J. Tigges
John A. Vann, CIMC

INSTITUTE FOR INVESTMENT MANAGEMENT CONSULTANTS © 1989   (Individuals) 8

Equity managers are relatively aggressive in their investing and generally seek long-term capital appreciation using a variety of equity investment approaches. Historically, equity managers have exhibited higher variability of returns (risk), but also have achieved higher returns over the long term relative to fixed-income or balanced portfolios.

Consider the differences between just two common equity approaches: growth and value. Growth managers focus on companies exhibiting superior earnings growth relative to the market in general, whereas value managers concentrate on whether a company's stock is undervalued relative to traditional financial characteristics, such as price-to-earnings and price-to-book ratios. Just as the stock market may be up when the bond market is down, growth managers tend to perform well when value managers are slumping and vice versa. Sometimes this divergence occurs over several consecutive years. Because such diversity exists among equity approaches it is essential to understand an equity manager's approach before investing.

Fixed-Income—Fixed-income portfolios in the wrap fee account programs are generally comprised of high-quality fixed income securities, such as U.S. government issues and/or investment-grade corporate bonds. Excess cash may be invested in cash equivalents such as money market funds.

Investors who are good candidates for fixed income management are generally long-term, risk-averse, and mainly interested in capital preservation, consistency of earnings, and regular cash flow.

Managers in this asset class have historically demonstrated lower variability of returns. Due to the lower risk, however, pure fixed-income portfolios have generally produced lower returns relative to equity or balanced portfolios.

Chapter 7

Balanced—Balanced portfolios are comprised of a mixture of equity and fixed income securities, thus creating a more balanced risk/return environment. The mixture of equity and fixed income in a balanced portfolio is generally expressed in terms of a target asset mix, with the understanding that the actual mix will naturally fluctuate around the target. A common target asset mix is 60/40, or a mix that fluctuates around 60% equity and 40% fixed income. Depending on market conditions and the investment approach employed, a variety of mixes, 50/50, 70/30, etc., may be used.

Investors who are good candidates for balanced management are relatively conservative, but also are willing to assume a moderate level of risk in order to achieve the potential for moderately higher returns.

Balanced managers allocate the portfolio's assets among stocks, fixed-income securities, and cash-equivalents, and emphasize both income generation and capital appreciation. Interest payments and equity dividends generate most of the income, while the potential for capital appreciation is sought through long-term fixed income and equity holdings. Balanced portfolios have historically earned higher returns than pure fixed income investments.

Making the Right Choice
Suppose your questionnaire indicates that you should consider an equity approach, but you know that in five years you will need to make sizeable withdrawals to help pay for your child's college tuition. If this were the case, you may select a balanced program, at least until your cash needs are no longer significant.

Having a trained investment management consultant evaluate your questionnaire and your investment objectives before you make your wrap fee manager decision can be invaluable (see Figures 7–2 and 7–3).

CHAPTER 8

THE HISTORY OF INVESTMENT RETURNS

The history of returns on investment, as documented in study after study, shows three basic characteristics:

- Common stocks have average returns higher than bonds, which in turn have higher returns than short-term money market instruments (see Figure 8–1)

- The daily, monthly, and yearly fluctuations in actual returns on common stocks exceed the fluctuations in returns on bonds, which in turn exceed the fluctuations on short-term money market instruments (see Figure 8–2)

- The magnitude of the period-to-period fluctuations in rate of return increases as the measurement period is shortened and decreases as the measurement period is lengthened. In other words, rates of return appear more normal over long periods of time (see Figure 8–3).

The really impressive characteristic of investment returns is that the variation in year-to-year rates of return on common stocks dwarfs the average annual rate of return on stocks.

We now know that it is nonsense to say, "Common stocks have produced an average rate of return of 10%." This is an incomplete and misleading statement (see Figure 8–4).

Figure 8–1   The Best Source of Total Return Asset Returns Since 1926

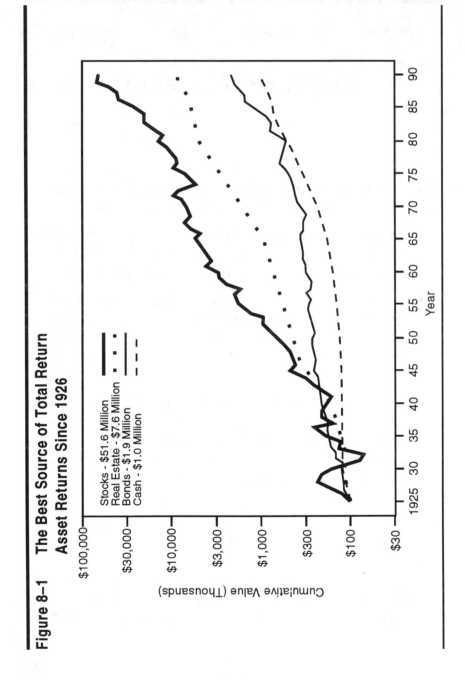

Figure 8–2 The Importance of Time
Stocks Are Considerably More Volatile

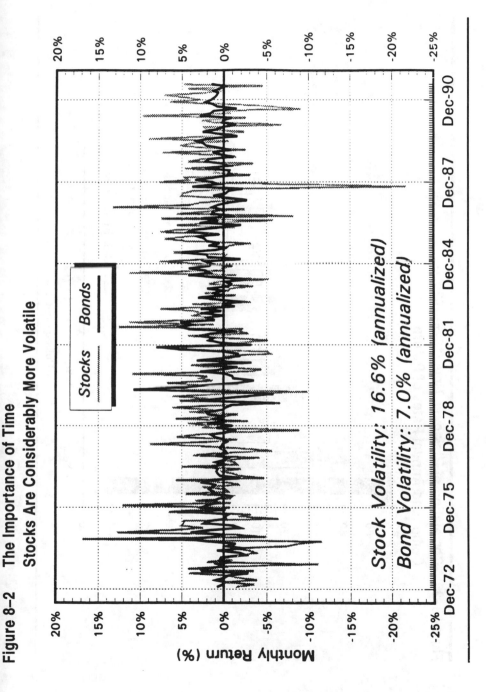

Stock Volatility: 16.6% (annualized)
Bond Volatility: 7.0% (annualized)

**Figure 8–3 Correlation of Risk over Time (1926–1990)
Compound Annual Rates of Return**

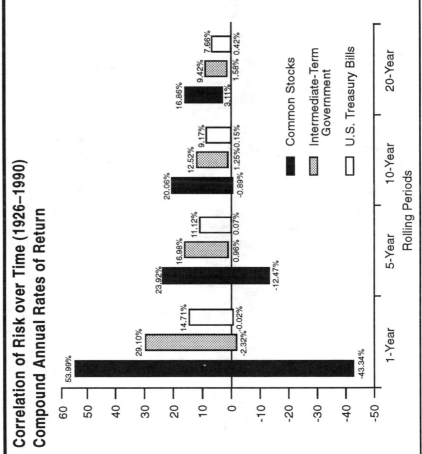

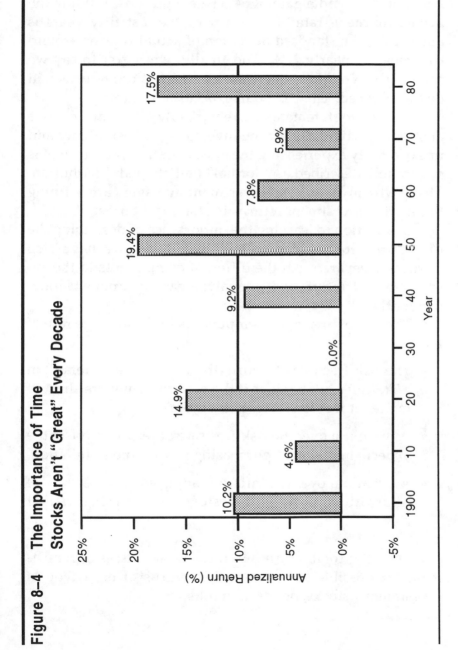

**Figure 8–4 The Importance of Time
Stocks Aren't "Great" Every Decade**

a loss of 43%, and a gain of 54% (see Figure 8–3). While the geometric mean rate of return over the last fifty years is about 10%, the standard deviation of actual returns around that mean is nearly 22%. And finally, we regret to say we cannot give you the sequence with which those returns will be experienced. They, of course, occur at random.

These two statements are remarkably different from one another—particularly for the investor who is suddenly and unexpectedly experiencing the most negative year in what is so serenely described as "normal" bell-shaped distribution. That's why investors and investment managers are learning to describe investment returns in statistical terms.

In addition to learning the importance of describing the distribution of returns around that mean, we have also learned to separate out the different components in the average rate of return and to analyze each component independently.

There are three main components in the average rate of return:

- The risk-free rate of return (there is no risk of default in a Treasury bill because if the government were short of money it would simply print more)

- A premium over the risk-free rate of return to offset the expected erosion of purchasing power due to inflation

- A premium over the inflation-adjusted risk-free rate of return to compensate investors for accepting market risk.

Dividing total return into these three classes of returns makes it possible to compare the returns of each type of investment—stocks, bonds, and bills.

Treasury bills appear quite safe and reliable—in nominal terms, not adjusted for inflation—with positive returns in 5 to 54 years. However, when adjusted for inflation, returns are positive just less than 60 percent of the time: Even more impressive, the average annual rate of return on bills, after adjusting for inflation, is zero.

In other words, Treasury bills are usually no more than a haven from inflation. Most of the time, you do get your money back—with its purchasing power still intact. But that is all you get. There is virtually no real return on your money, just the return of your money.

STANDARDS FOR REPORTING PERFORMANCE

Historically, there have been no mandated standards for reporting performance results for individually managed investment accounts. There are, however, three general methods used by investment advisors for reporting performance results to clients with individually managed accounts:

Gross Performance rates of return are calculated prior to deduction of any fees or costs associated with the management of the portfolio.

Net Performance rates of return are calculated after the deduction of transaction commissions, if any, but prior to the deduction of asset-based fees such as investment advisory and fees in lieu of commissions, if any.

Net-Net Performance rates of return are calculated after the deduction of ALL fees and commissions associated with the management of the client's portfolio.

Most investment advisors report performance results on either a gross or net basis, with the latter being predominant. Very few advisors are currently reporting rates of return to clients on a net-net basis.

Net reporting has been most widely used because it is preferred by institutional clients. Traditionally, institutional clients have paid for the services they receive in two ways:

1. A management fee paid to the investment advisor for portfolio management services based on a fixed percentage of the assets being managed, plus,

2. Commission charges paid to broker-dealers for the securities transactions that occur in their accounts.

This is referred to as "fee plus commission" pricing. Institutions have generally preferred having performance reported after the deduction of transaction-based commissions, but prior to the deduction of the investment advisor's management fee. Institutions prefer to compare their performance results before fees, as these fees may vary from one institutional account to another. Consequently, performance reporting systems were developed to accommodate this preference.

Gradually, as more individual investors entered this market, an alternative pricing mechanism was introduced—the "wrap fee." Wrap fee pricing enables the client to pay a single asset-based fee for the service provided by his broker-dealer (transaction execution, custody of securities, initial consultation, ongoing monitoring and advice, etc.), which is combined with the investment manager's fee for portfolio management services. This type of pricing is also referred to as "fee plus fee."

Since wrap fee clients do not pay for transaction commissions as trades are executed, the net reporting system relays results to these clients on a gross basis.

Fee plus commission clients, on the other hand, had their performance results presented on a true net basis (after the deduction of transaction commissions, which were paid as trades occurred, but prior to the deduction of the investment advisor's management fee). This difference in reporting performance rates of return to clients, depends on how clients were paying for the variety of services they received.

PART III

SELECTING A
WRAP MANAGER

CHAPTER 9

PICKING THE RIGHT WRAP FEE MANAGER

Selecting the right investment manager to meet your investment goals is said to be an art not a science. There is a group of investment professionals who decided to specialize in finding managers. These professionals are called Investment Management Consultants and they are dedicated to helping both individuals and institutions in the selection of money managers whose investment philosophy, organization, and performance are consistent with specific investment needs.

Most are highly trained, and the rest will say they are. We will discuss this in greater detail later. What this group of professionals do and how it relates to wrap programs is described in the following list of their ongoing services:

1. Assistance in setting investment parameters and performance goals.
2. Guidance in selecting the right money manager or managers to meet the client's specific investment needs, out of the more than 11,000 available today.
3. Continuing consultation, as needed.

This is what an Investment Management Consultant does. How it is done and exactly *who* does it, is what the balance of this book is about.

Chapter 9

SELECTING A WRAP FEE ACCOUNT
USING AN INVESTMENT MANAGEMENT CONSULTANT

Since it is the consultant's job to select the appropriate money manager, some serious thought must be given to the qualifications of the individuals who make this decision.

Aside from the obvious "track record" type of information, the investor/client will want to know the number of money managers with whom the consultant's firm is working. In this case, the higher number is not necessarily the better one. In the course of working with a limited number of money managers, the consultant is in a better position to maintain a higher degree of quality evaluation and service. It is the consultant's objective to identify the strengths and the weaknesses of the money manager's performance. This involves close examination and an ongoing relationship that is relatively close, as opposed to casual or infrequent contact.

The actual selection process (see Figure 9–1) includes:

1. Determining the client's objectives.
2. Assisting in the development of a preliminary list of potential money managers.
3. Assisting in the evaluation and final selection of a money manager.

Thereafter, the consultant carefully monitors both the portfolio and the performance of the management firm advising the client. It is imperative that this critical function be performed by an objective third party in order to ensure that the client's long-range goals will be effectively achieved.

Once an investor has established the need for a money manager, he or she will receive assistance from the consultant in all of the following areas:

1. Establishing realistic investment objectives and implementing a plan that assures the realization of those objec-

Figure 9–1   Selecting a Wrap Manager

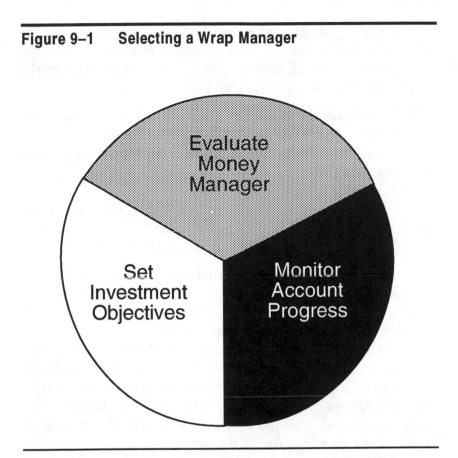

tives. All books on the subject of investing agree that you must have a plan. But they never tell you how to develop the plan—only that you must have one. The best way to develop a plan is to have access to viable information and to have someone on the other side of that information who can properly interpret it. Here we have one of the strongest arguments for seeking out a consultant, someone who will help you define investment objectives and institute a goal-setting process that will result in the most lucrative investment policy.

Chapter 9

A major part of achieving one's financial objectives requires an understanding of risk-adjusted returns. It is not uncommon to meet with a client and to have the initial conversation go something like this:

Consultant: "Now then, Mr. Jones, how may I help you?"
Client: "That's easy! By making me a lot of money."
Consultant: "How much would you hope to realize on your investment?"
Client: "Double."
Consultant: "And what amount of risk are you willing to take in order to realize such a return?"
Client: "I don't want to take any risk."

In the face of such an unrealistic objective, it is necessary to structure a plan that comes as close to meeting the client's objectives as possible, even as it introduces him to a more realistic means of achieving these ends.

The statement involving the desire to earn a lot of money is certainly understandable, as is the statement concerning a desire to take no risk. But once these two thoughts have been combined, they create a concept that is totally unworkable. At this juncture, it is the investment management consultant's job to take this unrealistic response and dissect it, in order that it may be reduced to reality.

Reality is not always an easy thing for the investor to hold onto, particularly in situations where he permits some past occurrence or future projection to affect his immediate judgment. Here again we have a legitimate need for a consultant who will not allow the investor's own biases to affect his business judgment.

2. Developing a reasoned perspective on the overall market outlook. The investor must not be permitted to believe that the market will always improve. Market fluctuations and their inherent risks are a fact of life.

3. Establishing a balanced portfolio policy by setting the relative parameters for conservative, aggressive, and speculative investments. An investor would find it rather difficult, perhaps even impossible, to determine if the consultant is conservative, aggressive, or speculative without first reviewing all of the consultant's information. This will serve to properly categorize the consultant according to the answers provided to each question. Completing simple questionnaires, which many money managers routinely use, may bring you closer to understanding your objectives, but nothing quite compares to having a professional assist you in clarifying your objectives and individual investment style in a truly professional way.

4. Selecting specific investments that meet the necessary criteria based on each investor's particular situation.

5. Monitoring overall performance against established objectives. For a client who would like his investment portfolio to perform as well as the market, but would like to take less risk than the market, the Consultant will attempt to find a money manager who takes a more conservative approach. To reduce risk, it is important to first determine what time period will be involved, and then to find the money manager whose past performance record and individual style is most suited to the investor's objectives.

UNDERSTANDING MANAGER STYLES

Many wrap investors, brokers, and pension sponsors often chase the performance history of investment managers in searching for their pot of gold. But like a rainbow, this is merely an illusion—refracted light hovering in the rain drops of past performance.

Rainbow chasing comes into play when an investor finds an investment manager who did exceptionally well in the past, and hires him only to find out later that it was the manager's style that did exceptionally well and not necessarily the manager himself.

When you hire a wrap fee money manager, it is important for you to understand the style of manager with whom you are working. It is also important to understand when a particular style works well and when it doesn't work at all.

A full understanding of which segment of the manager's performance cycle you are looking at is also important. As a wrap fee investor, you are also buying the opportunity that these managers will pick companies that will grow in adverse or stormy environments.

How do you quantify what good performance is without falling into the trap of rainbow chasing as a method of trying to "beat the market"?

Chapter 10

What you really need to evaluate is the level of risk and volatility that a manager is taking in order to get their performance (see Figure 10–1). This is something many investors tend to overlook. However, this is what a professional investment management consultant can bring to the table. A consultant should highlight the advantages of lower volatility, high relative returns, and exactly why a particular manager's performance is leading or lagging the market. This is a key element in identifying a trend and getting in front of it. This goes way beyond just identifying the managers who have had exceptionally good performance near term.

Figure 10–1   Investment Management Styles:
Expectations for Return and Risk Tolerance

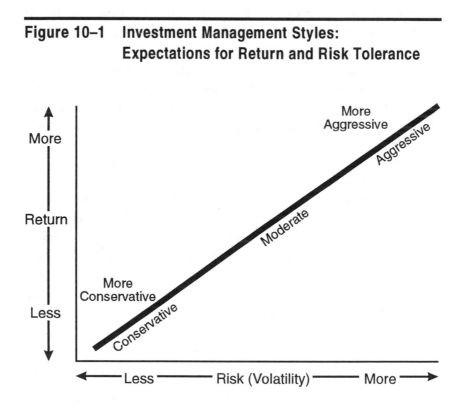

Therefore, when making a wrap fee manager selection, or when contemplating the termination of a manager, one must look at how long the manager's performance has lagged market averages. Keep in mind that the market average is a compilation of all the different stocks that fall into every one of the management disciplines. The segments that will be leading will actually be the ones that are influencing the averages in certain areas.

Example: Over the last few years, when the larger capitalization stocks did exceptionally well, the top 100 stocks in the S&P 500 represented over 60% of the market capitalization. Therefore, they influenced the S&P index considerably, whereas the bottom 100 stocks in the S&P 500 represented only about 2-3% of the market capitalization.

When the smaller cap stocks start to move, they really won't have much influence on the S&P 500 and consequently you will see a large percentage of small- and medium-cap managers actually outperforming the market averages. As a result some of the investors may be compelled to hire one of these managers well into the first leg of the cycle for small- and medium-cap managers.

An investor may actually be correct in identifying this trend. However, they may be identifying it after the first leg, only to ride down the correction phase before the second leg up for this particular style. If an investor is going to identify a manager solely on performance, then he'd better understand what portion of the cycle that manager is in. That is the fallacy of looking at a manager who has had great performance over 5 to 10 year periods.

Therefore, when making a manager selection or when contemplating the termination of a manager, it is important to understand investment style (see Figure 10–1). Let's look at individual manager's styles and how they relate to the investment process (see Figure 10–2).

103

Figure 10–2 A Single Style Can Produce Inconsistency

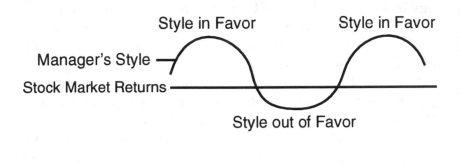

VALUE

Primary motivation is to select securities based on known information. This information may take the form of price/earnings screens or screens for various financial characteristics. When using a P/E screen for example, then the "P" in the ratio is today's price and the "E" is the trailing twelve month's earnings. This style is frequently associated with a strong emphasis or discipline based on the foregoing selection methods. The value manager tries to find stocks where the price is 30-50% less than breakup or replacement of the company assets.

Value managers would come into play predominantly after a long market decline or bottom of a market cycle. Also, in periods where market prices are cheaper, pessimism is very high and economic problems are very widespread. A value manager is not necessarily going to focus as much on the economy, but more on the pricing of individual securities relative to their book value or replacement costs, etc.

Relative Value Managers

An example of a relative value manager is Winrich Capital Management located in Lake Forest, California. Winrich believes that interest rate instruments and stocks represent two competing uses for investment dollars. And their movement, relative to each other, affects the investor's decision about which one is a better value. As interest rates go down, the relative attractiveness of stocks increases. For example, Winrich looks at different sectors and tries to determine the best value in each sector. One sector might be financial, another energy, and yet another consumer staples. This means that they might own a stock in one sector that has a much higher P/E ratio than a stock in another sector.

Relative value managers look within a sector, and do a bottoms-up analysis within that sector. This may sound like a sector rotator manager, only looking for values in each sector to determine which sector is going to do the best. A relative value manager does not want to be limited to one sector in case that sector goes out of favor. A relative value manager is trying to do something in between and not let absolute value force them to be overly concentrated. They look at the relative value of stocks in each sector.

GROWTH AND EMERGING GROWTH

Some people confuse growth managers with emerging growth managers. "Emerging means it is a smaller company that is emerging in size hence the smaller capitalization, whereas growth stocks are companies which have earnings that are generally above the average for the market," says Jim Awad of Awad & Associates, a small-cap emerging growth manager.

Chapter 10

Growth Managers

Growth managers are more attractive in periods when the market is doing well and the companies a growth manager buys are doing best within a market showing a very strong earnings growth. A high degree of volatility comes into play with growth managers because they manage higher multiple stock. The P/E multiples are higher, consequently the volatility of the stocks is greater.

Now let's break this into large-cap growth and small-cap growth. There will be periods where growth stocks in the large-cap sectors do exceptionally well because there is a high level of safety, meaning higher quality and better capitalized companies. Unfortunately, growth stocks with smaller capitalization will be overlooked to a wide extent, because small- or medium-cap stocks happen to be out of vogue with the market at that time.

One type of growth manager, such as Frontier Capital Management in Boston, Massachusetts, tracks growth of earnings using a thematic approach. They identify companies, both domestically and internationally, which will take advantage of trends that are unfolding, such as the growth of world communications, international telecommunications, health, and companies that have had good growth in these areas, not tied to cyclical business cycles. They had actually performed exceptionally well throughout the entire recession because their stocks were moving as a result of uninterrupted earnings growth.

When applying an earnings growth approach, you have to be more definitive about whether you are talking large-caps or small-caps. If you want to employ a value approach to the earnings approach and large-caps have already made their big move and small-caps haven't, and you are willing to accept a higher level of volatility, then perhaps smaller capitalized companies will be more attractive.

1991 was a perfect example: In the middle of 1990-91, smaller capitalization stocks were down significantly. January 1989 to October 1990 was devastating for the smaller cap type of stocks. For the period when the market declined in May of 1990 through October 1990, the S&P was down 14.5% while the NASDAQ was down 27.8%. However, from October 1990 through December 1991, the S&P was up 42.6% and the NASDAQ, over the counter, was up 81%.

So, we look at the year 1991 as a market year, the S&P was only up 30%, but the NASDAQ was up 59%.

Emerging Growth As the name suggests, these managers tend to buy stocks that have a high degree of price volatility. This is a bottom-up style of management in that the primary motivation for buying a particular stock is inherently found in the stock itself. These are the "stock pickers." Some buy based on price momentum or earnings momentum, but are not limited to a change in the way a company is perceived.

Quality Growth (Hybrid Index) The primary purpose is to replicate the performance of the market. An example would be a majority, if not all, of the stocks in the upper-half of the S&P 500. Many managers perform as well as the market with lower relative market risk. Some perform better than the market with equivalent market risk.

Balance Growth These managers typically do not buy overly aggressive stocks, but they do rely heavily on earnings forecasts. This is a style that is usually devoid of extremes, not too much income and not too much risk. One might say that if you were going to place all of the fund's assets with one manager, this style would most likely be selected.

Chapter 10

Another trend that is unfolding, which appears to be transparent to many investors, is the growth of the convertible bond market. It has been very attractive to own high-yield securities that can be converted into equities. The one inherent fact that goes with the ownership of the convertible securities is that more of your middle capitalization sized companies are the ones that issue convertible debt. They do so to reduce the yield on the bond that they are issuing. They give a little supercharge effect to the debt securities so that they don't have to pay as much in interest.

Income Growth The primary purpose in security selection is to achieve a current yield significantly higher than the S&P 500. The stability of the dividend and the rate of growth of the dividend is also of concern to the income buyer. These portfolios may own more utilities, less high-tech, and may also own convertible preferreds and convertible bonds.

Income growth is primarily used to fund higher income needs such as endowments and things of that sort. The growth portion is the exposure to equities to provide an increased amount of cash flow and to try to increase the value of the portfolio, perhaps to maintain or stay ahead of inflation.

One type of manager that falls under income growth, but utilizes its own asset category is Calamos Asset Management Company, in Oak Brook, Illinois. The firm utilizes its own subasset category known as convertible bonds. When the small-cap segment of the market is not doing well, Calamos is doing well because interest rates are going down. When the small-cap segment of the market takes off again, and the medium-cap segment follows by going up and interest rates rise causing bond prices to decline, the investor gets an added bonus and Calamos will outperform other fixed-income securities by far.

The downside protection of a convertible bond portfolio is exactly what makes it attractive. It is an effective way to take highly volatile stocks and reduce their volatility with the fixed income component.

But the performance of those types of securities in a market that was not necessarily favorable to medium- to small-cap stocks, meant that the convertible bond managers, like the small-cap managers, were making a lot of their return off the income and not necessarily getting as much advantage out of the equity side, until that portion of the market turned around.

Therefore, when you hire a convertible bond manager, you're actually getting a middle-cap equity manager who uses a bond component to do the investing. Currently income growth managers are enjoying a very strong return.

For a consultant analyzing these managers, predicting something like this isn't very difficult. The key here is to identify the primary components of the companies that make up the convertible bond market, and the basis on which the managers are investing. Are they investing for purposes of yield only or for the purpose of the opportunity of owning these medium- and small-cap stocks? Either way, convertible bonds are just a safer way to do it.

These particular managers can do a very good job, provided that they have a lot of analytical expertise in the industries in which the investor is interested.

Example: During the mid-80s, many industry rotator managers were in small-cap stocks, especially in the area of high-tech stocks, and their performance was way off. This was primarily due to the style of management to which they were adhering.

Fixed Income

This style uses strictly cash flow generating instruments, such as bonds, notes, CDs, preferred stocks, etc. The advisors will primarily try to maximize highest yields while attempting to protect principal by adjusting maturities to take advantage of rising and falling interest rates.

Cash Management

Short-term fixed instruments make up these portfolios, while liquidity and maximizing principal protection is their primary objective. Even though these accounts have short-term (one-day) liquidity, they typically pay more like the 90-180 day CDs, rather than passbook or one-week CDs.

Fixed income and cash management accounts are driven by the immediate need for money. If the need for money has a very short-time horizon for liquidity, that would be one of the major factors influencing a fixed income or cash manager.

INDUSTRY ROTATORS

Their primary emphasis is on finding industries that will outperform the market as a whole. They begin with a top-down approach which requires them to make projections and forecasts on general economic conditions. This "MACRO" approach then leads them to either over- or underweigh certain industries that are consistent with their economic scenario. The industry categories are filled with individual stocks believed to be the strongest in these industries.

An Industry Rotator is a manager who would identify specific industries that have moved (that are either under-valued or have moved into a trend the market is strongly supporting). For example, back in the early 1980s, when oil stocks had been doing exceptionally well as an industry, a rotator might have become heavily involved in owning those stocks. As the rotator managers moved further into the '80s, there was a heavy concentration in aerospace stocks, and a move away from oil and gas stocks.

SUMMARY

Every investor wants to beat the market. To do so, seek the help of a qualified and compatible wrap fee manager. To assess the manager's compatibility, ask what market they compare themselves to. What time period are they going to use for the comparison? If their objective is to beat the market, then do they want to beat the S&P 500, the value line index, or a convertible bond index? More importantly, do they really need to focus on determining their level of tolerance for volatility, as well as their longer-term return expectations or requirements? These are the key components you should use to identify a wrap fee manager's style.

The problem is that every investor has expectations of seeing immediate performance, and those expectations may not be compatible with a particular manager's style at different points in time. The object is to lengthen the time horizons beyond a 3-5 year period and then look at a manager's style, concentrating on the quality of securities and level of volatility and risk control to determine what makes the investor comfortable over a longer period of time.

Remember, if an investor has enough money to employ more than one investment manager, it can increase one's chance of being in the right place on more than one occasion during a complete market cycle, and with lower overall volatility (see Figures 10-2 and 10-3).

Figure 10–3 Combining Styles through Multi-Managers

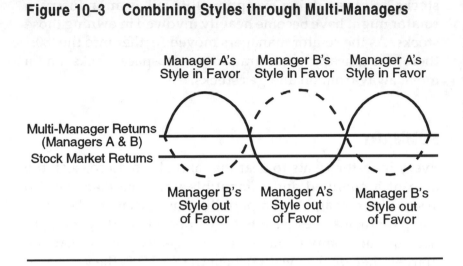

Instead of sprinting madly down the road in hope of finding the proverbial pot of gold at the end of the rainbow, why not be standing where the next rainbow appears?

CHAPTER 11

TYPES OF WRAP FEE MONEY MANAGERS

The selection of a wrap fee money manager is an exacting process since it affords many vital considerations. Exactly who manages money—and how do they do it?

BANKS

These financial institutions are abundant in number, existing in virtually every community. Nearly half of all smaller pension plans are managed by bank trust departments, their sponsors having selected them because of their own past associations with the bank. Broadening the relationship to include money management services seems both a wise and expedient thing to do. There may, however, be some under-lying disadvantages, one of which is that, historically speaking, banks have had a tendency to underperform. Also, their investment choices are frequently impeded or delayed by the need for committee approval which may prevent timely action. The investor, looking in from the outside, may not be in a position to evaluate a bank's performance in the proper light.

Example: While a bank may be able to come up with some really good performance numbers on their balanced account (perhaps through the conscientious efforts of a ris-ing superstar on the equity side of the ledger), the portfolio

113

may show an extremely poor fixed-income side, where another segment of the group is listlessly plodding along. The investor, who is concentrating on the balanced account, will not be in a position to see that the fixed-income numbers are actually being "propped up" by the equity numbers, which is an important thing to know and certainly justifies close monitoring of the portfolio's performance.

It is also important to remember that the bank's trust departments generate revenue based on the assets customers entrust to them and charge the customer a percentage fee for taking control of their money. They are, of course, obliged to provide the investor with something to do with his money, although they would just as soon provide the services connected with rolling it over into CDs and then reloaning it to make additional money on the spread. But for people who are interested in participating in some type of growth, the banks do provide money management services (primarily in order to appear accommodating).

Most banks are not in the money management business. Rather, they are in the business of borrowing money from you and lending it out to somebody else at a higher price. Realistically speaking, banks are remarketers of money as opposed to money managers.

Finally, banks have a relatively high turnover in personnel, which may result in inconsistent investment styles and mixed results.

INSURANCE COMPANIES

Unlike banks, who guarantee a full return on your investment, insurance companies will guarantee a certain rate of return (i.e., deferred annuities). They may place the money in a large commercial building, or use it to purchase some long-term bonds. Whatever their choice, you do not get to participate in the actual investment. They are investing your money for themselves. An insurance company will gladly pay you 8% so that they can make 12. This method of investment is popular during periods of economic instability, when investors are more interested in a "safe" return than a highly profitable one.

Insurance companies can be considered valid sources for investment management, provided the investor does not object to having a portion of his money "skimmed off the top."

The primary disadvantage in using an insurance company for money management purposes is its lack of individual account management and flexibility.

MUTUAL FUNDS

Current studies indicate that mutual funds and brokerage firms manage the smallest share of small pension monies. Mutual funds are preferable for accounts that can't meet the minimum requirements of independent money managers. They can also provide low-cost management and they do possess some of the industry's best investment talent.

Mutual funds are probably the closest thing available to professional money management, although they have some of the same drawbacks as banks, including a moderately high turnover in personnel.

As a potential investor, it is sometimes difficult to decide which fund to buy. If no investment objectives have been established by the investor, it can be very difficult indeed, since every mutual fund is listed by objective. With approximately ten different objective categories to choose from, it becomes necessary for the investor to categorize himself.

Those who purchase a no-load fund will have no salesperson or consultant to rely upon. They will need to determine on their own whether or not a given fund meets their particular investment requirements.

You should not confuse a no-load fund—one that you acquire on your own through a newspaper ad, credit union, etc.—with a non-front end loaded fund, which is being sold to you by a broker, since there is no way that the latter will be sold without the salesperson receiving a commission. In addition, you may expect to pay money management fees and a brokerage commission, all of which are paid by the money manager out of your fund.

Remember, too, that in the case of a loaded mutual fund, the broker will be compensated on a percentage basis going in, which means that, having been paid up front, there is no further incentive for him or her to continue any dialogue or consulting relationship with the investor.

Since it is relatively easy to obtain a license to sell mutual funds and since there is no requirement to be listed on the New York Stock Exchange, it is always wise for the investor to beware.

In cases where an investor is dealing with one of the larger banks or insurance companies, he or she may find themself confined to a very limited number of funds and in many cases, may only be offered a fund that is managed by the bank's or insurance firm's parent company.

Still, the greatest pitfall in buying a mutual fund exists in the fact that the investor has no way of knowing if the people who created the fund and its five-year performance record are still associated with the fund. The SEC is currently attempting to devise a way to require mutual fund companies to disclose such changes in personnel. At present, the broker does not have this information either, perhaps because the sales literature is not properly analyzed, or once again, because of a lack of full disclosure.

While there are services that will rate mutual funds for you, it is important to understand that they are only rating performance. They will not supply a complete breakdown or synopsis of everything and everyone involved since that is not what they are in business to do. And again, unless the salesperson has made a concerted effort to closely monitor the company, he will not be in a position to pass along this vital information to you.

BROKERAGE HOUSES

These investment management subsidiaries represent a growing segment of the investment management market. While they will certainly give individual attention to accounts and provide investment flexibility, they too have their drawbacks. Perhaps the most prevalent one is the fact that their research information comes from a parent company that can be somewhat biased. In addition, securities transactions are often arranged through the parent firm and this may result in substantially higher trading costs.

Another point to consider is, just as with banks and mutual funds, how can you really be sure that the broker is working in your best interest? He may not be if he does not also expose you to outside money managers, thereby giving you a greater choice and an opportunity to make some important comparisons.

There are a number of brokerage firms today that are nothing short of adamant on the subject of offering only their own money management services to potential investors, choosing not to give up a portion of their fee to outside professionals. Such decisions are made at the executive level or by national sales departments of each individual brokerage firm, and while they may strongly imply that their service includes individual attention, what they offer is actually "blanket" management for everybody. Although blanket management is not necessarily a bad thing, who is in a position to say that the brokerage firm's style of money management is the right style for everyone?

INDEPENDENT INVESTMENT MANAGEMENT FIRMS

These are fast becoming the largest groups to offer investment services. They provide the most flexible and complete array of personalized investment services for the intermediate-sized pension sponsor. Generally, they are owned by investment professionals who offer individual account management. Their highly competitive nature encourages them to strive for superior performance and, because these professionals are frequently well compensated, the firms experience little in the way of personnel turnover.

Back in the mid-70s, there were total of 2,500 independent money managers; at present, their numbers are approaching 20,000. Banks, insurance companies, mutual funds, and brokerage firms have all been spawning grounds for their independent talent, and so they are frequently referred to as the "best of the best."

On an individual basis, they are evaluated by the investment management consultant to ascertain their qualifications and overall compatibility with the client.

The consultant might begin his evaluation by asking for the money manager's largest account, smallest account, best performing account, worst performing account, and finally, his own personal account. From this, he will be able to determine if the money manager works more successfully with larger or smaller accounts, and compare the manner in which he runs his own account to how he runs those of his clients. In this way, the consultant can determine if the individual style of a particular money manager is suited to that of certain investors.

It is to the independent money manager's credit that his entrepreneurial spirit has taken him out of the corporate structure and encouraged him to strike out on his own. From this point on, it is clearly a case of "survival of the fittest."

There is ample evidence to support that many banks have begun to recognize the talents of the independent money manager. In more than one instance, banks have closed down their money management departments realizing they weren't doing a very efficient job. In one case, a Washington consulting firm was hired in place of a bank's own money management department, a firm that works regularly with forty of the top Fortune 500 companies in the country.

A number of years ago, a large New York banking institution dismissed all of its money managers and began buying up independent money management firms which they purchased through stock trades.

Independent money managers, the ultimate entrepreneurs, are highly motivated by the capitalistic system, and tend to do well for their clients and themselves. That is not to say that every single money manager is better than every brokerage firm or mutual fund, for that is hardly the case.

It is the consultant's job to sift through their professional backgrounds and past performance records in order to properly evaluate and categorize them. After selecting the "best of the best," these choices will be narrowed to those whose geographical locations are most favorable, to those who have shown a proficiency in larger or smaller accounts (again depending on the client's specific needs), and finally, to those whose individual style most effectively complements the investment objective of the client.

After three or four final candidates have been chosen, the consultant will assist the client in making an individual decision, based in large measure on the "chemistry" that exists between the money manager and his potential client. From the standpoint of compatibility, it must be a good marriage in order to work well on both sides.

CHAPTER 12

THE DUE DILIGENCE PROCESS

The process of choosing a money manager involves two broad-based considerations. The first concerns the client's investment objectives. These objectives address safety of principal and investment return. After defining these objectives, the investor can begin the search for an appropriate money manager.

This second step concerns the all-important issue of qualifying the manager, and is the subject of this chapter. This qualifying process, better known as due diligence by the investment industry, simply means that care has been taken to substantiate the suitability of a manager. However carefully done, what needs to be known before hiring a money manager is subjective in nature and difficult to learn.

All investors have individual investment requirements. Some investors have tax considerations, others do not. Some need income while others require growth of capital. Most importantly, investors seek out the knowledge of experts because they believe professional managers can do a better job than they can do themselves. These separate investment needs often cause managers to handle portfolios in different ways. The way managers choose to report on these portfolios leads to different performance results. Consequently, per-

We would like to thank Jerry Caswell, MBA, PhD, Investment Advisory Services, Raymond James & Assocates, Inc., for his contribution to this chapter.

formance numbers often tell less about a manager than the investor assumes.

Choosing a money manager once was a relatively simple process. The world of investment management was the private domain of large pension managers and bank trust departments. Selecting a manager for a pension depended more on the manager's client list than his investment track record.

For individual accounts, most investors felt bank trust departments were a safe and conservative place to keep their money. From the Great Depression to the late sixties, inflation remained low and the stock market had one of its biggest run-ups in history. During this period most people had few complaints about the growth of their money because the underlying buying power of their investment continued to increase.

Starting in the late seventies and early eighties, the number of investment managers grew rapidly. This was due to several factors. From the administrative side, new government regulations made administrating pensions of all sizes cumbersome. Under the new regulations, fiduciaries found themselves personally liable for lapses in their pension's administration. At this time, individuals and pension administrators also discovered that inflation was rising while the stock market was not. Passive investing no longer resulted in the rising purchasing power of savings. Investors began to look beyond the big pension managers and bank trust departments for outside talent to invest their money.

The demand for managers with new ideas spawned the rapid growth of what is now the independent investment manager. Both the large number of new managers and the rapid increase in the assets under their management reflect this rapid growth. But with the influx of new capital looking for managers, a large number of newly established managers have arisen. Many of these start-ups manage assets in the hundreds of millions of dollars. Today it is not uncommon to find management firms not even in existence just a decade ago controlling over half a billion dollars in assets.

How can you gather knowledge about these managers? Request a copy of the manger's ADV form. No matter how impressive the manager's general marketing information is, investors should keep in mind that this information serves the purposes of the manager and not the investor. Disclosures usually reflect what the manager wants the investor to know. Knowledgeable investors do have alternatives for gathering information about managers, because the Securities and Exchange Commission (SEC) regulates investment managers, and additional information from disclosure statements is on file with the government.

The most important of these disclosure documents is the ADV. By law the manager must provide Part II of the form (or equivalent disclosure) to prospective clients. While Part II is the only form legally required to be furnished to the public, it never hurts to request both parts (see Figure 19–6).

The ADV provides basic background information on the manager's state registrations, disciplinary or legal problems, ownership, potential conflicts of interest with fees or commissions, financial condition, and the background of the firm's principals. Investors should keep in mind that the SEC never passes on the merits or accuracy of the information provided in the ADV. Its purpose is to place basic information about the manager on the public record. By having an ADV, the investor has an opportunity to do some basic background checking. Obvious areas of interest are prior employment of the firm's principals and their educational backgrounds. When legal actions against the firm are discovered, investors should try to obtain copies of the court-filed complaints. By checking with the SEC's enforcement division, the investor may uncover actions taken by the SEC against the manager for regulatory violations.

THE FORM 13F FILING

If the manager manages $100 million or more in equities, SEC regulations require that a quarterly 13F filing be made. The filing states the equity positions and the number of shares held by the manager. Because the manager submits his portfolio positions quarterly, these reports often accurately predict the manager's performance for the coming quarter. Some managers may argue that, because portfolio adjustments often occur between filings, the 13F is an inaccurate performance measure. Most managers have portfolio turnovers of about 25% a year or higher. Even at 40% turnover a year rate; the average quarter has only a 10% change in portfolio positions—a relatively small amount. This gives the investor using the 13F filing another way of comparing the manager's publicly reported performance with his SEC 13F filings.

MANAGERS WITH PUBLIC FUNDS

While it's the exception rather than the rule, investors should always check to see whether the manager also manages a mutual fund in addition to his individual accounts. If he does, then compare the performance of the manager's individual composites with that of his mutual fund. The two should be similar in performance since it is unlikely that different investment styles are being applied to each. Because of regulations governing mutual funds, investors are safer using performance of the mutual fund rather than the manager's individual account composite.

THE BROKERAGE NETWORK

Most full-service brokerage houses have the in-house capability of tracking the performance of managers. Upon opening a managed account, the brokerage firm begins to monitor the account's performance. Quarterly reports compare the manager's performance with those of other managers. The broker assigned to the account often receives these reports. By tracking a large number of portfolios from a particular manager it becomes possible to measure the performance and consistency among the manager's accounts.

In addition to tracking performance, many full-service brokerage houses make on-sight inspections of the managers they monitor. By combining information from house accounts and visiting managers, these brokerage firms are often the best repository of information on managers. Investors should always try to find out whether a brokerage has excluded a manager from doing business with any brokerage firms. Similarly, it helps if a manager's name is on the brokerage's list of approved managers.

THE MANAGER

It is unlikely that most managers will voluntarily talk about reasons for not doing business with them. A manager's disclosure is, by nature, a one-sided viewpoint. There are numerous questions we could list here that would be prudent to ask the manager. For the sake of brevity, we will limit ourselves to two questions.

First, it is important to understand the history of the management team. If managers have come and gone, then it is important to know who they were and why they left. As with any organization, a management team must work well together if it is going to succeed. If there is dissension among

125

those making the decisions, then portfolio consistency might suffer.

The second question, if truthfully answered, is one of the most telling pieces of information about any manager. Ask the manager to state the total asset value and the number of new accounts acquired and lost during the past five years. A good manager has little to fear from this question. On the basis of this one piece of evidence alone, most investors can save themselves a lot of trouble.

Other factors that investors might want to know about are the size of the firm, how long they have been in business, their clientele list, and any references they might want to disclose.

Common sense dictates that these basic questions be explored. Investors should be careful of firms growing so fast that service and performance suffer. The faster growing manager must place additional time and attention on the administration of his business. This is sometimes to the detriment of securities research and portfolio performance.

IMPROVING STANDARDS

In 1991 the Association for Investment Management and Research (AIMR) Board of Governors endorsed a set of performance presentation standards designed to raise the ethical and professional practices of the investment management industry. The performance standards provide investment managers with a standardized format for calculation and presentation of their performance for clients after December 31, 1992.

Also the establishment of an independent, performance-monitoring clearinghouse formed by the brokerage community would benefit everyone. By collecting and pooling data from its members, a clearer picture of manager performance would occur. Knowing that an independent group has access to actual performance numbers, managers would be more likely to report their performance composites accurately.

Currently, most managers issue quarterly reports to their accounts. These reports are individual and are independent of their composite numbers. The SEC also should require managers to report composite numbers to their individual accounts. Managers reporting higher composite numbers than experienced by their investors would have to answer to their own clientele. This reporting method is both easy to implement and would be quite effective because managers must first answer to their own clients when issuing composite numbers.

By being selective, the investing public can force positive change on the investment management industry. No one wants to see greater government interference in the private sector unless truly warranted. The investment industry can avoid this if it comes up with solutions to its existing problems. This is best done by the public and investment community coming together through organizations like the Association for Investment Management and Research, and the Institute for Investment Management Consultants. Public confidence can only be maintained when voluntary and full disclosure is made by the investment management industry.

CHAPTER 13

WHAT YOU NEED TO KNOW ABOUT AN INVESTMENT MANAGEMENT CONSULTANT

An investment management consultant can match an investor with a compatible wrap fee account manager. He does this by establishing realistic, long-term investment objectives with the following considerations: an investor's return expectations, the amount of assets desired to have under management, risk tolerance, income/cash flow needs, appropriate asset allocation, and time horizons for the funds.

A consultant will help an investor complete a detailed questionnaire covering topics such as income needs, time horizon, risk tolerances, economic situation, and financial goals. The questionnaire is different for trustees of pension or profit sharing plans. But both types of questionnaires are designed to find out what the investor's preferences are and how they feel their assets should be managed.

The information obtained from the questionnaire will be used to write an investment policy statement based on an investor's return expectation and the amount of risk he is willing to accept. This investment policy statement is then used to help determine the appropriate investment manager candidates to be introduced.

This policy statement also serves as a written job description for the investment advisor managing your assets.

You don't want to just hire a manager and give him carte blanche with no understanding of your goals and objectives. The policy formally communicates your needs to the investment advisor and eliminates the possibility of a misunderstanding.

WHAT SERVICES WILL AN INVESTMENT MANAGEMENT CONSULTANT (IMC) PROVIDE FOR YOU?

An investment management consultant begins by following a structured process. The consulting process consists of the following six steps:

1. Analyzing your goals and objectives
2. Formulating a written investment policy document
3. Establishing appropriate asset allocations
4. Introducing suitable managers
5. Monitoring your portfolio's performance
6. Ongoing manager's evaluation and due diligence.

WHAT IS THE DIFFERENCE BETWEEN A WRAP FEE MONEY MANAGER AND AN INVESTMENT MANAGEMENT CONSULTANT?

A wrap fee money manager buys and sells securities on his client's behalf. The manager's investment decisions are based on his experience, training, and proven investment strategies in accordance with clearly stated investment objectives.

Investment management consultants do not directly manage their clients' money. Consultants analyze their clients' objectives, and establish appropriate asset allocations, introduce the clients to suitable money managers, monitor their clients' accounts, and evaluate the money managers on an ongoing basis.

WHY CAN'T I FIND A WRAP FEE MANAGER ON MY OWN?

You can! But, if done properly, it is very time consuming and cost prohibitive, and requires skilled experience. While there are many data bases available to the investment community, finding an investment manager is an art requiring more than simply looking at marketing brochures or the data published in financial magazines. The seasoned consultant goes beyond the raw performance numbers and analyzes the qualitative aspects by going on-site and continuously auditing the investment managers' firms.

WHAT EDUCATIONAL BACKGROUND AND CREDENTIALS WARRANT SOMEONE CALLING HIMSELF OR HERSELF AN INVESTMENT MANAGEMENT CONSULTANT?

Individuals who call themselves investment management consultants should have formal training, demonstrate that they have been in the consulting business for a number of years, and currently have assets under management.

Many investment management consultants are members of professional associations that have standards and/or examinations.

The Institute for Investment Management Consultants, "The Institute," which is a national nonprofit professional association for the consulting profession, provides training development and continuing education for its members. The Institute awards the following designations for achievements in the field of investment management consulting:

AIMC (Accredited Investment Management Consultant): This designation is granted to Institute members in good standing who have completed a detailed course in the process of investment management consulting. Subjects covered include: the development of investment policies; money manager analyses; asset allocation; performance monitoring and evaluation; and understanding ERISA (Employment Retirement and Income Securities Act of 1974). An AIMC is a highly trained consultant.

CIMC (Certified Investment Management Consultant): This designation is awarded to those Institute members who are seasoned in the consulting process and who meet several criteria developed by the Institute's Committee on Education and Certification. A CIMC is a highly seasoned consultant.

To earn the CIMC, a consultant must have five or more years as a registered representative of the New York Stock Exchange, or seven years of investment experience with no less than 25 separate consulting accounts and $15 million under management.

You should also try to determine whether the investment management consultant has a proven track record.

Questions to ask of a consulting firm under consideration:

- How long has the firm been in the consulting business?

- What is the number of professional consulting support staff and number of full-time analysts designated to conduct on-site manager visitations, account audits, and due diligence?

- In the firm's consulting history, how many managers have they thoroughly evaluated by face-to-face interviews (versus questionnaire mailing)?

- How many of the managers in the consulting firm database are audited on the manager's premises annually?

The following two questions will illustrate their depth of due diligence:

- Is the firm's database proprietary and self-developed or purchased from some other database? There is nothing inherently wrong with either database, although self-developed may imply that the consulting firm has taken more time and energy to evaluate money managers.

- Does the consulting firm provide and/or sell information to money managers? Do the managers in the database have to pay to be in the consulting firm's database or purchase data from the consulting firm? This will uncover potential and obvious conflicts of interest.

Does the firm have any affiliation with the money manager?
It is important that you know all of the financial industry activities or affiliations your investment management consultant's firm has. This will help you to determine whether your consultant may face any potential conflicts of interest and what his level of commitment is to the services you desire.

Typically an investment management consultant will fall into one of the following three categories: (1) representing a consulting group or department affiliated with a brokerage firm, (2) representing an independent firm with a broker affiliate, (3) representing an insurance company subsidiary.

Chapter 13

You should be aware of the relationship the investment management consultant has to the money management organization recommended by the consultant. Even though the association may be entirely appropriate, you should be aware of all the ways your investment management consultant and his/her firm are paid by you, the investor, and/or any fees paid by money management firms being recommended by the consultants.

Questions to ask of an individual consultant you are considering:

- What professional credentials or designations do they hold?
  Example: CIMC, AIMC, CFA, CIMA

- How long has the consultant been providing investment management consulting services?

- What percentage of the consultant's business is dedicated to providing consulting services to clients?

- What consulting services are provided?
  Examples:
  a) individually tailored investment policy statements
  b) manager search and selection
  c) objective performance monitoring and manager evaluation reports

- Consulting client experience (number of consulting relationships)? Ask for references.

- What types of accounts are consulted?
  Examples: pension plans, public funds, foundations and endowments, eleemosynary, Taft-Hartley, high net worth individuals.

What size accounts does the consultant handle?

Some investment management consultants focus primarily on servicing large, institutional investors, such as pension funds, which have $50 million in assets or more. Others specialize in "high net worth" individuals, foundations/endowments, small/medium size pension plans ($100,000 to $50 million).

What references does the investment management consultant have?

You should ask your investment management consultant for references from clients whose situations and objectives are similar to your own.

Ask your consultant how long most of his clients have been with him. If at all possible, try to get references from clients who have worked with a consultant for at least three to five years. Your consultant should also be willing to furnish references from other professional organizations. One good source is the Institute for Investment Management Consultants (602-265-6114).

What types of wrap fee money managers does the consultant recommend?

Rather than selecting a wrap fee manager who favors the latest fad, or the best return in the last quarter, investment management consultants select the managers who use a discipline or style that is most suitable to meeting the objectives established in your investment policy statement.

What are the monitoring and review procedures used by consultants?

Your investment management consultant updates, monitors, revises, and reviews your progress toward achieving your investment objectives quarterly. Depending on your needs and situation, follow-up sessions may be scheduled monthly, quarterly, or annually. Ask your prospective investment management consultants how frequently they will meet with you to review your portfolio, as well as how frequently you will receive written account statements.

Regardless of how often you personally meet with your investment management consultant, insist on a minimum of quarterly written reports that measure actual performance against established objectives that you have set forth in your investment policy.

Close communication increases the "comfort level" for both you and your investment advisors.

How is an investment management consultant compensated, and how do they set their fees?
The fees charged by investment management consultants vary greatly. Many consultants charge different fees depending on the size of the portfolio, the investment instruments used, and other factors. There are three major ways in which an investment management consultant is compensated: fees, commissions, or a combination of fees and commissions.

Fee-only. Fee-only investment management consultants set fees based on a percentage of the value of the assets under management, or according to a set hourly rate or flat fixed fee, and receive no other compensation for their services.

Those investment management consultants who offer basic hourly rates, charge from $75 to $300 an hour.

Some investment management consultants charge a fixed fee, also known as a flat fee for their services. Depending on the complexity of the plan and the services needed, fixed fees range from $500.00 and up.

Commissions. Investment management consultants who derive any part of their income from commissions, receive part of the funds you invest in a particular product or security, regardless of the investment results. If the investment management consultant does not charge a fee, he is likely to be receiving commissions from transaction decisions made by the investment managers he recommends.

Your fund expenses and performance will be directly influenced by how your consultant's income is determined. So be sure that your investment management consultant fully and completely discloses how he or she will be compensated, before you enter into any agreement.

Some investment management consultants use an "offset" fee structure, also known as "soft dollars" where the fee charged is reduced by the amount of commission. Using a commission to offset a fee may be entirely appropriate, as long as the relationship between an advisory company and the investment management consultant is fully disclosed.

Who will handle my wrap fee account?
Your investment management consultant will normally handle your wrap account. Find out if that's the case, and if not, who will handle it. Also get the names of all associates or others who work with your consultant in case you need information and can't reach your consultant.

Tell your consultant how much personal contact you're likely to need and whether it's important to you that you talk directly with the person actually managing your investment portfolio.

Who is the custodian of the assets in a wrap account?
Assets are not held by the registered investment manager (money manager). Your assets should be held in an insured

custodial account at the brokerage firm where your consultant is affiliated. The insured bank custodian or trust accounts protect you from fraud, embezzlement, financial failure, and such. Obviously it does not insure against market value loss or guarantee returns. In most cases, money managers only have authority to make the buy/sell decisions in your portfolio operating under the guidelines of your investment policy statement.

What is the difference between discretionary and non-discretionary money managers?

You can give a discretionary money manager either limited or full power of attorney over your account. Limited power of attorney (also called limited trading authorization) enables your advisor to buy and sell assets and reinvest the proceeds within the account without your approval of specific transactions. A limited power of attorney restricts the ability of your advisor to remove assets from the account.

On the other hand, full power of attorney means that your advisor may also withdraw assets from the account. While the vast majority of investment advisors manage their clients' accounts honestly, granting direct access to a client's assets creates an opportunity for the misuse of a customer's resources. You should know what bonding and insurance your advisor carries to cover such potential misuse.

You will need to be very clear on which power of attorney you will grant your financial advisor. Although rare, there are nondiscretionary advisors who provide advice to their clients but the clients make all the buy and sell transactions themselves. Should you have the time and inclination to do your own trading, you may decide not to grant any power of attorney.

CONCLUSION

As you can see, selecting an investment manager is not something to be done quickly or taken lightly. There is a great deal of information to obtain, a consultant can help you evaluate an investment manager's record and background very carefully. More importantly, the consultant will help you identify the manager(s) most appropriate for your individual circumstances.

By investing your time before you invest your money, you will be better able to select an appropriate consultant and investment advisor.

FORM ADV

Form ADV, a Uniform Application for Investment Advisor Registration, must be filed with the SEC to become a Registered Investment Advisor. Although registration with the SEC does not signify competence or training, the form provides important information for you to consider when choosing an advisor.

The Form ADV has two parts. Ask for both sections. Part 1 will tell you how long an advisor has been in business as well as his or her education, business, and disciplinary background (see Figure 14–1).

Question 11 in Part 1 shows whether or not an advisor has been disciplined for any violation of investment-related laws or regulations (see Figure 14–2). SEC rules required registration investment advisors to disclose whether or not in the past 10 years they have been declared bankrupt, ever had their license suspended, or violated any of the SEC's or Commodity Futures Trading Commission's regulations or statutes.

Check that the information your advisor gives verbally does not conflict with the ADV form. If you note any discrepancies, ask for a complete examination.

We would like to thank Frontier Capital Management Company, Inc., for a copy of their ADV application.

141

Chapter 14

Part 2 of Form ADV provides more detailed information on the way an advisor conducts business, services provided, account review procedures, fee structures, clients served, and investments offered.

The form also covers an advisor's methods of analysis, sources of information, and investment strategies. In addition, questions are asked about the advisor's other financial industry activities and affiliations.

The form is part of the public record, so your advisor should be willing to give you a copy. However, an advisor is not required by law to provide Part 1 of Form ADV.

The information covered in Part 2 may be presented to clients in some format other than a copy of Form ADV itself, but SEC rules require advisors to tell you, in writing, about their education and experience, the types of work they or their firms do, and how they are paid.

If an advisor does not wish to give you copies of both parts of the form, you can obtain any registered advisor's complete Form ADV from the SEC. (However, consider carefully any advisor who won't give you copies of his or her Form ADV, and be sure to ask, "Why not?")

Figure 14-1 ADV Form–Part I

<table>
<tr><td colspan="3">OMB APPROVAL</td></tr>
<tr><td>OMB Number:</td><td>3235-0049</td></tr>
<tr><td>Expires:</td><td>June 30, 1994</td></tr>
<tr><td>Estimated average burden hours per response ..... 8.96</td></tr>
</table>

FORM ADV
Part I - Page 1   **Uniform Application for Investment Adviser Registration**

This filing is an: ☐ Initial Application
or an: ☒ Amendment

If this filing is an Amendment:
• Give the Applicant's SEC File Number 801- 15724
• Is Applicant now active in business as an Investment Adviser?   Yes ☐ No ☒

WARNING: Failure to complete this Form accurately and keep it current subjects applicant to administrative, civil and criminal penalties.

1. A. Applicant's full name (If sole proprietor, state last, first and middle name):
      Frontier Capital Management Company, Inc.

   B. Name under which business is conducted, if different:

   C. If business name is being amended, give previous name:

2. A. Principal place of business: (Number and Street — Do not use P.O. Box Number)   (City)   (State)   (Zip Code)
      99 Summer Street   Boston   MA   02110

   B. Hours business is conducted at this location: C. Telephone Number at this location: (Area Code)   (Telephone Number)
      from 9:00 a.m.   to 5:00 p.m.   (617)   261-0777

   D. Mailing address, if different   (Number and Street or P.O. Box Number)   (City)   (State)   (Zip Code)
      from address given in 2A:

   E. Is the address in Item 2A or 2D being amended in this filing?........................   Yes ☐ No ☒

   F. On Schedule E give the addresses and telephone numbers of all offices at which applicant's investment advisory business is conducted, other than the one given in Item 2A.

3. A. If books and records required by Section 204 of the Investment Advisers Act of 1940 are kept somewhere other than at the principal place of business given in Item 2A, give the following information (if kept in more than one place, give additional names, addresses and hours of business on Schedule E):
      Name and address of entity where books and records are kept:

      (Number and Street)   (City)   (State)   (Zip Code)

   B. Hours business is conducted at this location: C. Telephone Number at this location: (Area Code)   (Telephone Number)
      from   to

EXECUTION

For the purpose of complying with the laws of the State(s) I have marked in Item 7 relating to the giving of investment advice, I hereby certify that the applicant is in compliance with applicable state surety bonding requirements and irrevocably appoint the administrator of each of those State(s), or such other person designated by law, and the successors in such office, my attorney in said State(s) upon whom may be served any notice, process or pleading in any action or proceeding against me arising out of or in connection with the offer or sale of securities or commodities, or out of the violation or alleged violation of the laws of those State(s) and I do hereby consent that any such action or proceeding against me may be commenced in any court of competent jurisdiction and proper venue within said State(s) by service of process upon said appointee with the same effect as if I were a resident in said State(s) and had lawfully been served with process in said State(s).

The undersigned, being first duly sworn, deposes and says that he has executed this Form on behalf of, and with the authority of, said applicant. The undersigned and applicant represent that the information and statements contained herein, including exhibits attached hereto and other information filed herewith, all of which are made a part hereof, are current, true and complete. The undersigned and applicant further represent that to the extent any information previously submitted is not amended, such information is currently accurate and complete.

Date: 3/22/23	Name of Applicant: Frontier Capital Management Company, Inc.	By (Signature): Nancy J. Smith
Typed Name and Title:	Nancy J. Smith, Vice President	

Subscribed and sworn before me this 22nd day of March 19 93

By: Janet B. Muirhead

My commission expires Dec. 13, 1996   County of Suffolk   State of Massachusetts

Figure 14–1   ADV Form–Part I

FORM ADV	Applicant:	Frontier Capital Management	SEC File Number:	Date:
Part I · Page 2		Company, Inc.	801- 15724	March, 1993

4. A. Persons to contact for further information about this Form: (Name) (Title)

Carla Herwitz or Allen Bornheimer   Counsel

B. Mailing Address (Number and Street, City, State, Zip Code):   Area Code and Telephone Number:

Choate, Hall & Stewart; 53 State Street; Boston, MA 02109   (617) 227-5020

5. A. Applicant consents that notice of any proceeding before the Securities and Exchange Commission or a jurisdiction in connection with its investment adviser registration may be given by registered or certified mail or confirmed telegram to: (Last Name) (First Name) (Middle Name)

Wimberly, John David; Chairman

B. (Number and Street)   (City)   (State)   (Zip Code)   **6.** Applicant's fiscal year ends: (Month)   (Day)

99 Summer St.; Boston, MA 02110   December   31

7. In the box below, give status of applicant's investment adviser registration by indicating:

"1" for pending   "3" for withdrawn before registration within the last 10 years
"2" for registered   "4" for previously registered within the last 10 years

Securities and Exchange Commission __2__

AL _2_ AK _2_ AZ ___ AR _1_ CA _2_ CO ___ CT _2_ DE _2_ DC ___ FL _2_ GA _2_ HI ___ ID _1_
IL _2_ IN _2_ IA ___ KS _2_ KY _2_ LA _2_ ME _2_ MD _2_ MA ___ MI _2_ MN _2_ MS _2_ MO _2_
MT _2_ NE _1_ NV _2_ NH _2_ NJ _2_ NM _2_ NY _2_ NC _2_ ND _1_ OH ___ OK ___ OR _2_ PA _2_
RI _2_ SC _1_ SD _2_ TN _2_ TX _2_ UT _2_ VT ___ VA _2_ WA _2_ WV _2_ WI ___ WY ___ Puerto Rico ___

Other (Specify):

8. Applicant is a (check box that applies and complete those items):

A. ☒ CORPORATION - Complete Schedule A. | (1) Date of incorporation (Month, Day, Year): Nov. 26, 1980 | (2) Jurisdiction where incorporated: Massachusetts

B. ☐ PARTNERSHIP - Complete Schedule B. | (1) Date of establishment (Month, Day, Year): | (2) Current legal address (Number, Street, City, State, Zip Code):

C. ☐ SOLE PROPRIETORSHIP | (1) Date business began (Month, Day, Year): | (2) Current residence address of proprietor: (Number, Street, City, State, Zip Code) | (3) Social Security No.

D. ☐ Other - Specify | (1) Date of establishment (Month, Day, Year): | (2) Current legal address (Number, Street, City, State, Zip Code):

Complete Schedule C

9. Is the applicant taking over the business of a registered investment adviser? (If yes, describe the transfer on Schedule E, including the transfer date, and predecessor's full name, IRS employer number and SEC file number)............................   Yes ☐ No ☒

10. A. Does any person not named in Item 1A or Schedules A, B, or C, through agreement or otherwise, control the management or policies of applicant?...............................   Yes ☐ No ☒

(If yes, state on Schedule E the exact name of each person and describe the basis for the person's control.)

B. Is the applicant financed by a person not named in Items 1A or Schedule A, B, or C other than by: (1) a public offering under the Securities Act of 1933; (2) credit given in the ordinary course of business by banks, suppliers or others; or (3) a satisfactory subordination agreement under Securities Exchange Act of 1934 Rule 15c3-1 (17 CFR 240.15c3-1)?...............................   Yes ☐ No ☒

(If yes, state on Schedule E the exact name of each person and describe the arrangement through which financing is made available including the amount.)

Answer all items. Complete amended pages in full, circle amended items and file with execution.

Figure 14–1 ADV Form–Part I

FORM ADV Part I · Page 3	Applicant: Frontier Capital Management Company, Inc.	SEC File Number: 801- 15724	Date: March, 1992

11. Disciplinary questions. Definitions:

- Advisory affiliate — A person named in Items 1A, 10A or Schedules A, B or C; or an individual or firm that directly or indirectly controls or is controlled by the applicant, including any current employee except one performing only clerical, administrative, support or similar functions.

- Investment or investment-related — Pertaining to securities, commodities, banking, insurance, or real estate (including, but not limited to, acting as or being associated with a broker-dealer, investment company, investment adviser, futures sponsor, bank or savings and loan association).

- Involved — Doing an act or aiding, abetting, counseling, commanding, inducing, conspiring with or failing reasonably to supervise another in doing an act.

A. In the past ten years has the applicant or an advisory affiliate been convicted of or pleaded guilty or nolo contendre ("no contest") to:

  (1) a felony or misdemeanor involving:
- investment or an investment-related business
- fraud, false statements, or omissions
- wrongful taking of property or
- bribery, forgery, counterfeiting, or extortion? .... Yes ☐ No ☒

  (2) any other felony? .... Yes ☐ No ☒

B. Has any court:

  (1) in the past ten years, enjoined the applicant or an advisory affiliate in connection with any investment-related activity? ..... Yes ☐ No ☒

  (2) ever found that the applicant or an advisory affiliate was involved in a violation of investment-related statutes or regulations? ..... Yes ☐ No ☒

C. Has the U.S. Securities and Exchange Commission or the Commodity Futures Trading Commission ever:

  (1) found the applicant or an advisory affiliate to have made a false statement or omission? ..... Yes ☐ No ☒

  (2) found the applicant or an advisory affiliate to have been involved in a violation of its regulations or statutes? Yes ☐ No ☒

  (3) found the applicant or an advisory affiliate to have been a cause of an investment-related business having its authorization to do business denied, suspended, revoked, or restricted? ..... Yes ☐ No ☒

  (4) entered an order denying, suspending or revoking the applicant's or an advisory affiliate's registration or otherwise disciplined it by restricting its activities?. ..... Yes ☐ No ☒

D. Has any other federal regulatory agency or any state regulatory agency:

  (1) ever found the applicant or an advisory affiliate to have made a false statement or omission or been dishonest, unfair, or unethical? ..... Yes ☐ No ☒

  (2) ever found the applicant or an advisory affiliate to have been involved in a violation of investment regulations or statutes? ..... Yes ☐ No ☒

  (3) ever found the applicant or an advisory affiliate to have been a cause of an investment-related business having its authorization to do business denied, suspended, revoked, or restricted? ..... Yes ☐ No ☒

  (4) in the past ten years, entered an order against the applicant or an advisory affiliate in connection with an investment-related activity? ..... Yes ☒ No ☐

  (5) ever denied, suspended, or revoked the applicant's or an advisory affiliate's registration or license, prevented it from associating with an investment-related business, or otherwise disciplined it by restricting its activities? Yes ☐ No ☒

  (6) ever revoked or suspended the applicant's or an advisory affiliate's license as an attorney or accountant? .. Yes ☐ No ☒

Figure 14–1 ADV Form–Part I

FORM ADV Part I - Page 4	Applicant: Frontier Capital Management Company, Inc.	SEC File Number: 801- 15724	Date: March, 1992

E. Has any self-regulatory organization or commodities exchange ever:

    (1) found the applicant or an advisory affiliate to have made a false statement or omission? .... Yes ☐ No ☒

    (2) found the applicant or an advisory affiliate to have been involved in a violation of its rules? .... Yes ☐ No ☒

    (3) found the applicant or an advisory affiliate to have been the cause of an investment-related business having its authorization to do business denied, suspended, revoked, or restricted? .... Yes ☐ No ☒

    (4) disciplined the applicant or an advisory affiliate by expelling or suspending it from membership, by barring or suspending its association with other members, or by otherwise restricting its activities? .... Yes ☐ No ☒

F. Has any foreign government, court, regulatory agency, or exchange ever entered an order against the applicant or an advisory affiliate related to investments or fraud? .... Yes ☐ No ☒

G. Is the applicant or an advisory affiliate now the subject of any proceeding that could result in a 'yes' answer to parts A-F of this item? .... Yes ☐ No ☒

H. Has a bonding company denied, paid out on, or revoked a bond for the applicant? .... Yes ☐ No ☒

I. Does the applicant have any unsatisfied judgments or liens against it? .... Yes ☐ No ☒

J. Has the applicant or an advisory affiliate of the applicant ever been a securities firm or an advisory affiliate of a securities firm that has been declared bankrupt, had a trustee appointed under the Securities Investor Protection Act, or had a direct payment procedure begun? .... Yes ☐ No ☒

K. Has the applicant, or an officer, director or person owning 10% or more of the applicant's securities failed in business, made a compromise with creditors, filed a bankruptcy petition or been declared bankrupt? .... Yes ☐ No ☒

If a 'yes' answer on Item 11 involves:

- an individual, complete a Schedule D for the individual
- a partnership, corporation or other organization, on Schedule E give the following details of any court or regulatory action:
  - the organization and individuals named
  - the title and date of the action
  - the court or body taking the action
  - a description of the action.

12. Individual's Education, Business and Disciplinary Background. Complete a Schedule D for each individual who is:

A. The applicant, named in Part I Item 1A

B. A control person named in Part I Item 10

C. An owner of at least 10% of a class of applicant's equity securities

D. An officer, director, partner, or individual with similar status of applicant, described in Schedule A Item 2a, Schedule B Item 2, or Schedule C Item 2

E. A member of the applicant's investment committee that determines general investment advice to be given to clients

F. If applicant has no investment committee, an individual who determines general investment advice (if more than five, complete for their supervisors only)

G. An individual giving investment advice on behalf of the applicant in the jurisdiction in which this application is filed

H. An individual reporting a 'yes' answer to the disciplinary question, Part I Item 11

Figure 14–1   ADV Form–Part I

FORM ADV Part I - Page 5	Applicant: Frontier Capital Management Company, Inc.	SEC File Number: 801- 15724	Date: March, 1992

13. Does applicant have custody (see definition in instructions) of any advisory client:

A. funds .... Yes ☐ No ☒

B. securities .... Yes ☐ No ☒

C. If either answer is yes, the value of those funds and securities at the end of applicant's last fiscal year was:

(1) ☐ under $100,000   (3) ☐ $1,000,0001 to $5,000,000

(2) ☐ $100,000 to $1,000,000   (4) ☐ Over $5,000,000

14. Do any of applicant's related persons have custody (see definition in instructions) of any advisory client:

A. funds .... Yes ☐ No ☒

B. securities .... Yes ☐ No ☒

If either is yes:

C. is that person a registered broker-dealer qualified to take custody under Section 15 of the Securities Exchange Act of 1934? .... Yes ☐ No ☒

D. the value of those funds and securities at the end of applicant's last fiscal year was:

(1) ☐ under $100,000   (3) ☐ $1,000,001 to $5,000,000

(2) ☐ $100,000 to $1,000,000   (4) ☐ Over $5,000,000

15. Does applicant require prepayment of fees of more than $500 per client and more than 6 months in advance? .... Yes ☐ No ☒

16. With a few exceptions, the "brochure rule" (Advisers Act Rule 204-3) requires that clients must be given information about the investment adviser. Will applicant be giving clients:

A. Part II of this Form ADV? .... Yes ☒ No ☐

B. Another document that includes at least the information contained in Form ADV Part II?..................... Yes ☐ No ☒

17. A. The number of employees of applicant who perform investment advisory functions (including research, but excluding unrelated functions such as accounting) is: (check only one box)

(1) ☐ 1 person, part time   (3) ☐ 2-9 persons

(2) ☐ 1 person primarily involved in providing investment advisory services   (4) ☒ 10 or more persons

B. The number of clients to whom applicant provided advisory services during the last fiscal year was:

(1) ☐ 14 or fewer   (4) ☒ 101 to 500

(2) ☐ 15 to 50   (5) ☐ over 500

(3) ☐ 51 to 100

Figure 14–1   ADV Form–Part I

FORM ADV Part I · Page 6	Applicant: Frontier Capital Management Company, Inc.	SEC File Number: 801- 15724	Date: March, 1993

18. Does applicant manage client securities portfolios on a discretionary basis? .... Yes ☒ No ☐

If yes, at the end of applicant's last fiscal year these accounts:

A. numbered ___221___.   B. totaled in aggregate market value, rounded to nearest thousand .... $ 1,344,000.00

---

19. Does applicant manage or supervise client securities portfolios on a non-discretionary basis? .... Yes ☐ No ☒

If yes, at the end of applicant's last fiscal year these accounts:

A. numbered _____.   B. totaled in aggregate market value, rounded to nearest thousand .... $ _____000.00

---

20. Does applicant hold itself out as providing financial planning or some similarly termed services to clients? .... Yes ☒ No ☐

If yes, during the last fiscal year applicant provided financial planning services to clients:

A. who numbered:

(1) ☒ 14 or fewer   (4) ☐ 101 to 500

(2) ☐ 15 to 50   (5) ☐ over 500

(3) ☐ 51 to 100

B. whose investments in financial products based on those services totaled:

(1) ☐ under $100,000   (3) ☒ $1,000,001 to $5,000,000

(2) ☐ $100,000 to $1,000,000   (4) ☐ over $5,000,000

---

21. Did applicant recommend securities to clients during its last fiscal year in which the applicant acted (itself or through a related person) as an underwriter, general or managing partner, or offeree representative, or had any ownership or sales interest (other than the receipt of normal and customary sales commissions as a broker or brokers representative)? .... Yes ☒ No ☐

If yes, the approximate value of securities so recommended during its last fiscal year is:

A. ☐ Under $50,000   C. ☒ $250,001 to $1,000,000

B. ☐ $50,000 to $250,000   D. ☐ over $1,000,000

---

22. Attach to this Form any financial statements required by the jurisdiction in which applicant is filing, other than the balance sheet required by Part II Item 14.

Figure 14-2   ADV Form–Part II

FORM ADV
Part II · Page 1

Uniform Application for Investment Adviser Registration

OMB APPROVAL
OMB No.:   3235-0049
Expires: June 30, 1988

Name of Investment Adviser:	Frontier Capital Management Company, Inc.					
Address:	(Number and Street)	(City)	State)	(Zip Code)	Area Code:	Telephone Number:
	99 Summer Street	Boston	MA	02110	(617)	261-0777

This part of Form ADV gives information about the investment adviser and its business for the use of clients.
The information has not been approved or verified by any governmental authority.

Table of Contents

149

Figure 14–2 ADV Form–Part II

FORM ADV	Applicant: Frontier Capital Management	SEC File Number:	Date:
Part II· Page 2	Company, Inc.	801- 15724	March, 1993

Definitions for Part II

Related person — Any officer, director or partner of applicant or any person directly or indirectly controlling, controlled by, or under common control with the applicant, including any non-clerical, non-ministerial employee.

Investment Supervisory Services — Giving continuous investment advice to a client (or making investments for the client) based on the individual needs of the client. Individual needs include, for example, the nature of other client assets and the client's personal and family obligations.

---

1. A. **Advisory Services and Fees.** (check the applicable boxes)

    For each type of service provided, state the approximate % of total advisory billings from that service. (See instruction below.)

    Applicant:

☒ (1)	Provides investment supervisory services	100 %
☐ (2)	Manages investment advisory accounts not involving investment supervisory services	0 %
☐ (3)	Furnishes investment advice through consultations not included in either service described above	0 %
☐ (4)	Issues periodicals about securities by subscription	0 %
☐ (5)	Issues special reports about securities not included in any service described above	0 %
☐ (6)	Issues, not as part of any service described above, any charts, graphs, formulas, or other devices which clients may use to evaluate securities	0 %
☐ (7)	On more than an occasional basis, furnishes advice to clients on matters not involving securities	0 %
☐ (8)	Provides a timing service..	0 %
☐ (9)	Furnishes advice about securities in any manner not described above .:...............................	0 %

    (Percentages should be based on applicant's last fiscal year. If applicant has not completed its first fiscal year, provide estimates of advisory billings for that year and state that the percentages are estimates.)

    B. Does applicant call any of the services it checked above financial planning or some similar term? ....   Yes ☒   No ☐

    C. Applicant offers investment advisory services for: (check all that apply)

☒ (1) A percentage of assets under management		☐ (4) Subscription fees
☐ (2) Hourly charges		☐ (5) Commissions
☐ (3) Fixed fees (not including subscription fees)		☐ (6) Other

    ---

    D. For each checked box in A above, describe on Schedule F:

    • the services provided, including the name of any publication or report issued by the adviser on a subscription basis or for a fee

    • applicant's basic fee schedule, how fees are charged and whether its fees are negotiable

    • when compensation is payable, and if compensation is payable before service is provided, how a client may get a refund or may terminate an investment advisory contract before its expiration date

    ---

2. **Types of Clients** — Applicant generally provides investment advice to: (check those that apply)

☒ A. Individuals	☒ E. Trusts, estates, or charitable organizations
☒ B. Banks or thrift institutions	☒ F. Corporations or business entities other than those listed above
☒ C. Investment companies	☒ G. Other (describe on Schedule F)
☒ D. Pension and profit sharing plans	

Figure 14–2 ADV Form–Part II

FORM ADV Part II- Page 3	Applicant: Frontier Capital Management Company, Inc.	SEC File Number: 801- 15724	Date: March, 1993

3. Types of Investments. Applicant offers advice on the following: (check those that apply)

A. Equity Securities
☒ (1) exchange-listed securities
☒ (2) securities traded over-the-counter
☐ (3) foreign issuers

☒ B. Warrants

☒ C. Corporate debt securities
   (other than commercial paper)

☒ D. Commercial paper

☒ E. Certificates of deposit

☒ F. Municipal securities

G. Investment company securities:
☐ (1) variable life insurance
☐ (2) variable annuities
☐ (3) mutual fund shares

☒ H. Unites States government securities

I. Options contracts on:
☒ (1) securities
☐ (2) commodities

J. Futures contracts on:
☐ (1) tangibles
☐ (2) intangibles

K. Interests in partnerships investing in:
☐ (1) real estate
☐ (2) oil and gas interests
☒ (3) other (explain on Schedule F)

☐ L. Other (explain on Schedule F)

4. Methods of Analysis, Sources of Information, and Investment Strategies.

A. Applicant's security analysis methods include: (check those that apply)

(1) ☐ Charting

(2) ☒ Fundamental

(3) ☒ Technical

(4) ☒ Cyclical

(5) ☐ Other (explain on Schedule F)

B. The main sources of information applicant uses include: (check those that apply)

(1) ☒ Financial newspapers and magazines

(2) ☒ Inspections of corporate activities

(3) ☒ Research materials prepared by others

(4) ☐ Corporate rating services

(5) ☐ Timing services

(6) ☒ Annual reports, prospectuses, filings with the Securities and Exchange Commission

(7) ☒ Company press releases

(8) ☐ Other (explain on Schedule F)

C. The investment strategies used to implement any investment advice given to clients include: (check those that apply)

(1) ☒ Long term purchases
   (securities held at least a year)

(2) ☒ Short term purchases
   (securities sold within a year)

(3) ☒ Trading (securities sold within 30 days)

(4) ☐ Short sales

(5) ☐ Margin transactions

(6) ☐ Option writing, including covered options, uncovered options or spreading strategies

(7) ☒ Other (explain on Schedule F)

Chapter 14

Figure 14–2 ADV Form–Part II

FORM ADV Part II · Page 4	Applicant: Frontier Capital Management Company, Inc.	SEC File Number: 801- 15724	Date: March, 1992

5. Education and Business Standards.

Are there any general standards of education or business experience that applicant requires of those involved in determining or giving investment advice to clients? .... **Yes** ☒ **No** ☐

(If yes, describe these standards on Schedule F.)

6. Education and Business Background.

For:

- each member of the investment committee or group that determines general investment advice to be given to clients, or
- if the applicant has no investment committee or group, each individual who determines general investment advice given to clients (if more than five, respond only for their supervisors)
- each principal executive officer of applicant or each person with similar status or performing similar functions.

On Schedule F, give the:

- name
- year of birth
- formal education after high school
- business background for the preceding five years

7. Other Business Activities. (check those that apply)

☐ A. Applicant is actively engaged in a business other than giving investment advice.

☐ B. Applicant sells products or services other than investment advice to clients.

☐ C. The principal business of applicant or its principal executive officers involves something other than providing investment advice.

(For each checked box describe the other activities, including the time spent on them, on Schedule F.)

8. Other Financial Industry Activities or Affiliations. (check those that apply)

☐ A. Applicant is registered (or has an application pending) as a securities broker-dealer.

☐ B. Applicant is registered (or has an application pending) as a futures commission merchant, commodity pool operator or commodity trading adviser.

C. Applicant has arrangements that are material to its advisory business or its clients with a related person who is a:

☐ (1) broker-dealer

☐ (2) investment company

☐ (3) other investment adviser

☐ (4) financial planning firm

☐ (5) commodity pool operator, commodity trading adviser or futures commission merchant

☐ (6) banking or thrift institution

☐ (7) accounting firm

☐ (8) law firm

☐ (9) insurance company or agency

☐ (10) pension consultant

☐ (11) real estate broker or dealer

☒ (12) entity that creates or packages limited partnerships

(For each checked box in C, on Schedule F identify the related person and describe the relationship and the arrangements.)

D. Is applicant or a related person a general partner in any partnership in which clients are solicited to invest? .... **Yes** ☒ **No** ☐

(If yes, describe on Schedule F the partnerships and what they invest in.)

152

Figure 14-2 ADV Form-Part II

FORM ADV Part II · Page 5	Applicant: Frontier Capital Management Company, Inc.	SEC File Number: 801- 15724	Date: December , 1992

9. Participation or Interest in Client Transactions.

Applicant or a related person: (check those that apply)

☒ A. As principal, buys securities for itself from or sells securities it owns to any client.

☐ B. As broker or agent effects securities transactions for compensation for any client.

☐ C. As broker or agent for any person other than a client effects transactions in which client securities are sold to or bought from a brokerage customer.

☒ D. Recommends to clients that they buy or sell securities or investment products in which the applicant or a related person has some financial interest.

☒ E. Buys or sells for itself securities that it also recommends to clients.

(For each box checked, describe on Schedule F when the applicant or a related person engages in these transactions and what restrictions, internal procedures, or disclosures are used for conflicts of interest in those transactions.)

10. Conditions for Managing Accounts. Does the applicant provide investment supervisory services, manage investment advisory accounts or hold itself out as providing financial planning or some similarly termed services *and* impose a minimum dollar value of assets or other conditions for starting or maintaining an account?...................................... Yes ☒ No ☐

(If yes, describe on Schedule F.)

11 Review of Accounts. If applicant provides investment supervisory services, manages investment advisory accounts, or holds itself out as providing financial planning or some similarly termed services:

A. Describe below the reviews and reviewers of the accounts. For reviews, include their frequency, different levels, and triggering factors. For reviewers, include the number of reviewers, their titles and functions, instructions they receive from applicant on performing reviews, and number of accounts assigned each.

Portfolios are reviewed on a daily basis by the portfolio manager responsible for the account. Each institutional portfolio manager reviews approximately 10-15 accounts. Each high net worth portfolio manager manages 40-50 accounts. Each account is reviewed on the basis of the individual client's goals and objectives. The reviewers/(portfolio managers) are:

    J. David Wimberly; Chairman, Portfolio Manager
    Thomas W. Duncan; President, Portfolio Manager
    Donald E. August; Executive Vice President, Portfolio Manager
    Grace K. Fey; Executive Vice President, Portfolio Manager
    James B. Howard; Senior Vice President, Portfolio Manager
    Elizabeth Ames Macdonald; Senior Vice President, Portfolio Manager
    George H. Kidder; Vice President, Portfolio Manager
    Michael A. Cavarretta; Vice President, Portfolio Manager
    Nancy B. Prial; Senior Vice President, Portfolio Manager

B. Describe below the nature and frequency of regular reports on their accounts.

Clients receive monthly or quarterly asset statements and quarterly strategy reviews from Frontier. They also receive phone calls from the portfolio managers on a regular basis, and quarterly meetings are held.

153

Figure 14–2   ADV Form–Part II

FORM ADV Part II · Page 6	Applicant: Frontier Capital Management Company, Inc.	SEC File Number: 801- 15724	Date: March, 1993

12. Investment or Brokerage Discretion.

    A. Does applicant or any related person have authority to determine, without obtaining specific client consent, the:

        (1) securities to be bought or sold? .... Yes ☒ No ☐

        (2) amount of the securities to be bought or sold? .... Yes ☒ No ☐

        (3) broker or dealer to be used? .... Yes ☒ No ☐

        (4) commission rates paid? .... Yes ☒ No ☐

    B. Does applicant or a related person suggest brokers to clients? .... Yes ☐ No ☒

        For each yes answer to A describe on Schedule F any limitations on the authority. For each yes to A(3), A(4) or B, describe on Schedule F the factors considered in selecting brokers and determining the reasonableness of their commissions. If the value of products, research and services given to the applicant or a related person is a factor, describe:

        • the products, research and services

        • whether clients may pay commissions higher than those obtainable from other brokers in return for those products and services

        • whether research is used to service all of applicant's accounts or just those accounts paying for it; and

        • any procedures the applicant used during the last fiscal year to direct client transactions to a particular broker in return for products and research services received.

13. Additional Compensation.

Does the applicant or a related person have any arrangements, oral or in writing, where it:

    A. is paid cash by or receives some economic benefit (including commissions, equipment or non-research services) from a non-client in connection with giving advice to clients? .... Yes ☒ No ☐

    B. directly or indirectly compensates any person for client referrals? .... Yes ☐ No ☒

        (For each yes, describe the arrangements on Schedule F.

14. Balance Sheet. Applicant must provide a balance sheet for the most recent fiscal year on Schedule G if applicant:

        • has custody of client funds or securities; or

        • requires prepayment of more than $500 in fees per client and 6 or more months in advance

        Has applicant provided a Schedule G balance sheet? .... Yes ☒ No ☐

Figure 14–2   ADV Form–Schedule F

Schedule F of Form ADV Continuation Sheet for Form ADV Part II	Applicant: Frontier Capital Management Co., Inc.	SEC File Number: 801- 15724	Date: March, 1993

(Do not use this Schedule as a continuation sheet for Form ADV Part I or any other schedules.)

I. Full name of applicant exactly as stated in Item 1A of Part I of Form ADV:

Frontier Capital Management Company, Inc.	IRS Empl. Ident. No.: 04-2715137

Item of Form (identify)	Answer
Part II Page 2 (1D)	The Firm manages institutional equity portfolios on a fully discretionary basis. The equity portion of the portfolios are generally concentrated in those sectors of the economy which we believe possess significantly above-average growth characteristics. In connection with its management services, the Firm has an active research program and provides clients with detailed appraisals of their portfolios, as well as quarterly reports outlining current investment strategy and plans for the future. The Firm manages balanced accounts in which a portion of the assets are invested in fixed income securities. The fixed income portion of the portfolio is invested in high quality securities of short to intermediate term maturities. The fees for the services described above are as follows, based upon a percentage of the amount of assets under management:

Growth and Mid Cap Growth Accounts:
$1-5 Million
  1% of total assets

Small Cap:
1% of all assets
under management

Accounts Over $5 Million	% Compensation
First $25,000,000	0.75%
Next $25,000,000	0.50%
Next $50,000,000	0.375%
Over $100,000,000	Negotiable

Fees are paid quarterly based on the average of the asset value of the account as of the last day of each month of each calendar quarter equal to one-fourth of the annual rate specified above. For the purposes of the calculation of the fees, the value of securities in each account is determined as of the last day of each month on which the New York Stock Exchange is open. If the Firm provides services for less than the whole of any calendar quarter, its compensation is determined as provided above on the basis of the value of assets in the account on the date of termination (or, if the New York Stock Exchange is not open on such date, as of the last preceding date on which it was open) and is payable on a pro rata basis for the last month during which the firm provided services.

The fees set forth above are not negotiable except under unusual circumstances.

The Firm or any client may terminate an investment advisory contract on 5 days' prior written notice or as mutually agreed to.

Figure 14–2   ADV Form–Schedule F

Schedule F of Form ADV Continuation Sheet for Form ADV Part II	Applicant: Frontier Capital Management Co., Inc.	SEC File Number: 801- 15724	Date: March, 1993

(Do not use this Schedule as a continuation sheet for Form ADV Part I or any other schedules.)

I. Full name of applicant exactly as stated in Item 1A of Part I of Form ADV: Frontier Capital Management Company, Inc.	IRS Empl. Ident. No.: 04-2715137

Item of Form (identify)	Answer

Part II
 	
Page 2
(1D)
Continued
	The Firm also manages equity and balanced portfolios on a fully discretionary basis for high net worth and institutional clients. Fees for those services are described below:
	
	Equity Accounts, $1-5 Million: **Bal. Accts. $1-5 Million:**
	    1% First $2 Million - 1.00%
	                  Next $3 Million - 0.75%
	
	Balanced and Equity Accounts Over $5 Million:
	  First $25,000,000 - .75%
	  Next $25,000,000 - .50%
	  Next $50,000,000 - .375%
	
	Fees are paid quarterly based on the asset value at the end of the quarter. In some cases where there exists a wrap fee agreement between the client-specified broker and Frontier, fees are paid 90 days in advance.
	
	The Firm currently has wrap fee arrangements with the following broker-dealers providing for the fees set forth below.
	
	1. Paine Webber Incorporated
	     Fee paid by client to broker - 3.0%
	     Portion of fee paid to Frontier - 1.0-1.5%
	
	2. Paine Webber Incorporated
	     Access
	       Fee paid to Paine Webber by client:
	          First $500,000 - 2.8%
	          Next $500,000 - 2.2%
	          Next $4,000,000 - 1.6%
	          Next $5,000,000 - 1.4%
	       Portion of fee paid to Frontier - 0.5%
	
	3. Advest, Inc.
	     Master Portfolio
	       Fee paid to Advest by client:
	          First $500,000 - 2.75%
	          Next $500,000 - 2.0%
	          Next $1,000,000 - 1.75%
	          Over $2,000,000 - 1.5%
	       Portion of fee paid to Frontier - 0.5%
	
	     Preferred Management
	       Fee paid to Advest by client:
	          First $500,000 - 3.0%
	          Next $500,000 - 2.0%
	          Next $1,000,000 - 1.5%
	          Over $2 million - 1.0%
	       Portion of fee paid to Frontier - 0.85%

Figure 14–2   ADV Form–Schedule F

Schedule F of Form ADV Continuation Sheet for Form ADV Part II	Applicant: Frontier Capital Management Co., Inc.	SEC File Number: 801- 15724	Date: September, 1992

(Do not use this Schedule as a continuation sheet for Form ADV Part I or any other schedules.)

I. Full name of applicant exactly as stated in Item 1A of Part I of Form ADV: Frontier Capital Management Company, Inc.	IRS Empl. Ident. No.: 04-2715137

Item of Form (identify)	Answer

Part II
 	
Page 2
 	
(1D)
Continued
	4. Investment Advisory Services of Raymond James & Associates, Inc.
	     Equity Accounts
	       Fee paid to Raymond James:
	         Under $200,000 - 3.0%
	         Over $200,000 - 2.5%
	       Portion of fee paid to Frontier - .5%
	
	     Balanced Accounts
	       Fee paid to Raymond James:
	         Under $200,000 - 3.0%
	         Over $200,000 - 2.5%
	       Portion of fee paid to Frontier - .5%
	
	5. Dean Witter
	     Access
	     Fee paid to Dean Witter:
	         First $500,000 - 3.0%
	         Next $500,000 - 2.5%
	         Next $1,000,000 - 2.0%
	         Over $2,000,000 - 1.6%
	     Portion of fee paid to Frontier - 0.5%
	
	6. Stockton Capital Management
	     Members Foresight & Members Trust
	     Fee paid to Stockton:
	
	|			

---	---	---	---
Account Size	Equity Only	Fixed Income Only	Balanced
$100,000-$250,000	2.70%	1.60%	2.10%
$250,001-$500,000	2.50%	1.50%	2.00%

$500,001-$1,000,000	2.30%	1.35%	1.75% |
			
			     Greater than $1,000,000 - Fee to be negotiated
			
			     Portion of fee paid to Frontier:
			| Account Size
				Fees

$0-$20,000,000	.50%

Above $20,000,000	.30% |
	
	     In certain situations, depending upon the level of activity in
	     the account, the client might be able to obtain similar services
	     at a lower aggregate fee by traditional rather than wrap
	     arrangements.

Figure 14–2   ADV Form–Schedule F

Schedule F of Form ADV Continuation Sheet for Form ADV Part II	Appucant: Frontier Capital Management Co., Inc.	SEC File Number: 801. 15724	Date: March, 1992

(Do not use this Schedule as a continuation sheet for Form ADV Part I or any other schedules.)

1. Full name of applicant exactly as stated in item 1A of Part I of Form ADV:	I.R.S. Empl. Ident. No.:
Frontier Capital Management Company, Inc.	04–2715137

Item of Form (Identify)	Answer
Part II 2G 3(K) 8C(12) 8D	Frontier acts as General Partner and Investment Advisor for two Limited Partnerships: The Frontier Growth Fund, L.P.; and the Frontier Small Cap Fund, L.P. Both funds invest in publicly traded corporate equity and debt securities, government and other securities and money market instruments. They may invest in options on individual stocks and stock index contracts. The funds are differentiated by their risk profiles, their asset allocation and by the segments of the equity market in which they invest.

Figure 14-2 ADV Form–Schedule F

Schedule F of Form ADV Continuation Sheet for Form ADV Part II	Applicant Frontier Capital Management Co., Inc.	SEC File Number: 801- 15724	Date: March, 1993

(Do not use this Schedule as a continuation sheet for Form ADV Part I or any other schedules.)

I. Full name of applicant exactly as stated in Item IA of Part I of Form ADV: Frontier Capital Management Company, Inc.	IRS Empl. Ident. No.: 04-2715137

Item of Form (identify)	Answer
Part II Page 3 4C(7)	In the construction of equity portfolios, the Firm seeks to consistently apply an approach that concentrates upon the identification of companies and industries likely to achieve significantly faster growth than the economy as a whole. Our portfolios will generally have the following characteristics: A. They will have a weighted earnings per share growth 2-3 times that of the Standard & Poor's 500 Stock Index or nominal GNP. B. They will be concentrated by sector and company. C. Securities of companies will be purchased primarily upon the basis of our analysis of the business prospects of the companies utilizing fundamental business analysis as opposed to technical analysis or other considerations. D. Our portfolios will not be widely diversified, and it is unlikely that there will be representation in the slower growing or mature areas of the economy. E. We attempt to anticipate change and will adjust industry weightings, as well as company holdings, based upon our analysis of key economic and structural forces. From time to time, we may determine that the equity market or individual securities are temporarily overpriced. Under such conditions, a portion of the portfolios may be invested in short-term securities normally consisting of Treasury Bills, commercial paper, and bank certificates of deposit. Under most circumstances, we do not plan to purchase fixed income securities which have maturities longer than ten years.

Figure 14–2   ADV Form–Schedule F

Schedule F of Form ADV Continuation Sheet for Form ADV Part II	Applicant: Frontier Capital Management Co., Inc.	SEC File Number: 801- 15724	Date: March, 1992
	(Do not use this Schedule as a continuation sheet for Form ADV Part I or any other schedules.)		

1. Full name of applicant exactly as stated in Item 1A of Part I of Form ADV: Frontier Capital Management Company, Inc.		IRS Empl. Ident. No.: 04-2715137

Item of Form (Identify)	Answer
Part II Page 4 (5)	Education and Business Standards: The Firm considers its people to be its most valuable asset. It therefore has demanding ethical and educational standards for all employees determining or giving investment advice. All employees must have the highest moral standards and be free of past criminal convictions involving securities violations. In addition, while not formally required, all employees rendering investment advice have many years of experience in investment advisory activities and extensive post-graduate educational degrees, generally a Masters Degree in Business Administration. All senior officers are expected to have completed the C.F.A. or equivalent program. New employees are encouraged to complete the C.F.A. program, for which the company provides funding, as quickly as possible.

Figure 14-2   ADV Form–Schedule F

Schedule F of Form ADV Continuation Sheet for Form ADV Part II	Applicant: Frontier Capital Management Co., Inc.	SEC File Number: 801- 15724	Date: March, 1992

(Do not use this Schedule as a continuation sheet for Form ADV Part I or any other schedules.)

I. Full name of applicant exactly as name in item 1A of Part I of Form ADV: Frontier Capital Management COmpany, Inc.	I.R.S. Empl. Ident. No.: 04-2715137

Item of Form (Identify)	Answer

Part II
 	
Page 4
 	
(6)
	J. David Wimberly, Born 1934
	    Southern Methodist University, Graduated 1955
	    University of Oklahoma, Graduated 1957
	    Harvard Business School, Graduated 1958
	
	    Frontier Capital Management Co., Inc. - 1981 to Present
	
	Donald E. August, Born 1942
	    Brown University, Graduated 1964
	    Harvard Business School, Graduated 1966
	
	    Frontier Capital Management Co., Inc. - 1981 to Present
	
	Thomas W. Duncan, Born 1943
	    St.Peter's College, Graduated 1965
	    Harvard Business School, Graduated 1969
	
	    Frontier Capital Management Co., Inc. - 1983 to Present
	
	James B. Howard, Born 1931
	    Amherst College, Graduated 1952
	    Harvard Business School, Graduated 1957
	
	    Frontier Capital Management Co., Inc. - 1984 to Present
	
	Grace K. Fey, Born 1946
	    Immaculate College, Graduated 1966
	    University of Maryland, Graduated 1970
	
	    Frontier Capital Management Co., Inc. - 1988 to Present
	    Investment Management Associates - 1986 to 1988
	    Winchester Capital Management - 1980 to 1986

Chapter 14

Figure 14–2   ADV Form–Schedule F

Schedule F of Form ADV Continuation Sheet for Form ADV Part II	Applicant: Frontier Capital Management Co., Inc.	SEC File Number: 801. 15724	Date: March, 1992

(Do not use this Schedule as a continuation sheet for Form ADV Part I or any other schedules.)

I. Full name of applicant exactly as stated in Item 1A of Part I of Form ADV: Frontier Capital Management Company, Inc.	IRS Empl. Ident. No.: 04-2715137

Item of Form (Identify)	Answer
Part II Page 5 9(A)	The Company serves as sole investment advisor, as well as general partner to the two limited partnerships described in the answer to Item 8D of Part II. Generally, the limited partners of these partnerships consist of individuals with whom the Company has existing client relationships. From time to time, the Company, certain related persons of the Company, including the Company's Pension and Profit Sharing Plans, and certain executive officers and directors of the Company and their families have purchased and intend to continue to purchase interests in these limited partnerships. All such purchases are made at the same price at which the interests are offered to outside investors at the time of purchase and are otherwise effected in a manner identical to purchases by outside investors. Because these occasional purchases of limited partnership interests may be deemed to constitute "purchases" of "securities" from a "client," the Company has checked the box opposite 9A. There are no other circumstances in which the Company, acting as a principal, may be deemed to buy securities from or sell securities to any client.

Figure 14–2 ADV Form–Schedule F

Schedule F of Form ADV Continuation Sheet for Form ADV Part II	Applicant: Frontier Cap. Management Co., Inc.	SEC File Number: 801- 15724	Date: March, 1992

(Do not use this Schedule as a continuation sheet for Form ADV Part I or any other schedules.)

1. Full name of applicant exactly as stated in Item 1A of Part I of Form ADV: Frontier Capital Management Company, Inc.	I.R.S. Empl. Ident. No.: 04-2715137

Item of Form (Identify)	Answer
Part II Page 5 (10)	The Firm manages institutional and high net worth portfolios on a fully discretionary basis. The minimum account size is $1,000,000. The Firm has discretion to make exceptions.

Chapter 14

Figure 14–2   ADV Form–Schedule F

Schedule F of Form ADV Continuation Sheet for Form ADV Part II	Applicant: Frontier Capital Management Co., Inc.	SEC File Number: 801- 15724	Date: March, 1992

(Do not use this Schedule as a continuation sheet for Form ADV Part I or any other schedules.)

I. Full name of applicant exactly as stated in Item 1A of Part I of Form ADV: Frontier Capital Management Company, Inc.	IRS Empl. Ident. No.: 04-2715137

Item of Form (identify)	Answer
Part II Page 6 12(A)	All accounts managed by the Firm will be fully discretionary. In this connection, the Firm will determine which securities will be bought or sold, and the commission rate to be paid when effecting such transactions. It is the intention of the Firm to seek competitive or "best execution" rates of commission from broker/dealers on all such transactions. However, it reserves the right to execute transactions through the broker/dealer whose transaction costs on an individual trade may not be the lowest available if, in the opinion of the Firm, such broker/dealer provides research or other services which enhance the probability of achieving the goals and objectives of the Firm's clients. In cases where Frontier is recommended to a client by a broker and the client instructs Frontier to execute transactions through the referral broker, Frontier's policy is to honor the client's request, even though the commission rates negotiated between the client and the broker may be higher or lower than rates negotiated between Frontier and the broker. With respect to research services provided by broker/dealers, the Firm will conduct an internal survey on a bi-monthly basis as a means of establishing the relative value of various research services available to it. This poll will serve as a basis for allocating brokerage commissions to various broker/dealers but will not supersede the primary objective of obtaining the best execution transactions, nor will it in any way serve as a contract or a pledge to deliver predetermined or minimum amounts of brokerage commissions to any Firm. The Firm will honor all client-directed brokerage transactions associated with beneficial and legal services provided to the client. The Firm also reserves the right to compensate brokerage firms for statistical or other services not directly related to research inputs on individual companies which, in its opinion, contributes to the proper management of client accounts. In assessing the importance of research inputs from various brokerage firms, the direct relationship between those inputs and transactions in any individual accounts will not be limiting in determining the allocation of commissions in each and every account.

164

Figure 14–2   ADV Form–Schedule F

Schedule F of Form ADV Continuation Sheet for Form ADV Part II	Applicant: Frontier Capital Management Co., Inc.	SEC File Number: 801- 15724	Date: March, 1993

(Do not use this Schedule as a continuation sheet for Form ADV Part I or any other schedules.)

I. Full name of applicant exactly as stated in Item 1A of Part I of Form ADV: Frontier Capital Management Company, Inc.	IRS Empl. Ident. No.: 04-2715137

Item of Form (identify)	Answer
Part II Page 6 13(A & B)	In 1992 the Firm did business with over 100 brokerage firms. At year-end 1992, the Firm's institutional policy was to pay a maximum of $.07 per share commission, or 50% off old rate (whichever is less) on all listed trades. Unless directed in writing by a client, the Firm will not do business with brokers charging higher rates than this figure. Consistent with best execution at this $.07 per share figure, approximately 75% of the Firm's listed commissions in 1992 were directed to brokers providing research and services to the Firm and/or its clients, 25% of this directed business involved requests made to the Firm by its clients in payment for services provided directly to the client by specific brokers, such as performance measurement services. It is the policy of the Firm, consistent with best execution, to honor such requests but with the understanding that only the commissions produced in the particular client's account will be utilized to satisfy these client-specific requests. Great care is taken to segregate these requests by the Firm's trading department. As of 12/31/92, the Firm has entered into numerous arrangements with brokers, again consistent with best execution and uniform commissions of $.07 per share, or 50% off the old rate (whichever is less) for general research and investment strategy services which can benefit all of the Firm's clients. A summary of the brokerage firms involved and a brief description of the related services is documented below:

Broker	Service/Description
Bear Stearns	Zacks
Bear Stearns	Herold Oil Service
Bear Stearns	ISI
J.C. Bradford	Research luncheons
Bridge	Bridge Data - Industry and company research data base and related computer equipment incident thereto.
Brick Securities	"Insider Trading" reports

165

Chapter 14

Figure 14-2   ADV Form–Schedule F

Schedule F of Form ADV Continuation Sheet for Form ADV Part II	Applicant: Frontier Capital Management Co., Inc.	SEC File Number: 801- 15724	Date: March, 1993

(Do not use this Schedule as a continuation sheet for Form ADV Part I or any other schedules.)

I. Full name of applicant exactly as stated in Item 1A of Part I of Form ADV: Frontier Capital Management Company, Inc.	IRS Empl. Ident. No.: 04-2715137

Item of Form (identify)	Answer
Part II Page 6 13(A & B) (Continued)	**Broker** **Service Description** Fidelity Billings Research Gordon Haskett Indata Portfolio Analysis Interstate First Call Jeffries Forum Research meetings with company managements McDonnell & Company Horizon Research - Industry and company earnings forecasts/surveys William O'Neil O'Neil Data Base - Investment strategy and data base screens Pershing SEI Carl H. Pforzheimer Oil News - Oil research S & P Securities S & P research reports Salomon Brothers Deemer Technical Research PIRA Oil Petrie Parkman Research (0.1) All else being equal, the value of products, research and services provided to the Firm for the benefit of its clients by the above brokers is a factor in the decision to effect transactions with them. Because of intense competition within the brokerage industry, the Firm has not found it necessary to "pay up" for any of the above research services. Individual Business: The majority of accounts in our individual business are broker directed, and the commission level is determined between the broker and the client, as described in Part II Page 12(A).

Figure 14–2   ADV Form–Schedule F

Schedule F of Form ADV Continuation Sheet for Form ADV Part II	Applicant: Frontier Capital Management Co., Inc.	SEC File Number: 801- 15724	Date: September, 1992

(Do not use this Schedule as a continuation sheet for Form ADV Part I or any other schedules.)

I. Full name of applicant exactly as stated in Item 1A of Part I of Form ADV:	IRS Empl. Ident. No.:
Frontier Capital Management Company, Inc.	04–2715137

Item of Form (identify)	Answer
Part II Page 5 9(D&E)	Additionally, under certain circumstances the Company's officers, directors, portfolio managers and other persons (collectively, "access persons") making investment decisions on behalf of Company clients are permitted to invest in securities in which the Company may have invested client funds. These circumstances are set forth in a Code of Ethics which the Company requires all of its access persons to review, sign and adhere to. The Code of Ethics generally prohibits all access persons from engaging in any transaction which would constitute a violation of Section 206 of the Investment Advisers Act of 1940, and Rules 204-2(a)(B) promulgated thereunder, and section 17(J) of the Investment Company Act of 1940, and Rule 17J-1 promulgated thereunder. Additionally, the Code specifically proscribes certain enumerated transactions as per se violations of the Code. Each access person is required to report to the Company all securities transactions engaged in for his or her account (except those over which such person has no control or which are in U.S. government securities). The President or any disinterested director (i.e., a director not involved in any way in the transaction) of the Company is authorized and empowered to review all such transactions against the requirements of the Code of Ethics and to report any violation of the Code to the Company's Board of Directors which may impose appropriate sanctions against the offender. Finally, access persons are permitted to trade in securities through outside broker/dealers engaged by the Company to execute client transactions.

Figure 14–2   ADV Form

HOW TO READ THE COVER PAGE

Relative Cycle Analysis

The Relative Cycle Analysis chart covers a 5 year time frame and shows how the investment adviser performed in calendar quarters when the S&P 500 or Bond Index rose in price and in those quarters when the S&P 500 or Bond Index declined in price. Equity and balanced accounts are compared to the S&P 500 market cycle, while fixed income accounts are compared to the Bond Index market cycle.

The unshaded bar on the left shows the percent of the market gain the manager realized during each of the up-market quarters (as measured by an appropriate index) in the analysis period. For instance, if the number is 70, the manager achieved 70% of the market gain during those periods. If the number is 150, the manager achieved 150% of the market gain during those periods.

The shaded bar on the right shows how the manager performed in down-market quarters. Again, if the number is -70, the manager lost 70% of the market decline. If the number is -120, the manager lost 20% more than the market decline.

What one generally looks for is an adviser who realizes a greater percentage rise in the rising markets than drop in the declining markets.

Long-Term Achievement

This chart compares the performance of the adviser's portfolios to a related market index during the period indicated and shows the relative growth of $1.00 invested by the adviser and the market index over that period of time.

Manager Evaluation

This table provides additional statistics on the manager's performance. The key refers to the symbols used in the Long-Term Achievement chart.

CUM ANL ROR

Cumulative annual rate of return.

RANK

The rank (in percentage) of this adviser versus other equity, balanced or fixed income advisers in the Performance Analytics universe over the time period indicated. A rank of 10 would indicate the adviser was in the top 10% of the universe.

BETA

Beta is a measure of volatility which is one means to measure risk. It associates the volatility of the portfolio with the volatility of the market. For equities, the market is the S&P 500; for balanced funds, the market is the Balanced Index; for fixed income, the market is the Merrill Lynch Master Bond Index. A beta of 1.20 implies volatility 20% greater than the market, since the market is, by definition, 1.00. A beta of .80 would imply 20% less volatility than the market.

QTR ALPHA

The alpha expresses the investment manager's superior or inferior performance after adjusting for the portfolio beta. Alphas are measured quarterly.

Managers that beat the market on a beta-adjusted basis have positive alphas (more than 0.0), and those that were beaten by the market have negative alphas (less than 0.0).

VAL ADDED

Value added is the return the manager achieved in excess of that which might have been expected, given the amount of volatility he or she assumed. The determination of value added is based on the assumption that there is an expected return on a portfolio, based on the return of the market and the volatility the manager is assuming. If the market advanced 10% and a manager had a beta of 1.50, the expected return for the portfolio would be 15%, or 50% greater than the market's return. If the manager achieved a return of 20%, his value added score would be 5% (his actual return of 20% minus his expected return of 15%).

QTR ST DEV

The standard deviation is a measure of the asset's volatility. The standard deviation is the dispersion of actual returns around the mean return. Since the standard deviation measures how much an asset's return fluctuates, it is often used as a measure of risk. For example, if OTC U.S. equities had a higher standard deviation than NYSE listed equities, 22.4% versus 16.3%, OTC equities would be more volatile.

R SQD

R SQD is both a measure of diversification and a gauge of the percentage of the portfolio's movement that is explained by the movement of the market. An R SQD of 0.90 would indicate that the portfolio is 90% as diversified as the market and that 90% of this portfolio's movement is explained by the market, while the other 10% is attributable to other factors that are stock- and not market-specific.

YEARS

The time period for which data is available for this investment adviser.

CYCLE ANALYSIS

Cycle Analysis is a numeric presentation similar to the Relative Cycle Analysis (RCA) charts except that the number of years of data represented may be different and the comparative index used for balanced funds is different.

The time period under review is indicated within the Manager Evaluation table. Balanced funds are compared to the Balanced Index market cycle rather than the S&P 500 as is the case in the RCA chart.

BOND INDEX

Merrill Lynch Government/Corporate Master Bond Index. Average maturity approximately 9 years.

BALANCED INDEX

An index comprised of 50% the S&P 500 for Equity and 50% the Shearson/Lehman Government/Corporate Bond Index for Fixed Income.

CHAPTER 15

MAKING THAT FINAL CHOICE

Although the material supplied by most wrap sponsor firms does an excellent job of quantifying the return objectives and the risk tolerance of the investor, it still leaves the investor with as many as two to six managers from which to choose! The information in the manager profiles goes a long way toward helping the investor, but it doesn't provide him with a structured approach to making that final choice. There are three key areas the investor and his prospect should examine as the field is narrowed down.

How can you tell explicitly if a manager gets enough extra return to justify the extra risk? Fortunately, there is a simple way to compare apples to apples in this situation. It is called the reward-to-risk ratio.

An analogy might be useful here. Consider automobiles for a moment. The range, in miles, of a car (on a single tank of gas) is somewhat like the returns of a manager. The size of the gas tank (or, more appropriately, the cost of filling that gas tank) is somewhat like the risk taken by a manager. The "market line" for this analogy would plot the range on the vertical axis and the gallons (or cost) on the horizontal axis. For certain drivers, the range would be more important than the cost of the fuel. For others, the reverse would be true. But

We would like to thank Kurt R. Winrich, Winrich Capital Management, Inc., for his contribution to this chapter.

169

the miles-per-gallon figure puts two cars on a comparable basis and, if cost is of any importance, allows the driver to determine which car is a better value (style and/or comfort aside).

You've probably already realized that the reward-to-risk ratio to the investor is nothing more than miles-per-gallon ratio to the driver. Most consultants can provide an investor with manager profiles and all the additional information needed to calculate reward-to-risk ratios. The returns are listed in Table 15–1, and the risk can be read from the market line chart. There's one refinement that should be made clear, however. The so-called "risk-free rate of return" (i.e., Treasury bills) should be subtracted from the manager's return. Why? Well, think back to the car analogy. If the first 50 miles of the trip were downhill, you could coast without using any gas (risk) at all, and your miles-per-gallon would be infinite! Obviously, what's important is how your car does after you reach level ground.

Since any car could coast at no cost, you should subtract those 50 miles from the total range. Likewise with the manager's returns.

Table 15–1 is an example of how to calculate the reward-to-risk ratio for Winrich Capital Management (using the March 1989 profile).

To put that into perspective, the reward-to-risk ratio for the S&P 500, over those same 8 years, was 0.27. Thus, Winrich Captial's reward-to-risk ratio was more than twice as good as the stock market.

Table 15–1   Reward-to-Risk Ratio

8-year return (annualized)	15.09%
Risk-free rate (T-Bills)	9.25%
Difference (excess return):	5.84%
8-year risk (from chart)	10.30 %
Reward-to-risk ratio:	0.57

Second, and more importantly, is the analysis of the philosophy and strategy. There are two important aspects of the philosophy to consider.

The first question should be, "Is it sound and is it logical?" Put in another way, does the manager's approach to investing make sense? Don't be fooled into believing that a successful investment philosophy must be incomprehensible (at least to us "mere mortals"). I'm not speaking of the details of investing—those may indeed be complex. What I'm talking about are the underlying principles that the manager goes by. And, as one investment consultant told me a few years ago, "If the manager can't explain how they invest, they probably don't understand it themselves!" That's not the kind of manager I'd be comfortable with!

The second question should be, "Is this manager's philosophy compatible with mine?" In other words, are you going to be forever anxious and uneasy with the manager's approach and activity? Or will you feel content and relaxed?

The manager should have goals that are consistent with your goals. The manager should also follow some basic principles in their strategy for reaching those goals. These are questions and areas that should be explored before anyone is disappointed or disillusioned.

Third, and most important, is an analysis of the investment process. This is so critical because it is the "link" to the future. If the process is systematic and disciplined, then the investor can have confidence that the great results of the past are more than likely to continue into the future. After all, the future is what's most important to the investor.

To analyze the investment process, I suggest that you look for five key elements.

The first is security selection criteria. Ask, for example, how they are determined, and what causes them to change.

171

In my opinion, explicit, well-defined criteria for security selection makes the most sense.

The second is the security selection process. Wonderful criteria is of little value if it is not applied. And that application should be to a sufficiently large "universe" of choices to make certain that few if any opportunities are missed.

The third is portfolio implementation. If the manager picks great securities, the investor should feel confident that they will own those securities in their portfolio. Otherwise, great security selections are meaningless.

The fourth is portfolio monitoring. Once the securities are in the portfolio, there should be an effective method for making certain that each portfolio stays invested according to the firm's policy and strategy in the context of client guidelines.

The fifth, and maybe most important, is security sell disciplines. After all, the bottom line is income and realized gains. Taking profits and minimizing losses is the goal, and though there is no perfect system, this has to be better than no system at all.

Always ask questions like, "Who or what keeps the system running?" Determine if it depends on one or more key individuals. If they own the firm, that may be all right, but if not, what happens if these people leave? Once again, your goal in analyzing the investment process is to gain the confidence that the results of the past are more than likely to continue into the future.

A 10% return may seem adequate but how does it compare to other similar investments? Did they earn 15%, 20%, or more? To accurately evaluate a portfolio's performance, you need a measurement that highlights those aspects of return that are due to the investment manager's performance—the time weighted rate of return (see Table 15–2). This measurement eliminates the effects on the portfolio of timing

Table 15–2   Time Weighted Rate of Return

Many factors influence portfolio return. Consider the following example:

Portfolio	Beginning Value	Ending Value	Percentage Increase
A	$100,000	$110,000	10%
B	$500,000	$550,000	10%
C	$2,000,000	$2,200,000	10%

In each of the portfolios, it appears that there is a 10% return on the funds invested, but this is not necessarily the case. Many factors affect portfolio performance. The increase of 10% could have resulted from:

The client's own contribution

Investment earnings (interest, dividends, market growth)

A combination of both

and magnitude of external cash flows (i.e., the client's own contributions and withdrawals). Because the manager does not typically have control on external cash flows it is important to factor them out. Thus, the time weighted rate of return more accurately reflects the manager's influence on the portfolio than would total return.

BUILDING A WRAP ACCOUNT RELATIONSHIP

If you currently are in a wrap program, you already know just how important the "value-added" service portion of the investment management equation really is. For those who aren't familiar with the importance of this aspect of consulting, it is simply this: The ability on the part of the broker to maintain, advise, protect, and evaluate all areas of the client's investment portfolio. Now, there is a big difference between brokers who, unfortunately, just give "lip service" and those who sincerely are interested in helping to maximize the performance of the investment portfolio. Let me explain.

All too often, well-meaning brokers think that good service means that they must try to please clients by carrying out their orders, or by doing what the clients want regardless of whether or not the particular investment idea is appropriate or safe. It's also very easy for some brokers to make the assumption that if a client is older—and therefore wiser—he certainly should know more and be able to make better decisions. This assumption may create an uneasiness on the part of the broker to dispute the investor's wishes.

We would like to thank Sydney LeBlanc, former editor of *Registered Representative*, for her contribution to this chapter.

175

Chapter 16

At times, a wealthy and successful investor will intimidate an inexperienced broker. The broker may not want to rock the boat for fear of losing a sizable account.

What many brokers fail to take into account is that some investors actually resist letting go of their authority to make their own decisions. The investor might be the president of his own company, an attorney, or a retired doctor—an individual who is used to making all of his own financial decisions. This type of investor needs direction, education, and advice that is simple, straightforward, and truthful. It's not at all uncommon for some brokers to think, "I'll make my client happy by asking for his preferences of investments. Then I'll sell him the products, make my commission and everybody wins." Sadly, this is a "keep 'em happy at any cost" attitude that just doesn't work. And most investors realize this in the long run. Let's use a specific example to illustrate this:

A client is with a broker for a year and a half. He is not yet on the wrap program and his broker is executing his trades. He'll make ten trades, trades that he instructed the broker to execute. Eight of them will be profitable and two of them will be losers. The excitement of the trading was fun for the client and the broker made a good commission. But, let's take a closer look at this transaction: The client probably made eight one-point profits and two 10-point losses. Human nature being what it is, the client might sit back and think, "Hmmm, I made a profit, and that's the eighth one this year—plus I've only had two losses." Well, it doesn't take a rocket scientist to figure out that it should be the other way around. So, then what happens?

The client soon tires of waiting for the profit to turn around and suddenly the broker becomes the scapegoat, even though the client directed the trades. The client accuses the broker of making most of the money. Now, think about it for a minute. Is the client right? Of course he is.

Even though the broker felt that he was properly servicing his client, the client lost. This scenario would never have occurred in the wrap program because the money manager directs the trades. Neither client nor broker is involved in the process. The broker rests easy because there exists no conflict of interest, and he can best service his client by monitoring the performance of the manager and offering regularly updated portfolio status reports. And the client rests easily because he knows that his money is being professionally managed by someone who has a track record of consistent performance, and someone who can be trusted to act in his (the investor's) best interest.

If an investor insists on making the decisions, it's perfectly okay to work through a discount brokerage to choose stocks, bonds, funds, and other products. But full service is generally not available—and it's the guidance and expertise that a client receives that can make that crucial difference between success and failure.

I would not recommend for an investor to plan his own portfolio or to invest his life savings without a full-service broker or an investment management consultant. I compare an inexperienced investor to the character in the story, "Telling the Surgeon How to Operate." If you've ever heard the one about the broker who was getting ready to undergo an operation who also had a previous discussion with his surgeon about investments, this analogy may hit home. Said the surgeon to his broker-patient, "Oh, no, I don't need an investment consultant. I've got subscriptions to the *Wall Street Journal* and *Forbes*, and I even read investment books from time to time. I can do it myself." The broker was disappointed with the doctor's attitude, but on the day of the operation, when they wheeled him into the operating room

Chapter 16

and he came face to face with the doctor, he pulled out a copy of *Gray's Anatomy* and the *American Medical Journal*. Confused, the surgeon said, "What are you doing bringing these books into the operating room?" To which the broker-patient replied, "Doc, I don't need you. With what I've learned from these medical books, I'm going to do the operation myself!" Brave man!

Now, what if a client wanted municipals (here, again, he is not in a wrap program). If the broker were to calculate mathematically he'd be better off compounding in an annuity—even after taxes—than he would be in tax-exempts. Wouldn't he recommend that course of action? Of course he would. But, again, many investment professionals are so eager to please that they will often make poor investment choices to avoid disagreeing with the client. So what happens? Just like clockwork, the client comes back after he experiences a loss in his account and asks what he should do with the bonds "the broker sold him." About the only thing the broker could do at this point is say (and hopefully he took notes at the time of the transaction), "I can see in my notes that I advised against these bonds and I warned you that you might have a loss, and it would have been a better investment choice to put your money into annuities."

The point is that the broker followed all the rules, executed the client's order to buy the bonds, made the client happy at the time, but now, the broker loses too. Even though the product was sold with full disclosure, relationships built on this type of foundation will eventually crumble. This is why the wrap program has been so successful on Wall Street, because everybody wins. The human nature factor has been taken away from both the investor and the broker and an effective investment management system has been put into place.

Building a Wrap Account Relationship

A large portion of the consultant's fee is based on determining what the investor's needs and goals are, as well as what his temperament and tolerance levels are. The consultant teaches the client about the discipline of having a system (such as the wrap program), and if the investor understands and trusts the broker and his system, then he will feel comfortable leaving the financial decision making to the money manager.

Occasionally, a broker may appear as though he is trying to win a popularity contest, that he really wants his clients to like and respect him. And they will, but only if he does his best to show his client how to obtain the best possible performance from his portfolio, and how to preserve that capital through the wrap program. As a result of the success of the system, popularity and respect will automatically follow.

Brokers lose clients when clients lose their money. And a client loses money when he doesn't fully understand the guts of any investment, when he gives in to human nature, or when he doesn't take advantage of the knowledge, the experience, and the systems that a dedicated, professional broker uses.

Investors need the elementary facts about the market and about their own financial goals. They need to be more open and willing to learn about investments and specific money management systems, including the wrap program.

Sometimes a client will ask himself, "Am I going to use a stockbroker or an investment management consultant to help me manage my money, or am I going to do it myself? If I use a broker, am I going to let him guide and teach me?" Here again, is where the broker will use discipline and will not hesitate to explain to the client the best system or the best money manager to use. The customer should be made aware that investment management is simply a system used to invest capital. The individual managing the investment becomes the most critical ingredient in the system, and can make or break the portfolio. This is where the client should pay the most attention to the broker's selection of a manager. That is what the broker is paid to do—evaluate the managers, choose one, monitor the performance and so forth. This is why the wrap program is so valuable.

Unfortunately, it has become almost a tradition in the securities industry to sell something that is popular or something that the firm is promoting. Successful brokers don't compromise their beliefs and their value system. To them, it's not what is popular, but what is in the best interest of the client.

The responsibility of choosing a money manager is also very important and clients should not lose sight of this. At times, a client will hear about a manager who has had a superior performance record for one or two years, and will ask his broker to set up the account with this manager. This is the time for the broker to explain to the client that advisors run hot and cold. Consistency is the most important factor in the selection process and performance should be judged over a five- to ten-year period.

It's awfully discouraging for some clients (and they often find out too late) to discover that they're only making 2-3% per year over a three- or four-year period, when just the year before they invested with the manager he gained fame for making a whopping 80% return. This makes a very good case for working with an investment consultant who can offer that "added value" to help choose the correct money manager for you.

Human nature plays an important role in the profit and loss adventure on Wall Street. Many investors fall prey to tempting investment situations that sound too good to be true—and usually are. These situations are usually speculative and should never be confused with the tried-and-true methods of investing. It's important for investors to know the difference between speculating and investing, and once again, this is where the broker steps in and advises against dangerous situations. Speculators usually fall victim to the basest elements of human nature because they thrive on the uncertainty of the roll of the dice, the danger of the all-or-nothing scheme, the risk of the get-rich-quick program.

The bottom line is that the conservative investor wants and needs a plan. He is driven only by the logic and the discipline of a system. He has done his homework and paid his dues. He deserves the best because he's earned it.

PART IV

MEASURING INVESTMENT PERFORMANCE

CHAPTER 17

INVESTMENT PERFORMANCE CONFUSION

Anyone who has heard a sales pitch about wrap programs from different stock brokerage firms may agree that there is a lot of confusion around investment performance. It seems that each brokerage house represents the number one manager in the country. How can this be? Everyone can't be number one, or can they?

One basic problem is letting the brokerage firm or money management firm pick the time period to represent their performance. There will be some period of time when a manager will show top quartile performance of all money managers in the country, just remember that even a broken clock is right twice a day.

Mutual funds, banks, brokers, insurance companies, and money managers use all sorts of methods to calculate investment returns. While the different approaches are usually perfectly legitimate, they can make comparisons difficult.

One thing to keep in mind—performance figures you see in brochures are there for one reason—marketing.

But as a wrap investor, you don't have to be helpless. Either you can solicit the help from an investment management consultant or take the time to get a better understanding of how performance is reported, and grasp just how risk-and-return statistics actually work. You can reduce the chance of falling victim to inflated sales pitches.

If a manager shows that three years of returns on an investment portfolio totals 33%, did the investment earn 11% a year or 10% a year? Both answers, and numerous others, are correct. How can this be?

The difference arises from the use of two types of return calculations. The simplest is the "average," where the returns for any number of past periods are added up and divided by the number of periods.

The second calculation, more widely used by investment firms, is the "compound," or annualized, rate of return. This figure is the rate at which $1 would have to grow in each of several periods to reach an ending amount.

Unlike the average, the compound return takes into account the sequence of earnings or losses. That's because a gain or loss in any one year, directly affects the amount of money left to build up in the next and subsequent years. Thus, a big gain in an earlier year generates a higher compound return than if the same gain had occurred more recently.

In addition, the bigger the swings in the returns from one period to the next, the lower the returns compared with average calculations.

Both return calculations can be useful in checking an investment's track record. The average return is going to give you some information about what is most likely to happen, but used together with the compound return, you also get the idea of the risk involved, so it's nice to look at both.

Time versus Dollar Weighting: While average and compound calculations produce different returns over several periods, the choice between so-called time-weighted and dollar-weighted calculations produces different return figures for the same period.

The dollar-weighted, or internal, calculations show the change in value of a portfolio for the average funds invested in the period, including cash added or withdrawn by the investor. That sounds like it covers all the bases, but those cash flows can be a problem in calculating the true performance of the investment manager. Because the manager can't control the size and timing of money flowing in and out of an account, a time-weighted calculation can be made to figure the value of $1 invested for the entire period, eliminating distortions from cash flows.

For the question of how your investment manager is doing, you want a time-weighted return. For the question of how your money is doing, you might want to calculate the dollar-weighted rate of return.

The difference between the return calculations is illustrated by two investors, each of whom opens a $100 account with a money manager. The manager buys a share of the same $50 stock for each client. A year later, each share has risen to $100. Client A adds $100, which the manager uses to buy another share of the same stock. Finally, after another year, the stock is back to $50.

On a time-weighted basis, the return on both accounts is zero because $1 invested at the start of the period was still $1 at the end. But on a dollar-weighted basis, Client A's account shows a negative 18.1% return, as the $150 invested fell to $100 Client B, with $100 at the start and the end of the period with no cash flows, had a zero dollar-weighted return.

Over short periods of, say, a month, or when there aren't cash flows, the differences between time-weighted and dollar-weighted calculations usually aren't significant. But they grow in importance as the time and cash flow increases.

Chapter 17

Per-share values of mutual funds are calculated on a time-weighted basis. Returns for savings accounts paying a constant rate are the same whether calculated on the time-weighted or dollar-weighted basis.

Volatility: It might appear that a 10% investment gain in one period, followed by a 10% loss the next period would leave you no worse off than when you started, but the math doesn't work out that way. What first grew to $110 in this example would then shrink to $99 in the next period.

The distortion is greater with bigger numbers. A 50% loss on $100 followed by a 50% gain leaves you at $75, still a long way from the original $100. In fact, it requires a 100% gain to get back to the original $100 investment.

Such big swings reflect high volatility that can eat deeply into portfolio results over time. Cautious investment professionals continuously warn that risk and returns are usually linked, as evidenced most recently by the performance of the high-risk, high-yield junk bond market. Because a loss in just one year will put a dent in investment results for years to come, it's well worth reviewing volatility as closely as returns.

By looking at only raw rates of return, you often have a very incomplete picture of why the manager earned what he did.

The important thing to know is the kinds of risk that a manager took to get that rate of return.

The AIMR Performance Presentation Standards can give you some insights into how managers report their results. They are a set of guiding ethical principles intended to promote full disclosure and fair representation in the reporting of investment results.

The objective of these Standards is to ensure uniformity in reporting so that results are directly comparable among investment managers. To this end, some aspects of the Standards are mandatory. These are listed below. However, not every situation can be anticipated in a set of guidelines. Therefore, meeting the full disclosure and fair representation intent means making a conscientious good faith interpretation of the Standards consistent with the underlying ethical principles.

MANDATORY REQUIREMENTS

- Presentation of total return using accrual as opposed to cash basis accounting (accrual accounting is not required for dividends, nor is it required for retroactive compliance).

- Time-weighted rate of return using a minimum of quarterly valuation (monthly preferred) and geometric linking of period returns.

- Size-weighted composites using beginning of period values to weigh the portfolio returns (equal-weighted composites are recommended as additional information, but are not mandatory).

- Inclusion of all actual, fee-paying, discretionary portfolios in one or more composites within the firm's management (no selectivity in portfolios, no simulation or portability of results within composites).

- Presentation of annual returns at a minimum for all years (no selectivity in time periods).

- Inclusion of cash and cash equivalents in composite returns.

Chapter 17

MANDATORY DISCLOSURES

- Prospective investors must be advised that a list of all of a firm's composites are available.

- For each composite, disclosure of the number of portfolios, the amount of assets, and the percentage of a manager's total assets which are represented by the composite. For composites containing five or fewer portfolios, disclosure of composite assets and percentage of firm assets, and a statement indicating that the composite includes five or fewer portfolios.

- Historical compliance is at the discretion of the manager. When the firm's historical performance record is presented, a disclosure must be made that identifies the in-compliance periods from the periods that are not in compliance. the firm must also disclose that the full historical performance record is not in compliance. If semi-annual or annual valuation periods are used to calculate returns and weight composites for retroactive compliance, this must also be disclosed.

- Disclosure of whether balanced portfolio segments are included in single-asset composites and, if so, how the cash has been allocated between asset segments.

- Disclosure of whether performance results are calculated gross or net of fees and inclusion of the manager's fee schedule in either case.

- Disclosure of whether leverage has been used in portfolios included in the composite and the extent of its usage.

- Disclosure of settlement date valuation if used in place of trade date.

- Disclosure of any non-fee paying portfolios included in composites.

STRONGLY RECOMMENDED GUIDELINES AND DISCLOSURES

- Reevaluation of the portfolio whenever cash flows and market action combine to distort performance (cash flows exceeding 10% of the portfolio's market value often cause such distortions). The methodology should be disclosed.

- Dispersion of returns across portfolios in the composite.

- Standard deviation of composite returns across time or other risk measures as determined by the manager.

- Comparative indices appropriate to the composite's strategies.

- Presentation of returns on a cumulative basis for all periods.

- Median size portfolio and portfolio size range for each composite (unless five or fewer portfolios).

- Percentage of total assets managed in the same asset class as represented by the composite. For example, percentage of total equity assets managed.

- Trade date preferred. Settlement date is acceptable but must be disclosed.

- If leverage has been used, results on an all-cash (unleveraged) basis are provided, where possible.

- Convertible securities which are not reported separately are assigned to an asset class (equities, under

191

most circumstances) and cannot be shifted without notice being given to clients concurrently or prior to such shifts.

- Presentation of performance may be either gross or net of fee as long as method is disclosed and the fee schedule is attached. AIMR prefers performance gross of fees.

- Accrual accounting for dividends and for retroactive compliance.

- Equal-weighted composites presented in addition to the mandatory presentation of asset-weighted composites.

What about when a manager uses the total return of a balanced composite to market a balanced account strategy?

- When a manager uses the total return of a balanced composite to market balanced account strategy, but wishes to present the portion of the balanced composite as supplemental information in presenting the balanced strategy, the segment returns can be shown without making a cash allocation as long as the returns for each of the composite's segments (including the cash portion or segment) are shown along with the composite's total return.

- In fixed-income strategies, or other single-asset strategies, a cash allocation to each of the segments must be made at the beginning of the reporting period.

For example, if a manager is using the equity-only returns of the equity portion of the balanced composite as an indication of expertise in managing equity-plus-cash portfolios, the manager must assign a cash allocation to the equity part at the beginning of each reporting period. That segment can then be included on the firm's list of composites.

For retroactive compliance, a manager must make a reasonable and consistent cash allocation to each of the composite segments and must disclose the methodology used for assigning cash.

- When the results of the balanced segments are added to single-asset composites, a cash allocation needs to be made to each of the segments. This prevents a manager from mixing asset-without-cash returns to asset-plus-cash-returns.

CHAPTER 18

AIMR INVESTMENT MANAGER STANDARDS

Compliance with the new AIMR Performance Presentation Standards took effect January 1, 1993. These standards are a hot topic in the investment community. Many investment managers have questions about the Standards. We hope that this chapter will help clarify the issues for you, and if your money manager will help you plan how to comply with the Standards.

In 1987, a special committee of the Financial Analysts Federation delivered their report on uniform performance reporting standards. After incorporating comments from various segments of the investment industry, the AIMR Board of Governors endorsed the Standards in August 1990.

An Implementation Committee then began to develop guidelines for investment managers to use in putting the Standards into practice in their own firms. The Implementation Committee published its report in December 1991, and reaffirmed the timetable for adoption of the Standards:

During 1992, AIMR members and their firms should be implementing the Standards.

Compliance with the Standards became effective on January 1, 1993.

We would like to thank John Griffin at Advent Software, Inc., for providing this copy of AIMR's Checklist for Standards for Performance Measurement.

195

The Implementation Committee has clearly stated that the Standards apply to performance presentation, not performance measurement. Except for the requirements that a time-weighted rate of return be used to calculate return and that total return be used, managers may choose their own performance calculations, within guidelines.

The AIMR has stated that the Standards were developed to close the door on misrepresentation, and to reduce confusion and mistrust among clients and potential clients. They have stressed the seriousness of the need for the Standards in establishing and maintaining consistent, sound, and ethical industry practices.

Besides the AIMR's deadline for compliance, market pressures from clients are building. Many plan sponsors now use compliance with the Standards as a screen for selecting managers. Clearly, noncompliance is becoming a competitive barrier for investment managers.

What does compliance with these Standards entail? How will you comply? Will your portfolio management system allow you to comply? How much work will compliance require? This chapter will help you answer these questions.

As with any major set of new standards, there are a number of issues of interpretation and implementation to consider. These AIMR Standards will have a direct impact on the way in which you manage your business and the systems upon which you rely.

FIVE ISSUES IN AIMR STANDARDS

Five issues in the AIMR Standards have attracted the most attention and questions:

- The use of time-weighted returns

- Presentation of returns before and after fees

- Dollar-weighting of composites

- Assignment of cash balances to asset classes in balanced portfolios

- Verification of performance

Calculate Time-Weighted Returns

Portfolios should be valued at least quarterly. Monthly valuation and linking is preferred.

Daily accounting for contributions and withdrawals is preferred. Portfolios should be revalued whenever a cash flow over 10 percent of the latest market value occurs.

Make sure that your portfolio management system's calculation of performance accounts for cash flows on a daily basis.

Show Returns Net and Gross of Fees

Results should be shown before fees, except when the SEC position on advertising requires that they be shown after fees.

To serve the two masters of SEC regulations and AIMR Standards, your portfolio management system must allow you to calculate and store returns two ways.

Use Dollar-Weighted Composites

Composites should be constructed to show the performance of groups of accounts with similar investment styles, risks and controls.

Composites should be weighted by account size. Your system should allow you to construct size-weighted composites easily and flexibly.

Chapter 18

Assign Cash Balances in Balanced Portfolios
When presenting a composite that represents a single asset class of your balanced portfolios, each asset class segment should be assigned its own cash balance.

When the asset mix is changed, bookkeeping transfers of cash among the asset classes should be made.

This is perhaps the most controversial aspect of the Standards since, for many managers, the assignment of cash to other asset classes presents an operational nightmare.

Verification of Performance
Composite performance should be verified by an independent party.

Your system should use only methods which conform to the Standards and which can be easily verified.

CHECKLIST REVIEW AND IMPLEMENTATION

The AIMR has published a 45-point checklist for compliance with the Standards.

Questions which may be of interest include:

- Must all portfolios be included in composites?

- How many composites do we need to comply?

- How do you define discretionary portfolios?

- What if we don't have historical performance records?

- How are balanced portfolio returns presented?

- How should cash be allocated?

- Must results be audited?

198

- How will the Standards be enforced?

CHECKLIST

I. Performance calculations

A. Performance results have been calculated on a time-weighted basis.

B. Returns combine income and current market valuations (thus presenting total returns).

C. Manager fee levels have been disclosed along with performance records so that after-fee results can be measured.

D. Performance results of broad security classes, such as equities or fixed-income, have been included with cash or substitute securities. If cash has been excluded from the calculations, then returns with cash have been presented with the statement that AIMR Standards consider performance with cash to be most representative of managerial results and most representative compared with other managers.

E. All exclusion from performance calculations and presentation by the manager have been disclosed.

F. The method of linking interim performance results (daily, monthly, quarterly) has been explained. AIMR Standard is for monthly linking.

G. Balanced account performance.

  1. The manager has assigned cash and substitute securities to the specific asset category to which they belong, thereby allowing a clear division of the performance record for each asset managed.

  2. If cash and substitute securities are not assigned to a separate asset, comparison should not be made

199

against other managers' performance figures for assets where cash returns have been included.

3. The manager has supplied information on risk, volatility, and/or measures that allow for reasonable performance evaluation.

H. Convertible securities have been consistently assigned to either equities or fixed-income, and have not been shifted without notice being given to clients concurrent or prior to such shift.

I. Managers have provided the indexes against which their submitted performance records have normally been compared.

J. If managers' assets have been leveraged, and performance returns calculated on this basis, results on an all-cash (unleveraged) basis have been provided.

II. Investment manager composites of performance results

A. The manager has submitted a composite of all accounts managed for each period submitted; the composite includes results from any and all accounts no longer clients of the firm.

B. If a manager has separate composites, all have been submitted. A prospect should be able to account for the performance of all the manager's assets managed.

C. Composites are not "survivors only" compilations; they include results of all accounts ever managed, including those of clients no longer with the firm.

D. All performance results contained in the composite include cash and substitutable securities, as per I.D. above.

E. All individual years and cumulative performance results for all periods have been supplied. The composite covers every year of the past 10 years, along with longer-term results if the manager has been in the business this long.

F. Compounded annualized returns have been provided for all periods.

G. A clear statement from the manager indicates that no selectivity of account results for partial periods exists.

H. Composite or other data have not been altered for reasons of personnel changes or any other reasons.

I. Composite results are:

   1. Weighted for the dollars under management (the AIMR Standard).

   2. Presented on a median (unweighted) basis (recommended only as additional information, not as the primary disclosure).

J. Data includes:

   1. Number of client relationships in the composite.

   2. Assets under management for each period.

   3. Average and median size of accounts in the composite.

   4. Assets shown as a percentage of the manager's total accounts, which share very comparable investment guidelines and risks; and as a percentage of the manager's total funds under management. (All clients and related performance data for this asset type can be accounted for.)

K. Fee information is clear, so that pre- and post-fee results can be determined.

L. Composites include typical indexes against which the manager has been judged.

M. Alpha, beta, standard deviation of returns, and other measures of risk, quality, variability, etc., within the composite for each year have been indicated.

N. Other information provided.

III. Verification of performance data.

A. Results have been audited by reputable auditors.

B. Results are not audited, but include statements that calculations and presentation of individual accounts and composites conform to AIMR Standards.

CHAPTER 19

MONITORING THE PORTFOLIO

There are reports which inform you of management statistics and investment status, display transaction summaries, produce billing and commission data, support trading activities, and present performance results. Reports are your vehicle for communication.

The following Report/Monitor is compliments of "The Professional Portfolio" from Advent Software.*

---

*We would like to thank Advent Software for their contribution to this chapter.

Chapter 19

Table 19–1   Portfolio Monitor
Statement of Management Fees

December 31, 1992

Larry Chambers Wrap Account
P.O. Box 1810
Ojai, CA   93024

Advent Asset Management
Statement Of Management Fees
For The Period October 1, 1992 to December 31, 1992

Portfolio Valuation with Accrued Interest as of 12-31-92	$	610,446.29
610,446 @ 3.000% per annum		4,578.35
Quarterly Wrap Fee	$	4,578.35
Total Due And Payable	$	4,578.35

Table 19–1   Portfolio Monitor
Cash and Equivalent Inventory

Advent Asset Management
Cash & Equivalent Inventory
Larry Chambers Wrap Account
December 31, 1992

Quantity	Security	Total Cost
Cash		
Money Market Fund		59,471.92
		59,471.92
Total Portfolio		59,471.92

Table 19–1   Portfolio Monitor
Fixed Income Inventory

Advent Asset Management
Fixed Income Inventory
Larry Chambers Wrap Account
December 31, 1992

Quantity	Security	Total Cost
Corporate Bonds		
5,000	Gencorp Inc 11.875% Due 09-15-93	4,975.00
5,000	K Mart Corp 12.125% Due 03-01-95	5,612.50
30,000	General Elec Co 8.625% Due 04-01-16	30,309.00
5,000	Toys R Us 8.250% Due 02-01-17	4,872.00
		45,768.50
Municipal Bonds		
5,000	S.F. Hsg Auth 5.000% Due 08-01-01	4,840.00
5,000	Portland Hsg Auth 5.375% Due 02-01-06	4,802.00
5,000	California St 3.625% Due 09-01-09	3,604.50
		13,246.50
Government Bonds		
5,000	U.S. Treasury Bonds 10.500% Due 02-15-95	5,636.00
5,000	U.S. Treasury Bonds 7.000% Due 05-15-98	5,058.00
5,000	U.S. Treasury Bonds 7.625% Due 02-15-07	5,093.50
		15,787.50
Total Portfolio		74,802.50

Table 19–1   Portfolio Monitor
Equity Inventory

Advent Asset Management
Equity Inventory
Larry Chambers Wrap Account
December 31, 1992

Quantity	Security	Total Cost
Common Stock		
1,000	Abbott Labs	29,000.00
270	American Tel & Tel	11,610.00
700	Anheuser Busch	38,500.00
2,750	Atkinson Guy F Co Cal	27,500.00
290	Baxter International	10,440.00
1,100	CML Group Inc	26,950.00
160	Consolidated Edison	4,480.00
280	Duke Power Co	9,520.00
330	General Electric	25,410.00
160	Gillette	7,520.00
480	Harley Davidson	12,480.00
1,100	Heinz H J	41,800.00
700	McDonalds	32,200.00
300	Norfolk Southern	18,900.00
700	Pepsico	24,718.00
500	Procter & Gamble	23,000.00
380	Southern	13,300.00
90	Texas Utilities	3,510.00
880	Time Warner	24,420.00
60	Unilever N V	6,480.00
160	Union Pacific	8,000.00
630	Walt Disney	22,680.00
		422,418.00
Total Portfolio		422,418.00

Table 19–1   Portfolio Monitor
Industry Diversification

Advent Asset Management
Industry Diversification
Larry Chambers Wrap Account
December 31, 1992

Code	Industry	Market Value	Pct.
N/A	Non-Industry Cash Securities	$ 59,471.92	9.8%
N/A	Non-Industry Securities	76,667.82	12.6
60	Conglomerates	34,470.00	5.7
80	Consumer - Other	70,000.00	11.5
90	Consumer - Personal Care	35,912.50	5.9
150	Food	82,662.50	13.6
190	Health - Products & Services	77,438.75	12.7
210	Leisure Time Products	70,890.00	11.6
370	Telecommunications	13,770.00	2.3
375	Transportation	53,516.25	8.8
380	Utilities	33,790.00	5.6
		$ 608,589.74	100.0%

Table 19-1 Portfolio Monitor
Unrealized Gains and Losses

Date	Quantity	Security	Unit Cost	Total Cost	Price	Market Value	Unrealized Gain/Loss	% G/L
Health - Products & Services								
06-30-92	1,000	Abbott Labs	29.00	29,000.00	30.37	30,375.00	1,375.00	4.7
06-30-92	290	Baxter International	36.00	10,440.00	32.37	9,388.75	-1,051.25	-10.1
06-30-92	1,100	CML Group Inc	24.50	26,950.00	34.25	37,675.00	10,725.00	39.8
				66,390.00		77,438.75	11,048.75	16.6
Leisure Time Products								
06-30-92	480	Harley Davidson	26.00	12,480.00	37.62	18,060.00	5,580.00	44.7
06-30-92	880	Time Warner	27.75	24,420.00	29.25	25,740.00	1,320.00	5.4
06-30-92	630	Walt Disney	36.00	22,680.00	43.00	27,090.00	4,410.00	19.4
				59,580.00		70,890.00	11,310.00	19.0
Telecommunications								
06-30-92	270	American Tel & Tel	43.00	11,610.00	51.00	13,770.00	2,160.00	18.6
				11,610.00		13,770.00	2,160.00	18.6
Transportation								
06-30-92	2,750	Atkinson Guy F Co Cal	10.00	27,500.00	9.37	25,781.25	-1,718.75	-6.2
06-30-92	300	Norfolk Southern	63.00	18,900.00	61.25	18,375.00	-525.00	-2.8
06-30-92	160	Union Pacific	50.00	8,000.00	58.50	9,360.00	1,360.00	17.0
				54,400.00		53,516.25	-883.75	-1.6

Table 19–1   Portfolio Monitor
Unrealized Gains and Losses

Date	Quantity	Security	Unit Cost	Total Cost	Price	Market Value	Unrealized Gain/Loss	% G/L
Utilities								
06-30-92	160	Consolidated Edison	28.00	4,480.00	32.62	5,220.00	740.00	16.5
06-30-92	280	Duke Power Co	34.00	9,520.00	36.12	10,115.00	595.00	6.2
06-30-92	380	Southern	35.00	13,300.00	38.50	14,630.00	1,330.00	10.0
06-30-92	90	Texas Utilities	39.00	3,510.00	42.50	3,825.00	315.00	9.0
				30,810.00		33,790.00	2,980.00	9.7
		Common Stock TOTAL		422,418.00		472,450.00	50,032.00	11.8
Corporate Bonds								
06-30-92	5,000	Gencorp Inc 11.875% Due 09-15-93	99.50	4,975.00	100.12	5,006.25	31.25	0.6
06-30-92	5,000	K Mart Corp 12.125% Due 03-01-95	112.25	5,612.50	112.25	5,612.50	0.00	0.0
06-30-92	30,000	General Elec Co 8.625% Due 04-01-16	101.03	30,309.00	105.06	31,518.75	1,209.75	4.0
06-30-92	5,000	Toys R Us 8.250% Due 02-01-17	97.44	4,872.00	100.50	5,025.00	153.00	3.1
				45,768.50		47,162.50	1,394.00	3.0

Table 19–1   Portfolio Monitor
Unrealized Gains and Losses

Date	Quantity	Security	Unit Cost	Total Cost	Price	Market Value	Unrealized Gain/Loss	% G/L
Municipal Bonds								
06-30-92	5,000	S.F. Hsg Auth 5.000% Due 08-01-01	96.80	4,840.00	99.51	4,975.65	135.65	2.8
06-30-92	5,000	Portland Hsg Auth 5.375% Due 02-01-06	96.04	4,802.00	99.67	4,983.50	181.50	3.8
06-30-92	5,000	California St 3.625% Due 09-01-09	72.09	3,604.50	74.24	3,711.80	107.30	3.0
				13,246.50		13,670.95	424.45	3.2
Government Bonds								
06-30-92	5,000	U.S. Treasury Bonds 10.500% Due 02-15-95	112.72	5,636.00	111.66	5,582.81	-53.19	-0.9
06-30-92	5,000	U.S. Treasury Bonds 7.000% Due 05-15-98	101.16	5,058.00	100.87	5,043.75	-14.25	-0.3
06-30-92	5,000	U.S. Treasury Bonds 7.625% Due 02-15-07	101.87	5,093.50	104.16	5,207.81	114.31	2.2
				15,787.50		15,834.37	46.87	0.3
Cash								
Money Market Fund				59,471.92		59,471.92		
				59,471.92		59,471.92		
Total Portfolio				556,692.42		608,589.74	51,897.32	9.3

Table 19-1 Portfolio Monitor Unrealized Gains and Losses

Date	Quantity	Security	Unit Cost	Total Cost	Price	Market Value	Unrealized Gain/Loss	% G/L
Common Stock								
Conglomerates								
06-30-92	330	General Electric	77.00	25,410.00	85.50	28,215.00	2,805.00	11.0
06-30-92	60	Unilever N V	108.00	6,480.00	104.25	6,255.00	-225.00	-3.5
				31,890.00		34,470.00	2,580.00	8.1
Consumer - Other								
06-30-92	700	Anheuser Busch	55.00	38,500.00	58.50	40,950.00	2,450.00	6.4
06-30-92	700	Pepsico	35.31	24,718.00	41.50	29,050.00	4,332.00	17.5
				63,218.00		70,000.00	6,782.00	10.7
Consumer - Personal Care								
06-30-92	160	Gillette	47.00	7,520.00	56.87	9,100.00	1,580.00	21.0
06-30-92	500	Procter & Gamble	46.00	23,000.00	53.62	26,812.50	3,812.50	16.6
				30,520.00		35,912.50	5,392.50	17.7
Food								
06-30-92	1,100	Heinz H J	38.00	41,800.00	44.12	48,537.50	6,737.50	16.1
06-30-92	700	McDonalds	46.00	32,200.00	48.75	34,125.00	1,925.00	6.0
				74,000.00		82,662.50	8,662.50	11.7

Table 19–1   Portfolio Monitor
Portfolio Appraisal

Quantity	Security	Unit Cost	Total Cost	Price	Market Value	Pct. Assets	Yield
Total Portfolio			556,692.42		610,446.29	100.0	2.9

Table 19–1 Portfolio Monitor Portfolio Appraisal

Quantity	Security	Unit Cost	Total Cost	Price	Market Value	Pct. Assets	Yield
Municipal Bonds							
5,000	S.F. Hsg Auth 5.000% Due 08-01-01	96.80	4,840.00	99.51	4,975.65	0.8	5.5
5,000	Portland Hsg Auth 5.375% Due 02-01-06	96.04	4,802.00	99.67	4,983.50	0.8	5.8
5,000	California St 3.625% Due 09-01-09	72.09	3,604.50	74.24	3,711.80	0.6	6.3
	Accrued Interest				276.56	0.0	
			13,246.50		13,947.51	2.3	5.8
Government Bonds							
5,000	U.S. Treasury Bonds 10.500% Due 02-15-95	112.72	5,636.00	111.66	5,582.81	0.9	5.2
5,000	U.S. Treasury Bonds 7.000% Due 05-15-98	101.16	5,058.00	100.87	5,043.75	0.8	6.8
5,000	U.S. Treasury Bonds 7.625% Due 02-15-07	101.87	5,093.50	104.16	5,207.81	0.9	7.4
	Accrued Interest				384.32	0.1	
			15,787.50		16,218.69	2.7	6.4
Cash							
	Money Market Fund		59,471.92		59,471.92	9.7	4.0
			59,471.92		59,471.92	9.7	4.0

Table 19–1   Portfolio Monitor
Portfolio Appraisal

Quantity	Security	Unit Cost	Total Cost	Price	Market Value	Pct. Assets	Yield
Utilities							
160	Consolidated Edison	28.00	4,480.00	32.62	5,220.00	0.9	5.9
280	Duke Power Co	34.00	9,520.00	36.12	10,115.00	1.7	5.0
380	Southern	35.00	13,300.00	38.50	14,630.00	2.4	5.9
90	Texas Utilities	39.00	3,510.00	42.50	3,825.00	0.6	7.2
			30,810.00		33,790.00	5.5	5.8
	Common Stock TOTAL		422,418.00		472,450.00	77.4	1.9
Corporate Bonds							
5,000	Gencorp Inc 11.875% Due 09-15-93	99.50	4,975.00	100.12	5,006.25	0.8	12.3
5,000	K Mart Corp 12.125% Due 03-01-95	112.25	5,612.50	112.25	5,612.50	0.9	7.0
30,000	General Elec Co 8.625% Due 04-01-16	101.03	30,309.00	105.06	31,518.75	5.2	8.5
5,000	Toys R Us 8.250% Due 02-01-17	97.44	4,872.00	100.50	5,025.00	0.8	8.5
	Accrued Interest				1,195.66	0.2	
			45,768.50		48,358.16	7.9	8.7

Table 19-1 Portfolio Monitor
Portfolio Appraisal

Quantity	Security	Unit Cost	Total Cost	Price	Market Value	Pct. Assets	Yield
Health - Products & Services							
1,000	Abbott Labs	29.00	29,000.00	30.37	30,375.00	5.0	2.2
290	Baxter International	36.00	10,440.00	32.37	9,388.75	1.5	3.1
1,100	CML Group Inc	24.50	26,950.00	34.25	37,675.00	6.2	0.2
			66,390.00		77,438.75	12.7	1.4
Leisure Time Products							
480	Harley Davidson	26.00	12,480.00	37.62	18,060.00	3.0	0.0
880	Time Warner	27.75	24,420.00	29.25	25,740.00	4.2	1.0
630	Walt Disney	36.00	22,680.00	43.00	27,090.00	4.4	0.6
			59,580.00		70,890.00	11.6	0.6
Telecommunications							
270	American Tel & Tel	43.00	11,610.00	51.00	13,770.00	2.3	2.6
			11,610.00		13,770.00	2.3	2.6
Transportation							
2,750	Atkinson Guy F Co Cal	10.00	27,500.00	9.37	25,781.25	4.2	0.0
300	Norfolk Southern	63.00	18,900.00	61.25	18,375.00	3.0	2.9
160	Union Pacific	50.00	8,000.00	58.50	9,360.00	1.5	2.5
			54,400.00		53,516.25	8.8	1.5

Table 19–1   Portfolio Monitor
Portfolio Appraisal

Quantity	Security	Unit Cost	Total Cost	Price	Market Value	Pct. Assets	Yield
Common Stock							
Conglomerates							
330	General Electric	77.00	25,410.00	85.50	28,215.00	4.6	2.9
60	Unilever N V	108.00	6,480.00	104.25	6,255.00	1.0	2.6
			31,890.00		34,470.00	5.6	2.9
Consumer - Other							
700	Anheuser Busch	55.00	38,500.00	58.50	40,950.00	6.7	2.2
700	Pepsico	35.31	24,718.00	41.50	29,050.00	4.8	1.3
			63,218.00		70,000.00	11.5	1.8
Consumer - Personal Care							
160	Gillette	47.00	7,520.00	56.87	9,100.00	1.5	1.3
500	Procter & Gamble	46.00	23,000.00	53.62	26,812.50	4.4	2.1
			30,520.00		35,912.50	5.9	1.9
Food							
1,100	Heinz H J	38.00	41,800.00	44.12	48,537.50	8.0	2.7
700	McDonalds	46.00	32,200.00	48.75	34,125.00	5.6	0.8
			74,000.00		82,662.50	13.5	1.9

Chapter 19

Table 19–1　Portfolio Monitor
　　　　　　　　Portfolio Summary

Advent Asset Management
Portfolio Summary
Larry Chambers Wrap Account
December 31, 1992

Security Type	Cost Value	Market Value	Pct. Assets	Yield	Est.Annual Income
Equities					
Common Stock					
Conglomerates	31,890.00	34,470.00	5.6	2.9	993.66
Consumer - Other	63,218.00	70,000.00	11.5	1.8	1,260.00
Consumer - Personal Care	30,520.00	35,912.50	5.9	1.9	665.20
Food	74,000.00	82,662.50	13.5	1.9	1,600.00
Health - Products & Services	66,390.00	77,438.75	12.7	1.4	1,058.00
Leisure Time Products	59,580.00	70,890.00	11.6	0.6	403.90
Telecommunications	11,610.00	13,770.00	2.3	2.6	356.40
Transportation	54,400.00	53,516.25	8.8	1.5	776.80
Utilities	30,810.00	33,790.00	5.5	5.8	1,958.00
	422,418.00	472,450.00	77.4	1.9	9,071.96
Fixed Income					
Corporate Bonds	45,768.50	47,162.50	7.7	8.7	4,200.00
Municipal Bonds	13,246.50	13,670.95	2.2	5.8	700.00
Government Bonds	15,787.50	15,834.37	2.6	6.4	1,256.25
Accrued Interest		1,856.54	0.3		
	74,802.50	78,524.37	12.9	7.7	6,156.25
Cash					
Cash	59,471.92	59,471.92	9.7	4.0	2,378.88
Total Portfolio	556,692.42	610,446.29	100.0	2.9	17,607.09

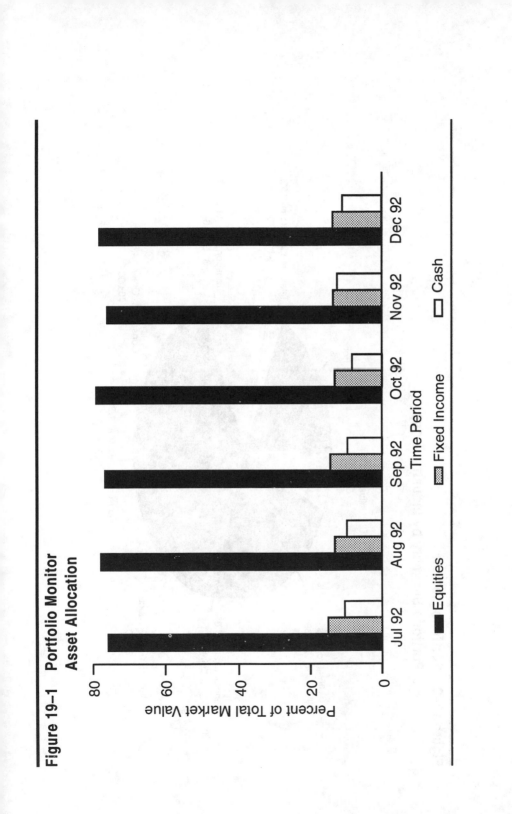

Figure 19–1 Portfolio Monitor Asset Allocation

Figure 19–2   Portfolio Monitor
Portfolio Summary by Industry Group

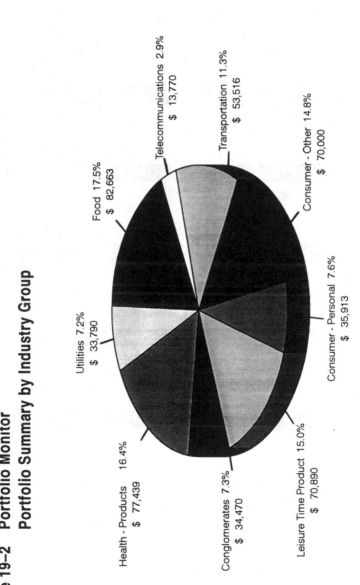

Figure 19–3   Portfolio Monitor
Portfolio Summary by Security Type

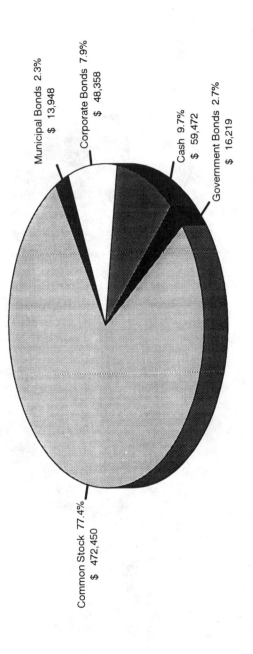

Municipal Bonds 2.3%
$ 13,948

Corporate Bonds 7.9%
$ 48,358

Cash 9.7%
$ 59,472

Government Bonds 2.7%
$ 16,219

Common Stock 77.4%
$ 472,450

Figure 19–4   Portfolio Monitor
Portfolio Summary by Asset Class

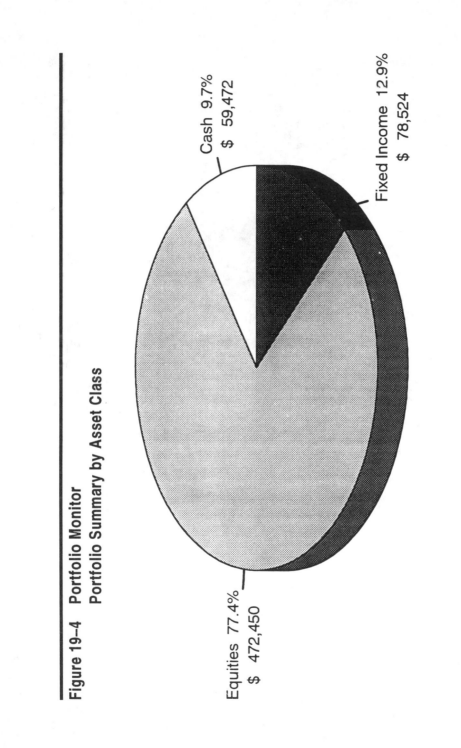

Cash 9.7%
$ 59,472

Fixed Income 12.9%
$ 78,524

Equities 77.4%
$ 472,450

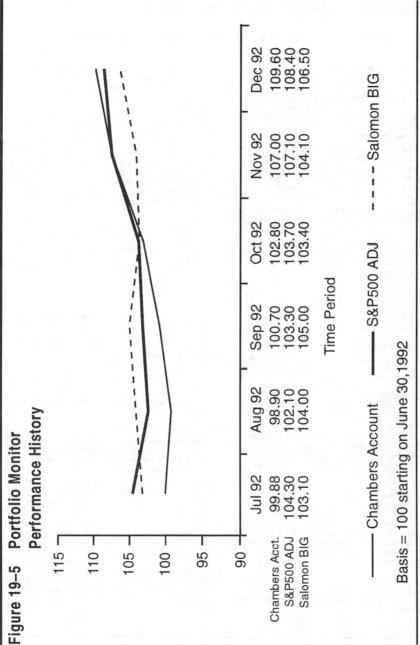

Figure 19-5   Portfolio Monitor Performance History

	Jul 92	Aug 92	Sep 92	Oct 92	Nov 92	Dec 92
Chambers Acct.	99.88	98.90	100.70	102.80	107.00	109.60
S&P500 ADJ	104.30	102.10	103.30	103.70	107.10	108.40
Salomon BIG	103.10	104.00	105.00	103.40	104.10	106.50

Time Period

—— Chambers Account   —— S&P500 ADJ   - - - - Salomon BIG

Basis = 100 starting on June 30, 1992

Figure 19-6   Asset Performance Monitor

HOW TO READ THE COVER PAGE

Relative Cycle Analysis

The Relative Cycle Analysis chart covers a 5 year time frame and shows how the investment adviser performed in calendar quarters when the S&P 500 or Bond Index rose in price and in those quarters when the S&P 500 or Bond Index declined in price. Equity and balanced accounts are compared to the S&P 500 market cycle, while fixed income accounts are compared to the Bond Index market cycle.

The unshaded bar on the left shows the percent of the market gain the manager realized during each of the up-market quarters (as measured by an appropriate index) in the analysis period. For instance, if the number is 70, the manager achieved 70% of the market gain during those periods. If the number is 150, the manager achieved 150% of the market gain during those periods.

The shaded bar on the right shows how the manager performed in down-market quarters. Again, if the number is -70, the manager lost 70% of the market decline. If the number is -120, the manager lost 20% more than the market decline.

What one generally looks for is an adviser who realizes a greater percentage rise in the rising markets than drop in the declining markets.

Long-Term Achievement

This chart compares the performance of the adviser's portfolios to a related market index during the period indicated and shows the relative growth of $1.00 invested by the adviser and the market index over that period of time.

Manager Evaluation

This table provides additional statistics on the manager's performance. The key refers to the symbols used in the Long-Term Achievement chart.

CUM ANL ROR
Cumulative annual rate of return.

RANK
The rank (in percentage) of this adviser versus other equity, balanced or fixed income advisers in the Performance Analytics universe over the time period indicated. A rank of 10 would indicate the adviser was in the top 10% of the universe.

BETA
Beta is a measure of volatility which is one means to measure risk. It associates the volatility of the portfolio with the volatility of the market. For equities, the market is the S&P 500; for balanced funds, the market is the Balanced Index; for fixed income, the market is the Merrill Lynch Master Bond Index. A beta of 1.20 implies volatility 20% greater than the market, since the market is, by definition, 1.00. A beta of .80 would imply 20% less volatility than the market.

QTR ALPHA
The alpha expresses the investment manager's superior or inferior performance after adjusting for the portfolio beta. Alphas are measured quarterly.

Managers that beat the market on a beta-adjusted basis have positive alphas (more than 0.0), and those that were beaten by the market have negative alphas (less than 0.0).

VAL ADDED
Value added is the return the manager achieved in excess of that which might have been expected, given the amount of volatility he or she assumed. The determination of value added is based on the assumption that there is an expected return on a portfolio, based on the return of the market and the volatility the manager is assuming. If the market advanced 10% and a manager had a beta of 1.50, the expected return for the portfolio would be 15%, or 50% greater than the market's return. If the manager achieved a return of 20%, his value added score would be 5% (his actual return of 20% minus his expected return of 15%).

QTR ST DEV
The standard deviation is a measure of the asset's volatility. The standard deviation is the dispersion of actual returns around the mean return. Since the standard deviation measures how much an asset's return fluctuates, it is often used as a measure of risk. For example, if OTC U.S. equities had a higher standard deviation than NYSE listed equities, 22.4% versus 16.3%, OTC equities would be more volatile.

R SQD
R SQD is both a measure of diversification and a gauge of the percentage of the portfolio's movement that is explained by the movement of the market. An R SQD of 0.90 would indicate that the portfolio is 90% as diversified as the market and that 90% of this portfolio's movement is explained by the market, while the other 10% is attributable to other factors that are stock- and not market-specific.

YEARS
The time period for which data is available for this investment adviser.

CYCLE ANALYSIS
Cycle Analysis is a numeric presentation similar to the Relative Cycle Analysis (RCA) charts except that the number of years of data represented may be different and the comparative index used for balanced funds is different.

The time period under review is indicated within the Manager Evaluation table. Balanced funds are compared to the Balanced Index market cycle rather than the S&P 500 as is the case in the RCA chart.

BOND INDEX
Merrill Lynch Government/Corporate Master Bond Index. Average maturity approximately 9 years.

BALANCED INDEX
An index comprised of 50% the S&P 500 for Equity and 50% the Shearson/Lehman Government/Corporate Bond Index for Fixed Income.

Figure 19–6 Asset Performance Monitor

ASSET PERFORMANCE MONITOR

A.G.Edwards

January 1993

FRONTIER CAPITAL MANAGEMENT CO., INC.
99 Summer Street
Boston, MA 02110
(617) 261-0681

Style: Core Growth

Account Type: Balanced, Equity

Minimum Account: $ 100,000

Client Contact: Ginny Morse,
Catrina Corey

Dollars Under Management: $1.3 Billion

Number of Clients: 223

Net Dollars Added Last Year: None

Net Clients Added Last Year: 32

Founded: 1980

Core Growth: Core Growth managers invest in stocks of companies that have demonstrated long periods of earnings growth and provide favorable prospects for above-average long-term growth. One variation of this style is the rising dividends philosophy.

Investment Philosophy

Frontier uses a thematic approach to core growth equity management. Based on a "top down" approach combined with "bottom up" stock analysis, Frontier identifies investment themes which direct their investments. Stock selection is based on the earnings and dividend growth, high return on equity, and attractive valuation levels. Price targets are set for 18 months in the future based on anticipated earnings and projected P/E ratios. Stocks are sold when they become fully valued, when fundamentals deteriorate, or they no longer fit the thematic orientation.

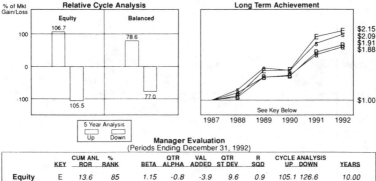

Manager Evaluation
(Periods Ending December 31, 1992)

	KEY	CUM ANL ROR	% RANK	BETA	QTR ALPHA	VAL ADDED	QTR ST DEV	R SQD	CYCLE ANALYSIS UP	DOWN	YEARS
Equity	E	13.6	85	1.15	-0.8	-3.9	9.6	0.9	105.1	126.6	10.00
S&P 500	s	16.1	28	..	..	..	7.8	..	..	..	10.00
Balanced	B	13.8	44	1.48	-0.6	-2.9	6.8	0.9	140.5	179.0	10.00
Bal. 50/50	a	14.1	34	..	..	..	4.5	..	..	..	10.00

© 1993 Performance Analytics, Inc.

Figure 19–6   Asset Performance Monitor

FRONTIER CAPITAL MGT - EQUITY ACCOUNTS

ANNUAL RATES OF RETURN

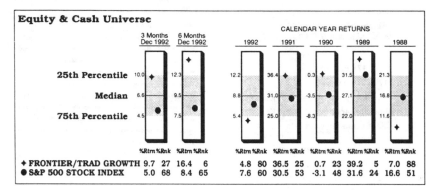

Equity & Cash Universe

| | 3 Months Dec 1992 | 6 Months Dec 1992 | CALENDAR YEAR RETURNS |
			1992	1991	1990	1989	1988
25th Percentile	10.0	12.3	12.2	36.4	0.3	31.5	21.3
Median	6.6	9.5	8.8	31.0	-3.5	27.1	16.8
75th Percentile	4.5	7.5	5.4	25.0	-8.3	22.0	11.6

	%Rtrn %Rnk	%Rtrn %Rnk	%Rtrn %Rnk	%Rtrn %Rnk	%Rtrn %Rnk	%Rtrn %Rnk	%Rtrn %Rnk
✦ FRONTIER/TRAD GROWTH	9.7 27	16.4 6	4.8 80	36.5 25	0.7 23	39.2 5	7.0 88
● S&P 500 STOCK INDEX	5.0 68	8.4 65	7.6 60	30.5 53	-3.1 48	31.6 24	16.6 51

QUARTERLY RATES OF RETURN

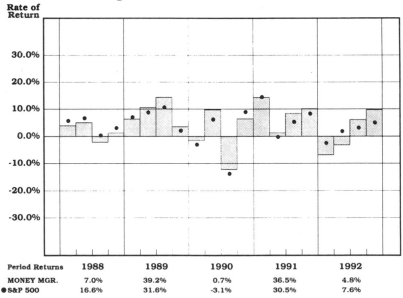

Period Returns	1988	1989	1990	1991	1992
MONEY MGR.	7.0%	39.2%	0.7%	36.5%	4.8%
● S&P 500	16.6%	31.6%	-3.1%	30.5%	7.6%

226

Figure 19–6　Asset Performance Monitor

CUMULATIVE RATES OF RETURN

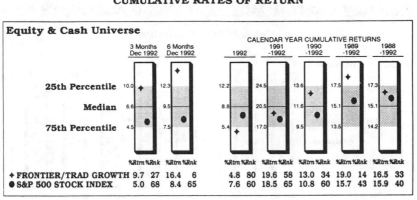

Equity & Cash Universe

	3 Months Dec 1992		6 Months Dec 1992		1992		1991 -1992		1990 -1992		1989 -1992		1988 -1992	
25th Percentile	10.0		12.3		12.2		24.5		13.6		17.5		17.3	
Median	6.6		9.5		8.8		20.5		11.6		15.1		15.1	
75th Percentile	4.5		7.5		5.4		17.0		9.5		13.5		14.2	

CALENDAR YEAR CUMULATIVE RETURNS

	%Rtrn	%Rnk	%Rtrn	%Rnk	%Rtrn	%Rnk	%Rtrn	%Rnk	%Rtrn	%Rnk	%Rtrn	%Rnk	%Rtrn	%Rnk
✦ FRONTIER/TRAD GROWTH	9.7	27	16.4	6	4.8	80	19.6	58	13.0	34	19.0	14	16.5	33
● S&P 500 STOCK INDEX	5.0	68	8.4	65	7.6	60	18.5	65	10.8	60	15.7	43	15.9	40

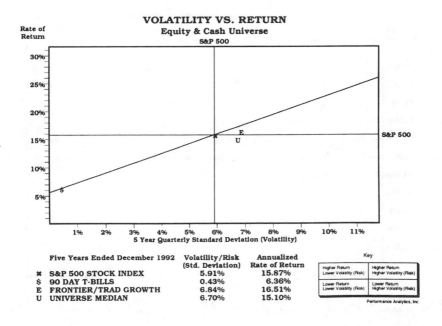

VOLATILITY VS. RETURN
Equity & Cash Universe
S&P 500

Five Years Ended December 1992	Volatility/Risk (Std. Deviation)	Annualized Rate of Return
✖ S&P 500 STOCK INDEX	5.91%	15.87%
$ 90 DAY T-BILLS	0.43%	6.36%
E FRONTIER/TRAD GROWTH	6.84%	16.51%
U UNIVERSE MEDIAN	6.70%	15.10%

Key

Higher Return Lower Volatility (Risk)	Higher Return Higher Volatility (Risk)
Lower Return Lower Volatility (Risk)	Lower Return Higher Volatility (Risk)

Performance Analytics, Inc.

227

Figure 19–6   Asset Performance Monitor

FRONTIER CAPITAL MGT - BALANCED ACCOUNTS

ANNUAL RATES OF RETURN

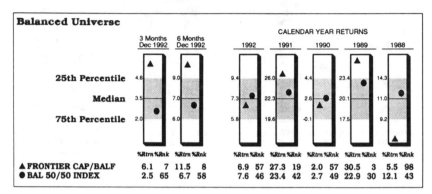

	3 Months Dec 1992		6 Months Dec 1992		1992		1991		1990		1989		1988	
	%Rtrn	%Rnk	%Rtrn	%Rnk	%Rtrn	%Rnk	%Rtrn	%Rnk	%Rtrn	%Rnk	%Rtrn	%Rnk	%Rtrn	%Rnk
▲ FRONTIER CAP/BALF	6.1	7	11.5	8	6.9	57	27.3	19	2.0	57	30.5	3	5.5	98
● BAL 50/50 INDEX	2.5	65	6.7	58	7.6	46	23.4	42	2.7	49	22.9	30	12.1	43

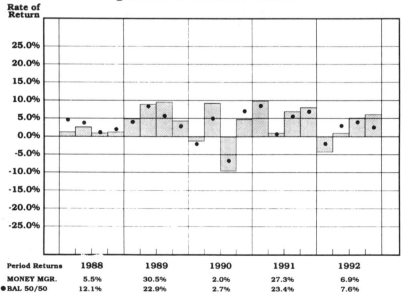

QUARTERLY RATES OF RETURN

Period Returns	1988	1989	1990	1991	1992
MONEY MGR.	5.5%	30.5%	2.0%	27.3%	6.9%
● BAL 50/50	12.1%	22.9%	2.7%	23.4%	7.6%

228

Figure 19-6 Asset Performance Monitor

CUMULATIVE RATES OF RETURN

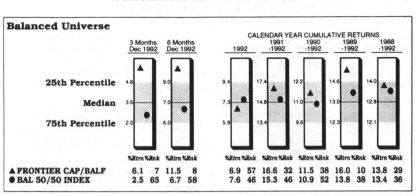

Balanced Universe

CALENDAR YEAR CUMULATIVE RETURNS

	3 Months Dec 1992	6 Months Dec 1992	1992	1991 -1992	1990 -1992	1989 -1992	1988 -1992
25th Percentile	4.6	9.0	9.4	17.4	12.2	14.6	14.0
Median	3.5	7.0	7.3	14.8	11.0	13.0	12.8
75th Percentile	2.0	6.0	5.8	13.4	9.6	12.3	12.1

	%Rtrn	%Rnk	%Rtrn	%Rnk	%Rtrn	%Rnk	%Rtrn	%Rnk	%Rtrn	%Rnk	%Rtrn	%Rnk	%Rtrn	%Rnk
▲ FRONTIER CAP/BALF	6.1	7	11.5	8	6.9	57	16.6	32	11.5	38	16.0	10	13.8	29
● BAL 50/50 INDEX	2.5	65	6.7	58	7.6	46	15.3	46	10.9	52	13.8	38	13.4	36

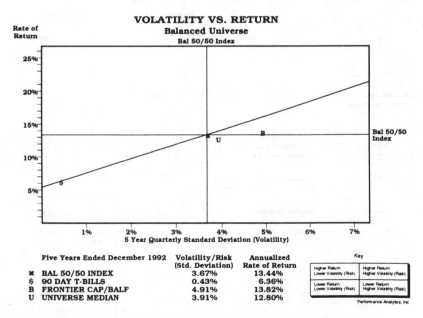

VOLATILITY VS. RETURN
Balanced Universe
Bal 50/50 Index

Rate of Return

5 Year Quarterly Standard Deviation (Volatility)

Five Years Ended December 1992		Volatility/Risk (Std. Deviation)	Annualized Rate of Return
✻	BAL 50/50 INDEX	3.67%	13.44%
$	90 DAY T-BILLS	0.43%	6.36%
B	FRONTIER CAP/BALF	4.91%	13.82%
U	UNIVERSE MEDIAN	3.91%	12.80%

Key

Higher Return Lower Volatility (Risk)	Higher Return Higher Volatility (Risk)
Lower Return Lower Volatility (Risk)	Lower Return Higher Volatility (Risk)

Performance Analytics, Inc

The Balanced Index is comprised of 50% the S&P 500 and 50% the Lehman Brothers Government/Corporate Bond Index.

229

Chapter 19

Figure 19–6   Asset Performance Monitor

HOW TO READ THE CHARTS

Bar Charts

These charts can be used to review the "class ranking" of the money manager compared with other managers having the same account type. The heading at the top of the page indicates the type of Universe used for the measure (such as Equity and Cash or Bond and Cash).

BAR GRAPHS

The bar columns show the percentage ranking of a manager and an index in the applicable (equity, fixed income or balanced) Performance Analytics data base. High is the top 5% of investment advisers in the data base during the period, 10% means the top 10%, Median is the middle of all advisers, etc. There is a column for the last (or latest) quarter, as well as other periods indicated.

The performances of the specific investment adviser and an index are shown by symbols (see the bottom of each page for symbols identification) in the bar columns so you can determine the class ranking of the adviser relative to other advisers and the index in each of the periods.

UNIVERSE RETURNS

Below each bar are the returns reported by advisers in a Performance Analytics data base. They provide a numeric ranking of the comparative universe, divided into quartiles to correspond with the shading of the bars and to help you see exactly how your account ranks. The percentage return after "High" shows the minimum your portfolio had to earn in order to have ranked in the top 5% of the universe. The percentage shown after "First Quartile" is the minimum a portfolio had to earn in order to rank in the top 25% of the universe.

ADVISER RETURNS

Below the Universe percentage returns, the percentage return and percentile rank are shown for the adviser and an index for each corresponding period.

Rates of Return by Quarter Charts

The objective of the "Rates of Return By Quarter" chart is to show the volatility of the manager's quarterly rates of return.

Each bar shows the absolute percentage return the manager achieved in the accounts he managed in each quarter over the past five years.

Scatter Charts

The scatter chart compares the return and volatility (as measured by standard deviation) for the manager with the returns and volatility of other similar managers in a related (equity, fixed income or balanced) Performance Analytics universe.

As one moves higher in the chart, the rate of return increases. Similarly, as one moves to the right, the volatility (as measured by the standard deviation) increases. The crossing point of the two lines is the median of the returns and volatility of all the managers in the sample.

Thus, what one would like is a manager in the upper left quadrant, i.e., high return with low volatility (risk).

The upper right quadrant indicates higher returns but higher volatility (risk) than the median of the universe.

The lower left quadrant indicates lower returns but lower volatility (risk) than the median of the universe.

The lower right quadrant indicates lower returns and higher volatility (risk) than the median of the universe.

The calculations for equity, fixed-income and balanced managers differ, since they are compared only against similar managers.

Figure 19–6   Asset Performance Monitor

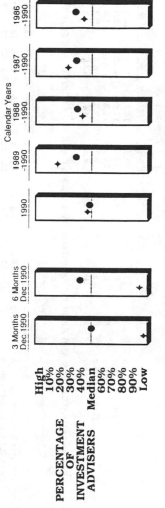

PERCENTAGE RETURNS ACHIEVED BY INVESTMENT ADVISER UNIVERSE

	3 Months Dec 1990	6 Months Dec 1990	1990	Calendar Years 1989-1990	Calendar Years 1988-1990	Calendar Years 1987-1990	Calendar Years 1986-1990
High	16.3	2.3	14.8	24.9	18.6	16.5	17.5
First Quartile	10.5	-4.7	0.3	14.7	14.8	12.4	13.6
Median	8.9	-7.0	-3.5	10.9	13.2	10.9	12.5
Third Quartile	7.2	-9.8	-8.3	6.2	10.6	8.8	10.6
Low	3.3	-16.1	-17.4	-3.2	0.8	2.9	6.3

PERCENTAGE RETURNS AND RANK OF FRONTIER CAPITAL MGT AND S&P 500

	3 Months Dec 1990		6 Months Dec 1990		1990		Calendar Years 1989-1990		Calendar Years 1988-1990		Calendar Years 1987-1990		Calendar Years 1986-1990	
	% Rtrn	% Rnk	% Rtrn	% Rnk	% Rtrn	% Rnk	% Rtrn	% Rnk	% Rtrn	% Rnk	% Rtrn	% Rnk	% Rtrn	% Rnk
FRONTIER/TRAD GRWTH +	2.6	100	-13.3	96	-2.8	46	16.6	17	13.7	41	12.4	27	12.7	42
S&P 500 STOCK INDEX ●	9.0	50	-6.0	39	-3.1	48	12.5	35	14.1	36	11.8	35	13.1	34

Figure 19–6 Asset Performance Monitor

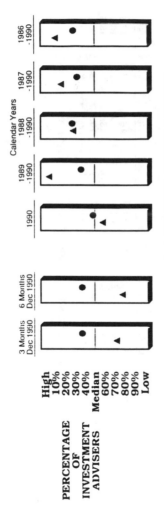

PERCENTAGE OF INVESTMENT ADVISERS

High 10% 20% 30% 40% Median 60% 70% 80% 90% Low

Calendar Years

3 Months Dec 1990 | 6 Months Dec 1990 | 1990 | 1989 -1990 | 1988 -1990 | 1987 -1990 | 1986 -1990

PERCENTAGE RETURNS ACHIEVED BY INVESTMENT ADVISER UNIVERSE

	3 Months Dec 1990	6 Months Dec 1990	1990	1989 -1990	1988 -1990	1987 -1990	1986 -1990
High	13.1	7.3	11.3	17.1	14.8	14.3	15.3
First Quartile	7.6	0.8	4.4	13.0	12.3	10.8	12.0
Median	6.2	-0.8	2.6	11.5	11.3	9.7	11.0
Third Quartile	5.3	-3.2	-0.1	9.3	10.2	8.5	10.2
Low	2.6	-10.1	-7.2	4.6	4.1	3.7	7.7

PERCENTAGE RETURNS AND RANK OF FRONTIER CAPITAL MGT AND BALANCED INDEX 50/50

	3 Months Dec 1990		6 Months Dec 1990		1990		1989 -1990		1988 -1990		1987 -1990		1986 -1990	
	% Rtrn	% Rnk	% Rtrn	% Rnk	% Rtrn	% Rnk	% Rtrn	% Rnk	% Rtrn	% Rnk	% Rtrn	% Rnk	% Rtrn	% Rnk
FRONTIER ADV/BALF ▲	5.4	72	-3.5	78	1.8	58	15.5	4	12.2	28	11.3	16	13.0	10
BALANCED INDEX 50/50 ●	7.0	37	0.0	37	2.8	48	12.3	36	12.2	27	10.5	32	11.8	28

* The Balanced Index is comprised of 50% the S&P 500 and 50% the Shearson Lehman Government/Corporate Bond Index

Figure 19-6   Asset Performance Monitor

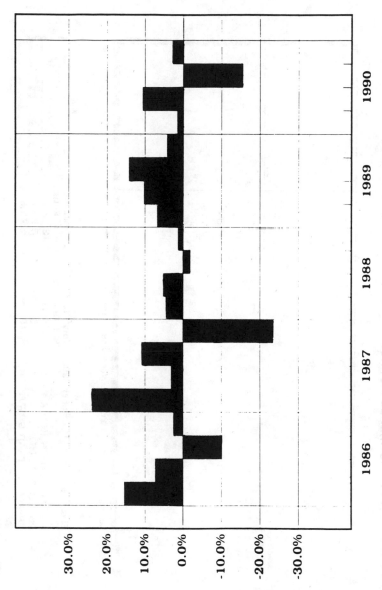

Figure 19-6 Asset Performance Monitor

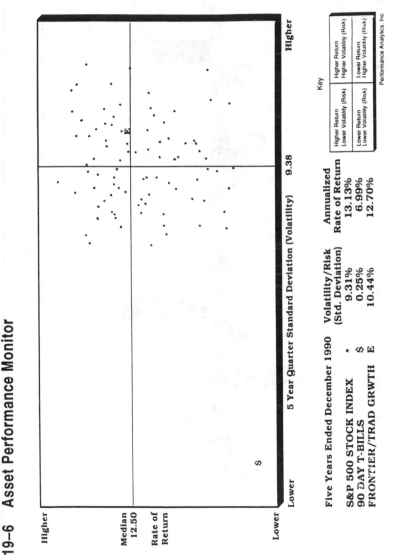

Five Years Ended December 1990		Volatility/Risk (Std. Deviation)	Annualized Rate of Return
S&P 500 STOCK INDEX	*	9.31%	13.13%
90 DAY T-BILLS	$	0.25%	6.99%
FRONTIER/TRAD GRWTH	E	10.44%	12.70%

Key

Higher Return Lower Volatility (Risk)	Higher Return Higher Volatility (Risk)
Lower Return Lower Volatility (Risk)	Lower Return Higher Volatility (Risk)

Performance Analytics, Inc.

Figure 19–6 Asset Performance Monitor

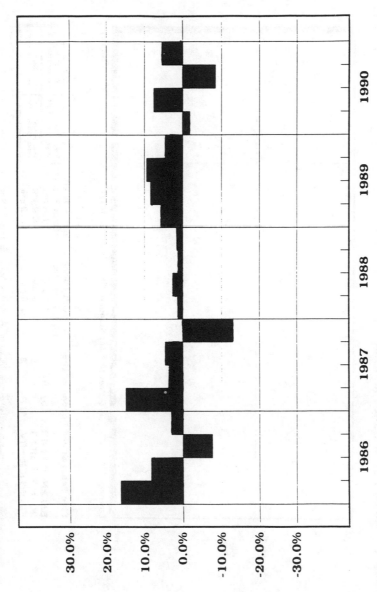

Figure 19–6 Asset Performance Monitor

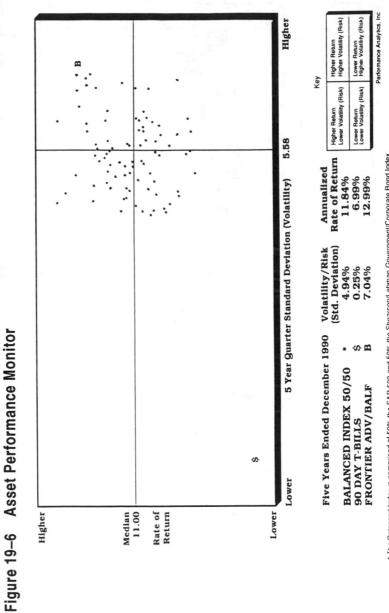

Five Years Ended December 1990		Volatility/Risk (Std. Deviation)	Annualized Rate of Return
BALANCED INDEX 50/50	*	4.94%	11.84%
90 DAY T-BILLS	$	0.25%	6.99%
FRONTIER ADV/BALF	B	7.04%	12.99%

* The Balanced Index is comprised of 50% the S&P 500 and 50% the Shearson/Lehman Government/Corporate Bond Index.

Figure 19–6   Asset Performance Monitor

State Registration Information

Frontier Capital Management Co., Inc. represents that they are registered as an investment advisor in the states of: IL, KS, MI, NH, OR and TX. They may be exempt from registration in other states and/or have filed new registrations. Please contact the money manager directly for current state registration information.

As of 12/31/92

The information in this report is intended for one-on-one discussions between A.G. Edwards Investment Brokers and their clients and prospects.

1. Performance data is generally after commissions and before fees charged by the investment manager, but this may not always be the case.
2. If the performance data provided is before investment management fees and/or commissions, client returns will be reduced by the advisory fees and any other expenses that may be incurred in the management of the investment advisory account.
3. The fees of the investment advisors are described in Part II of the advisor's Form ADV which is obtainable from the advisor and should be reviewed by each client or prospect considering the advisor before the advisor is hired.
4. An investment advisor should provide to each client or prospect the effect of an investment advisory fee, compounded over a period of years, on the total value of a portfolio.
5. There are no fees or commissions reflected in the performance information on the indices shown for comparisons.

Past results are not a guarantee of future performance.

Disclaimer of Warranties and Limitation of Liability

The investment performance data, the characterizations of fund managers' investment styles, and the investment portfolio information set forth in publications issued by Performance Analytics, Inc. are based upon information provided to Performance Analytics, Inc. by the fund managers identified therein or by other third parties, and Performance Analytics, Inc. has not undertaken any independent investigation or audit to confirm the accuracy or completeness of such information. Accordingly, Performance Analytics, Inc. makes no warranties whatsoever, whether express or implied regarding the accuracy or completeness of such information. In no event shall Performance Analytics, Inc. be liable for any damages whatsoever, including without limitation direct damages, incidental damages, consequential damages and punitive damages, as a result of the inaccuracy or incompleteness of any such information, and each user of such publications, by such use, waives any and all claims against Performance Analytics, Inc. relating to, arising out of, or in connection with any inaccuracy or incompleteness of any such information.

This information is obtained from Performance Analytics, Inc., and is considered reliable, but the information's accuracy is not guaranteed by A.G. Edwards & Sons, Inc. Neither the information nor any opinion that may be expressed constitutes the solicitation by A.G. Edwards & Sons, Inc. for the purchase or sale of any security.

B67-9303

PART V

WRAP AND PENSION PLANS

Figures V–1, V–2, and V–3 show typical pension plan banking relationship and the major service areas for which a fiduciary must be responsible. The last chart shows how a simple tactic like moving the monitoring and investment management out of the bank to an independent manager can actually improve performance.

Part V

Figure V–1   Typical Bank Relationship

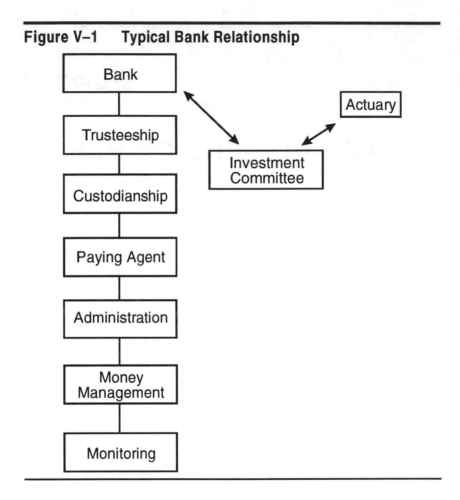

Figure V–2   Major Service Areas

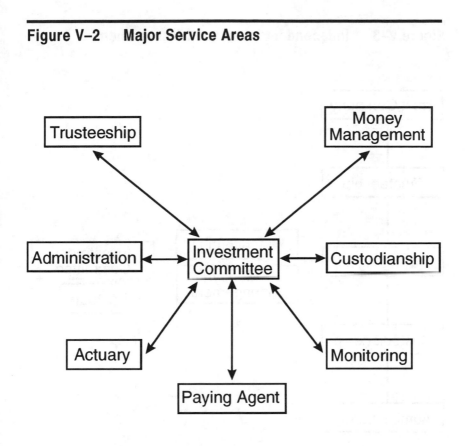

Figure V–3   Independent Investment Management

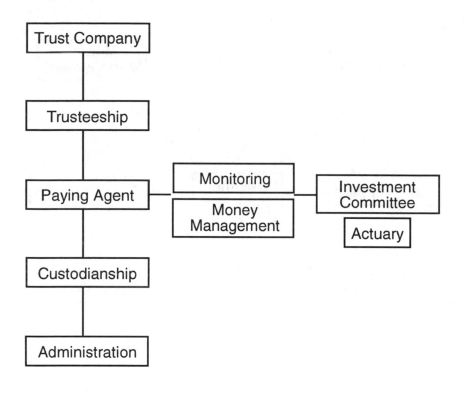

CHAPTER 20

WRAP MANAGEMENT IN PENSION PLANS

Most sponsors of pension plans, an estimated two-thirds, have not developed a written statement of investment objectives. Usually, they have no system for reporting portfolio performance and can be personally liable should a loss result from failure to act prudently. In other words, plan sponsors have a real need for an organized system of professional money management. Most wrap fee account programs offer many of these requirements as a part of their packages.

Given these realities, pension plan sponsors have to manage smart if they are to accomplish their objective of securing the future for their employees and/or members. And since successful investment management depends on direction and discipline, one of the best ways to do this is by utilizing one of the wrap account or wrap fee consulting programs.

Trained consultants will establish criteria to which investment managers are held accountable. They will select managers who follow an approach to investing consistent with the objectives and risk tolerance level of the plan.

Unfortunately, too many plan sponsors believe that the best method of operating conservatively is by investing in short-term CDs (certificates of deposit) or other passive

We would like to thank Randy A. Zimmermann, Vice President-Investments, A.G. Edwards & Sons, Inc., for his contribution to this chapter.

money market instruments that produce income but no growth.

This is saving, not investing. By accepting the security of short-term passive growth, potential is lost because inflation wipes out minimal growth.

Investment returns over a number of time periods indicate that equities (common stocks) have produced returns that offset inflation and provide real growth in principal sufficient to allow some funds to be perpetual. For example, if you examine the investment returns for four fixed periods, you will find that common stocks overwhelmingly out-performed corporate bonds, government bonds, Treasury bills, and inflation over most time periods.

The "prudent man" knows higher returns sometimes require the assumption of higher risks. Measuring the level of risk to be taken with a retirement fund is a matter of great concern. Many consultants have developed a set of standards or a business plan to mitigate the risks in managing the investment of these funds.

How does one go about writing an investment policy that will endure? The first step in preparing such a policy is understanding the long- and short-term needs of the retirement fund. Outside consultants can assist investment committees in developing a statement of investment objectives. The investment policy should establish realistic investment expectations and include a method of measurement to evaluate variations of risks. Results can be measured against the rate of return on the S&P 500, a corporate bond index, or a blended index of the two.

One important criterion that can be established in the statement of investment objectives is the level of volatility that the plan's portfolio and its trustees are willing to incur as they seek to provide an employee retirement fund.

Managing pension funds is no easy feat, especially given the confusing maze of regulations. Here's a brief look at some of the key requirements of the Employee Retirement Income Security Act 1974 (ERISA), which governs the activities of fiduciaries—persons responsible for handling or controlling the assets of qualified retirement plans.

1. Fiduciaries are required to perform their duties for the exclusive benefit of plan participants.
2. Fiduciaries are required to act with the care, skill, and diligence that a prudent person, acting in the same circumstances, would exercise.
3. Assets must be diversified to minimize the risk of large losses unless it is clearly not prudent to do so.
4. Fiduciaries must perform their duties in accordance with the documents and instruments governing the plan to the extent the documents are consistent with the provisions of ERISA.

Many consultants today use a regression analysis to compare the risk and return offered by many different investment vehicles and managers. As long as an account is achieving value-added return for the variability of risk it is incurring, many consultants feel comfortable with the consistency of that style.

Properly balanced accounts should have the flexibility of utilizing many types of conservative investment vehicles, realistic investment guidelines and the predefined quality and rating of those vehicles.

Additionally, the committee should recognize that investment philosophies differ among investment managers. Some of these may not be appropriate for your particular retirement fund.

For example, investment objectives should determine whether discretion to invest funds will be granted to an investment manager. If an investment manager is retained on an advisory basis without being granted discretion, the investor risks a loss of valuable time when faced with fast-moving markets. Other items that should be addressed are liquidity requirements, diversification policies, asset distribution, and supervision of the investment manager.

REVIEW IS CRITICAL

Establishing a quarterly review of the investment manager is vital. In this review, the investment manager should be held accountable for communicating progress toward accomplishing the objectives.

Trustees should be able to review the book and market values of investments in the account, as well as understand the investment management's philosophy toward changes in the economy that may affect the portfolio. This quarterly review must provide a forum for open discussion with the investment manager regarding any problems that may be developing.

Here are some questions that can help you evaluate whether you're on the right track to successful investment management of your pension plan:

- Has your pension plan grown to a size that now requires full-time professional management?

- Does your pension plan have a written statement of investment guidelines and objectives?

- Have you established asset allocation guidelines?

- Do you have objective standards by which you can judge the performance of your pension plan?

- Have you determined an acceptable level of risk, based upon your expectations or return?

- Are you receiving value-added services for your plan from a trained consultant?

- Have you developed a questionnaire that will determine whether the investment manager meets your needs, not his or hers?

- Is there an objective process in place to monitor and evaluate performance?

THE DEPARTMENT OF LABOR AND ERISA

The Department of Labor is actively pursuing pension plan administrators for violations of ERISA, the Employee Retirement and Income Act.

It is all part of a "get-tough" policy the government is using to impose stiff fines on fiduciaries who are not complying with the 15-year-old law.

Last year the U.S. Court of Appeals for the Eleventh Circuit imposed a $537,000 judgment against the manager of a company's profit-sharing plan's assets. The crime? The manager had put 70% of the plan in 30-year Treasury bonds, exposing plan holders to price volatility. The court held that the manager's investment strategy didn't fit the plan's objectives. Many small businesses seem especially likely to run afoul of ERISA's rules.

One small business owner in New York City was recently assessed $637,000 plus interest for losses his company's pension plan suffered at the hands of an investment advisor who had not registered with the Securities and Exchange Commission.

Chapter 20

Businessmen don't seem understand that to the Department of Labor, there is no excuse. If you don't seek professional help, you may run a significant risk of personal liability from lawsuits and enforcement actions. Plan participants have the right to sue to recover money lost due to mismanagement.

It is estimated that nearly 60% of the 735,000 pension plans violate some aspect of ERISA. This complex law covers the entire $2 trillion worth of pension plans in the private sector, from 401(k) plans to multimillion dollar defined benefit plans of major corporations. Personal liability can extend from the investment committee all the way to the board of directors.

The crackdown started building momentum in 1989 when the Labor Department complained that steps must be taken to strengthen enforcement. While other federal government agencies have been experiencing cutbacks, the Department of Labor has doubled its enforcement division and its litigation staff to crack down on violations.

There are now 500 full-time enforcement staffers and about 75 full-time litigators working in 15 regional centers across the U.S. The Department of Labor has redesigned their forms, making it easier for them to get information into their $40 million computer database. Their new computer can now flag violations, monitor plan expenses, and match up asset diversification for aberrations.

You used to be able to hide in a bank, but banks also will get a watchful eye from the DOL. The banking industry is facing big problems from mounting losses, heavy regulations, and competition. I have seen bank trust pension accounts earning less than the same bank's CDs. And still banks want Congress to lift prohibitions on selling insurance, stocks, and bonds. As a group, banks have not been the most alert in anticipating and solving these problems, and because of this, many sophisticated accounts have been leaving the banks recently.

Managing money effectively is an intuitive skill and it's not accomplished successfully in an institutional environment. Anyone in banking who has that talent will eventually leave, and a good investment manager who understands the business can earn five times what a bank trust officer can make.

There must be an incentive for the manager to make the most money possible for his clients. It doesn't make sense for a poorly paid manager to have much incentive. An investment counseling firm is able to offer its employees a piece of the firm, whereas a bank cannot.

How can pension managers stay out of trouble? For starters, a pension manager can protect himself by working with an investment management consultant. A consultant can draw up a written policy statement outlining the plan's investment objectives and then independently monitor the performance of the account.

CHAPTER 21

WRAP INVESTING AND FIDUCIARY LIABILITY

The Employee Retirement Income Security Act (ERISA) of 1974, the cornerstone of pension protection, has radically altered Wall Street. It institutionalized the way capital is raised, invested, and managed. It has been reported that in 1990 ERISA pension funds held 20% of all U.S. equities, up from 6% in 1970. Its requirements have also spawned the investment consulting industry.

ERISA was enacted to protect the interests of participants in employee benefit plans from abuses and discriminatory practices that evolved throughout the 1950s and 1960s. The magnitude and complexity of ERISA has led to a widespread lack of understanding of its basic principles and a commensurate lack of understanding of liabilities under it. Moreover, a high level of apathy has developed among fiduciaries who seek comfort in claiming they are "covered" by strictly worded plan documents.

This chapter is designed to assist plan sponsors in becoming aware of responsibilities they have as fiduciaries and the penalties that could be imposed for noncompliance with ERISA. Most importantly, it provides a framework which allows plan sponsors to develop a system of compliance, properly fulfilling their fiduciary obligations. It is in the

We would like to thank Drew Washburn, AEGON USA Investment Management, Inc., for his contribution to this chapter.

251

implementation and maintenance of the ERISA standards that the plan sponsors can also protect their personal liability.

I. INTRODUCTION

Anyone who is a trustee, sponsor, or otherwise exercises any authority or control over any type of employee benefit plan is a "fiduciary." A fiduciary who does not act according to the precepts of ERISA is not only subjected to personal liability but also could subject a plan to loss of its tax-free status.

Standard employee retirement plans include profit-sharing, pension, and 401(k)s. However, any plan maintained by an employer for the benefit of employees is covered by ERISA, including stock bonus plans, insurance plans (life, health, and disability), and vacation and scholarship funds.

II. BASIC PRINCIPLES OF ERISA

ERISA outlines five broad areas which set the standards of fiduciary conduct in administering a plan. In essence, anyone who exercises any authority over management, administration, disposition of assets or who renders advice will be held as a fiduciary.

1. The fiduciary's duties must be discharged solely in the interest of plan participants and their beneficiaries.

2. Reasonable expenses may be paid if the fiduciary's duties are discharged for the exclusive purpose of providing benefits to participants and their beneficiaries. Transactions for the benefit of any other entity are prohibited.

3. The benefit plan must be formalized in writing and must have written investment objectives. Fiduciaries must discharge their duties according to these plan documents and may rely on professional assistance to meet this obligation.

4. The Prudent Man Rule defines the standard of competence to which a fiduciary will be held responsible with respect to plan investment decisions. ERISA states that a fiduciary must discharge his duties "with the care, skill, prudence and diligence under the circumstances then prevailing that a prudent person acting in a like capacity and familiar with such matters would use in the conduct of an enterprise of a like character with like aims." In other words, fiduciaries can be held to the same level of skill as that of a professional money manager in making investment decisions. It is important to remember that pension dollars belong to employees and beneficiaries, not the sponsoring company. Hence, ERISA holds fiduciaries to as high an investment standard as possible—that of a "professional expert."

5. A fiduciary must diversify the investments of a plan so as to minimize the risk of large losses unless it is clearly not prudent to do so.

III. FIDUCIARY RESPONSIBILITY

It is extremely important for all plan fiduciaries to understand the graveness of their responsibilities and the potential penalties. Fiduciaries can be held personally liable for breach of violation of these responsibilities, even to the extent of having to restore lost profits to the plan.

Investment advisors are fiduciaries if they provide advice on the value and advisability of owning investments and have the discretionary authority to purchase or sell investments with plan assets.

It is important to note that if trustees or named fiduciaries properly select and appoint a qualified money manager, they will not have a co-fiduciary responsibility for acts and omissions of the advisor, unless they knowingly participate or try to conceal any such acts or omissions.

IV. THE WRITTEN PLAN OF INVESTMENT OBJECTIVES

All employee benefit plans should establish and maintain a written set of investment objectives for the plan. This is the only way a fiduciary can meet obligations and legally defend future actions. When the objectives and purposes of the plan are specified, it provides standards against which the fiduciary's conduct will be judged.

The Investment Policy Statement is the foundation upon which investment goals, manager evaluation, and monitoring will be based. It must be clear and specific enough to be a working document. Broad-based generalities will not serve as investment objectives. Being specific is the key to providing a proper working investment plan. "Long-term appreciation" is a nebulous goal; a better example might be "average growth of inflation plus 6% over three years." Qualitative aspects also are important; therefore, at a minimum the following items should be covered when designing an investment policy statement:

1. Nominal return benchmarks (with consideration of the "real" rate of return)

2. Definition of *risk*

3. Risk tolerance

4. Time period for review and evaluation

5. Allowable investments and quality standards

6. Liquidity requirements

7. Policy asset allocation

8. Procedure for selecting and dismissing money managers

9. Cash flow of the plan (both in and out)

10. Company finances, etc.

   The written plan of investment objectives does not have to be overly complex as long as the objectives are specific enough to meet the needs and goals of the plan participants. Some very comprehensive investment policy statements have been contained within three pages. Written objectives are as integral a part to a three-person pension plan as they are to massive plans such as that at General Motors. Fiduciaries in both cases will be held to standards defined by ERISA as well as by plan documents.

Example: ERISA fund investment policy (see Chapter 22).

V. DIVERSIFICATION OF PLAN ASSETS

It is an investment axiom that diversification is the key to reaching long-term goals, yet this area is one often violated by pension plans. Many benefit plans have too many eggs in one basket in an effort to seek maximum return or perhaps because of plain apathy on the part of the fiduciary. While ERISA does not specify recommended percentages among asset classes, diversification is the only prudent action a fiduciary can take to protect the long-term health of the plan.

   The following should be considered when evaluating diversification of the plan's portfolio:

1. The amount of plan assets

2. Type of investments (stocks, bonds, real estate, etc.)

3. Projected portfolio returns versus funding objectives

4. Volatility of investment returns

5. Liquidity and future cash flows

6. Maturity dates and retiree pension distributions

7. Economic conditions affecting the company and plan investments

8. Company and industry conditions

9. Geographic distribution of assets

There is not a specific minimum nor maximum for each asset class. ERISA states that a fiduciary should not invest an unreasonably large part of the funding in any one investment type.

A corollary to this is whether the fiduciary has considered enough comparable investments to ensure that the best alternative was chosen for the plan. This may involve a formal search for a money manager. The plan's investment committee should review and consider enough investment alternatives to make the most suitable choices for the plan, given inflation, comparable yields, risk vs. return, etc.

VI. AN EVALUATION OF RISK VERSUS RETURN

The concept of risk vs. return is pervasive in the investment business, and nowhere is it weighted more heavily than in the management of employee benefit plans. Specifically, the fiduciary must "minimize the risk of large losses, unless it is clearly not prudent to do so." This would be a rare phenomenon indeed, and the Department of Labor has yet to review a case in which it was not prudent to minimize losses. Importantly, this responsibility applies to the entire portfolio, not every single investment.

ERISA specifies four criteria to use in evaluating the risk and return characteristics of investment alternatives:

1. In terms of liquidity, diversification, return and safety, the individual investment should be appropriate to the total portfolio.

2. Once the asset class is selected (stock, bond, etc.), the fiduciary is required to find the prevailing rate of return of that market given the appropriate levels of risk. In other words, the choice must be made in the context of overall risk; and the investment choice should represent the "fair" return, not necessarily the "highest."

3. A fiduciary faced with investments of equal risk should not choose the one with the lower returns if a higher return is available.

4. In order to evaluate alternatives, some objective standards must be set forth against which to measure them.

VII. THE INVESTMENT PROFESSIONAL

It is obvious from the foregoing discussion, that the typical fiduciary will be unable to meet many of ERISA's requirements without professional assistance. The Prudent Man Rule alone is a sobering mandate, but the writing of investment objectives and fund monitoring are also key areas.

ERISA encourages fiduciaries to use financial professionals, especially money managers. The stress on using professional money managers is tacit recognition by the

Department of Labor that most fiduciaries do not possess the necessary skills to adequately discharge their duties; therefore, working with a money manager is often the only prudent course of action. While the fiduciary has the exclusive authority to manage plan assets, that authority can be delegated to a professional if the plan provides so in writing. Moreover, only a named fiduciary can delegate responsibility for management of plan assets.

The delegation of plan asset management provides two specific benefits to the plan and fiduciary. First, it fulfills the obligation under the Prudent Man Rule. Second, the trustee is not liable as a co-fiduciary for any acts or omissions of the investment manager. However, the fiduciary (trustee) must maintain an oversight obligation; therefore adequate monitoring, evaluating, and reporting procedures must be in place to fulfill this responsibility.

The plan sponsor should be aware of the fact that suitable money managers:

1. Must be registered with the SEC under the Investment Advisors Act of 1940 (unless exempt, as would be most banks and insurance companies).

2. Must acknowledge their fiduciary status in writing. Any professional providing advice must do so pursuant to a written agreement and an oral (preferably written) understanding of the plan.

VIII. THE INVESTMENT MANAGEMENT CONSULTANT

An investment management consultant can play a meaningful role in helping plan sponsors satisfy their responsibilities to the plan's participants. The following are a few of the important duties a good investment consultant can provide:

1. **RESEARCH**—The consultant can bring to the plan sponsor a variety of firms, and will help evaluate historical performance, philosophies, and other information of firms with different areas of expertise (small-cap, international, balanced, etc.).

2. **SELECTION**—The plan sponsor ultimately makes the decision as to which firm to hire, but the investment consultant can be helpful in this process. Manager selection should be based on comprehensive criteria such as risk vs. return, total years of investment experience, dollars under management, staff size, level of communication, etc. Most important, however, is the suitability question. The investment manager being considered must be well suited on all levels to work with the plan sponsor. A good consultant will bring objectivity into the selection process and make it easier for the plan sponsor to understand the differences of the investment managers being considered.

3. **MONITORING**—A qualified consultant will have reliable monitoring capabilities in place before selection is made. Monitoring criteria should be consistent with plan investment objectives, while allowing enough flexibility so the manager can practice his specialty. This is important especially with respect to time frames. Most managers need at least three years, and preferably five years, to prove themselves. This can seem too long to many plan sponsors but it underlines the importance of the selection process. It is imperative that the plan sponsor understands and feels comfortable with the advisor's philosophy, otherwise the customer will never have the patience to allow the manager's discipline to produce the desired results.

Specifically, a good monitoring system will contain some of the following information:

1. Time frame and frequency of review will be established.

2. Benchmarks will be established against which the manager will be judged.

3. Real versus nominal rates of return will be reviewed.

4. Risk and return objectives will be defined.

5. Manager performance relative to peers will be reviewed.

6. Degree of personal attention desired will be considered.

7. Qualitative aspects such as change of philosophy or personnel turnover will be established. (Sometimes these fundamental changes can be positive improvements.)

IX. LIABILITIES AND PENALTIES

Any fiduciary who breaches his fiduciary obligation will be held personally liable for losses caused by the breach of duty. Penalties may be imposed for up to six years after the fiduciary violation, or three years after the party bringing suit had knowledge of the breach. A willful violation carries personal criminal penalties of up to $5,000 ($100,000 for corporations) and up to one year in prison. Civil actions can be initiated by plan participants, beneficiaries, other fiduciaries, and the Department of Labor. Losses to the plan as well as profits made from the improper use of plan assets must be restored. Failure to disclose information to plan participants can result in a daily penalty of $100. The Department of Labor also can remove the fiduciary and take control over plan assets.

Bonding of the fiduciary is recommended to provide some protection against plan losses resulting from dishonest activities.

X. CORPORATE GOVERNANCE AND PROXY VOTING

Corporate governance covers proxy voting, shareholder rights, and the role the plan takes as "part owner" of a public corporation. The major issue in management is the voting of stock held by the plan, which can sometimes be rife with conflicts of interest. The best way to eliminate conflicts is to ensure that the fiduciary with voting responsibility is totally independent of the plan sponsor.

Fiduciaries have a legal obligation to evaluate carefully all sides of governance issues which affect the value of plan assets and shareholder rights. Stock should be voted in the best interest of plan participants and a system of voting for oversight and policies is the best way to ensure compliance with ERISA.

XI. PROHIBITED TRANSACTIONS

ERISA's prohibited transaction rules basically state that a fiduciary may not deal with plan assets in his own interest nor act in a manner adversely affecting plan participants. Prohibited transactions must be identified and eliminated in order to ensure a retirement plan's qualifications. Here are some general transactions that fall into this category.

1. Sale, lease, or exchange of property between plan and party-in-interest

2. Lending of money between plan and party-in-interest (Other than legal participant loans)

261

3. Transferring any plan assets to, or use of plan assets by, party-in-interest

4. Acquiring employer assets in excess of 10% of plan assets, including real estate (limits may be exceeded through special letter ruling from the IRS)

5. Self-dealing by fiduciary

6. Compensation paid to fiduciary by party involved in transaction with plan assets.

HOW TO AVOID PERSONAL PENSION LIABILITY

Do not take fiduciary liability lightly. Court records show many cases in which a fiduciary became personally liable, perhaps for acts for which he was unaware or in areas he did not know were within his responsibility. Not knowing one's responsibilities is no defense, and the cost of defense will probably be paid by either the plan or the company. However, this liability can be relatively easy to avoid if one understands his or her fiduciary responsibility as has been outlined in this booklet.

FIDUCIARY GUIDELINES

Here is a simple fiduciary check list. It does not cover every point possible. But it can serve as a guideline to help employers satisfy their fiduciary responsibility.

1. Know and understand the plan documents. Make sure they are kept current with the laws and have been properly filed and approved.

2. Make sure plan participants are kept fully informed as to:

A. Their account balances, or accrued benefits

B. Investment options

C. The plan's provisions (via the summary plan description)

D. Any other features of their employee benefit package that may require disclosure to the plan participants.

3. Have a working knowledge and a legal understanding of being a plan fiduciary.

4. If appropriate, hire a plan consultant to assist in:

A. Creating a written set of investment objectives (a sample has been enclosed)

B. Selecting a qualified investment manager

C. Devising an appropriate investment monitoring benchmark

D. Setting up periodic reviews of both investment performance and the plans objectives

E. Making sure that the plan administration is running smoothly. Tax forms should be filed on a timely basis, and participants should be receiving regular participant statements

F. Making sure that all fiduciaries are bonded with the appropriate insurance coverage

G. Most important, keeping a written record of the decisions made by the plans or the investment committee.

SUMMARY

The protection of employee benefit plan participants under ERISA is forthright, but the Department of Labor has realized that rules without compliance are meaningless. Additionally, the Pension Benefit Guarantee Corporation (PBGC) is running a significant deficit. This government agency, analogous to the Federal Savings and Loan Insurance Corporation (FSLIC), can no longer be supported by taxpayer dollars. Pressure is being increasingly applied on private pensions to meet ERISA's rules in order to minimize the U.S. government's liability in this area. Increasing surveillance and audits of small and medium-sized plans are inevitable since it has been estimated that approximately 80% of small plans (under $3 million) are currently in violation of ERISA regulations. Extensive understanding of ERISA is mandatory and the role of the independent investment management firm will emerge as a key to long-term success.

We do not hold ourselves out to be attorneys or specialists in pension legislation, nor are we attempting to offer any legal advice. We do advise employers to deal with their retirement plan consultants, attorneys, or CPAs if they have specific questions regarding their retirement funds.

ERISA FUND INVESTMENT POLICY STATEMENT

This represents the investment objectives, guidelines, and restrictions, otherwise known as the investment policy statement, for the XYZ Corporation Employee Profit Sharing Plan. This statement was developed to give the investment manager a clear understanding of the investments, restrictions, objectives, directions, and framework for evaluating performance.

The assets of the fund are to be managed and invested with the objective of achieving the greatest return consistent with the fiduciary character of the fund and to maintain a level of liquidity sufficient to meet the need for timely distributions to participants. The investment manager should strive to prevent the long-term erosion of capital and avoid a high degree of fluctuation in the value of the fund.

TRUSTEE RESPONSIBILITY

The trustees are obligated, by law, with the responsibility for the investment of the assets of the plan. The trustees shall discharge their duties solely in the interest of the participants and their beneficiaries. They shall discharge their duties with the care, skill, prudence, and diligence under the circumstances then prevailing that a prudent man acting in a like capacity and familiar with such matters would use in the conduct of an enterprise of a like character and with like aims.

Chapter 22

DELEGATION OF INVESTMENT MANAGEMENT

The management of the profit sharing plan fund assets and the responsibility for investment decisions shall be delegated to an SEC registered investment manager. The investment manager will be given full discretion in managing the funds within the guidelines of this investment statement. Accordingly, the trustee(s) require the investment manager to adhere to the Prudent Man Rule under such federal laws as now apply, or may in the future apply, to investment of the plan assets.

INVESTMENT GUIDELINES

1. As it relates to asset allocation/diversification, the trustee(s) believe that common stocks should have a place in the investment portfolio. The trustee(s) also believe that bonds should be included in this portfolio for adequate diversification. The trustee(s) also believe that the stock market is currently offering enough potential over the next year to compensate for the increased risk in using stocks versus the bond market.

   The trustee(s) believe the economic and market outlook should be evaluated first and the percentage in stocks should reflect that outlook and that the economic and market outlook should be considered in making bond investments. The percentage held in bonds should vary with this outlook.

2. As it relates to investment philosophy, the trustee(s) believe that the portfolio manager would invest in both established companies and in new companies which are considered to have good growth potential and that the portfolio manager will generally sell individual stocks when compared to other companies.

ERISA Fund Investment Policy Statement

The trustee(s) generally categorize this portfolio as a balanced portfolio with equal emphasis on capital growth and income. The trustee(s) tend to view risk as long-term erosion of capital with the possibility of a high degree of fluctuation in the value of the portfolio over a full market cycle. The trustee(s) would not be comfortable being fully invested during a weak market environment. The trustee(s) also would not be comfortable in attempting to anticipate and take advantage of market swings. Finally, the trustee(s) would expect the portfolio to have slightly less fluctuation than the market.

3. The following are acceptable asset classes:

   A. Common stocks

   B. U.S. government securities

   C. Convertibles

   D. Commercial paper

   E. Bonds—with no rating below A

   F. Money market funds

Investments may be chosen from the NYSE, ASE, regional exchanges and the national over-the-counter market. All assets must have readily ascertainable market value and be easily marketable.

4. The following are prohibited transactions or assets:

   A. Commodity trading, including all futures contracts

   B. Purchasing of letter stock

   C. Short selling

   D. Option trading

   E. Foreign securities

5. The investment shall be so diversified as to minimize the risk of large losses unless, under particular circumstances, it is clearly prudent not to do so. The trustee(s) believe the equity portion of the portfolio should have 20 to 30 positions.

INVESTMENT OBJECTIVE

It is the intention of the trustee(s) that the investment manager make reasonable efforts to preserve the principal of the funds delegated. However, preservation of the principal shall not be imposed on each individual investment.

The investment objective is to produce a total return, net of expenses, of at least 10% per year or 5% per year in excess of the rate of inflation, whichever is greater, over a rolling five-year period. It is expected that the total fund returns will surpass the market index, on average, over full market cycles.

In addition, the fund will be compared to:

A. A balanced composite of the S&P 500 Index and the SLH Govt./Corp Index in rations equal to that of the fund or comparable indices

B. S&P 500 Index

C. SLH Govt./Corp Index

D. Consumer Price Index

E. Comparable universe of advisors with similar risk levels

F. Risk-adjusted analysis

Disclaimer: The preceding policy is a speciman policy and should not be construded as being appropriate for every situation. Investors should seek help from a qualified consultant.

WRAP INVESTING FOR
SIMPLIFIED EMPLOYEE PENSION (SEP)

If you are a small business owner or self-employed professional, a Simplified Employee Pension (SEP) could be the answer to your retirement.

A Simplified Employee Pension is a nonqualified retirement plan which is best suited to small and medium-sized partnerships and corporations in which each participant has a self-directed individual retirement account. A hybrid between a profit-sharing plan and an IRA, a SEP offers the advantages of simplified administration—IRS Form 5500 is required—and the option to integrate your program with existing retirement plan assets and Social Security.

A SEP, which operates in much the same way that larger companies' 401(k) plans do, can be easily established with the help of a qualified financial advisor and administered by your bookkeeper or tax advisor.

Eligible participants can contribute up to 15% of their compensation or $30,000 to the plan on a tax-deferred basis until withdrawal and, in some cases, salary reduction features may be available.

An added tax feature of a SEP is that it is the only type of employer-funded retirement plan that can be established and funded following the end of the 1991 tax year. You can initiate a SEP through April 1992 (or later—if you qualify for an extension) to allow tax-deductible, tax-deferred growth.

The option of salary reduction is also available as part of a SEP. These plans are known as Salary Reduction/Simplified Employee Pensions or SAR/SEPs. Under the 1986 Tax Reform Act, employees can elect to set aside pretax dollars, and employers can make contributions on behalf of plan participants.

To utilize the salary reduction features or a SAR/SEP, sponsoring employers must have 25 or fewer employees and at least 50% of those eligible for the plan must elect to participate. Eligibility rules also require that employees meet certain minimum age and salary requirements and that they must have worked a minimum of three of the last five years.

To establish a SAR/SEP, an employer must contribute a minimum of three percent of total compensation for all eligible employees, whether or not they are enrolled in the salary reduction option.

Participants who choose the salary reduction option may contribute up to $8,475 in 1991, the same amount as in a 401(k). Following years are adjusted higher to account for inflation. Overall, the contribution limit per participant from all sources, including pretax deferrals and employer minimum and matching contributions cannot exceed the lesser of 15% of compensation or $30,000. Because contributions can vary from year to year, the SEP is as flexible as a profit-sharing plan.

A SAR/SEP is subject to a "nondiscrimination" test, which means that the amount that can be deferred through salary reduction by highly compensated employees is limited by the average amount the lower paid employees elect to defer.

Wrap Investing for Simplified Employee Pension

Each participant's funds are set aside in a SEP/IRA, which can be used to consolidate all retirement contributions from existing IRAs, and rollover money from qualified plans. All investment decisions are controlled by the individual participant.

A qualified financial advisor will be able to describe SEPs and SAR/SEPs to you in greater detail and will also explain how a plan will benefit your business.

Obviously, once the SEP has been established and some funding has begun, the wrap fee account approach can be utilized for an SEP just the same as a large retirement plan.

CONCLUSION

Wrap account investing is delivered in two approaches; (1) a product by a salesman or (2) a service by a consultant.

Product salespersons who shift from the oversimplified "packaged" approach to wrap account consulting will beat their competition. Those who are already providing this service in a meaningful way are the firms doing over half of the $40 billion wrap account business. These firms recognize the value provided by consulting the wrap investor, and offer a better all-around service than does a pre-package wrap sales program. Prepackage wrap programs can be likened to a suit off the rack, as compared to the custom tailoring of investment consulting. We fully admit that a suit off the rack sometimes fits perfectly.

Most investment professionals have not been taught how to deliver a wrap package to an investor the way it was intended. Working with a professional is the critical step in the process. If the investor believes in the program, under-

Conclusion

stands it, and stays with it, over time the investor will win at the investment game.

You can create the best investment package in the world, but if the person delivering it doesn't thoroughly understand it, his or her client won't either. The broker will think of wrap as just another Wall Street investment product, and so will the investor. The true value of the wrap account will be missing and no one-page questionnaire or one-page computer-generated investment policy will explain it.

Selling wrap accounts as a prepackaged product may be a good moneymaker for Wall Street, but it is not the best use of this service. The men and women selling wrap accounts in the 1990s are simply going to have to learn the money management business and thoroughly understand and implement the consulting process.

This will not happen across the board with everyone or every brokerage house selling wrap accounts. We all have our own level of enthusiasm and proficiency. It appears that many brokers are content at being adept at selling the wrap package rather than in being well-versed in how to use it. Since any professional broker or financial planner registered to sell investments can sell wrap accounts, it is incumbent upon the investor to demand a high level of competence and service.

The perfect wrap fee situation in the 1990s is when the individual investor understands the value of professional money management, and demands it, and when investment consulting professionals who provide services and access to money managers understand the process they are representing. Investors' objectives should be matched to manager styles. And investors need to understand when and why certain styles are in or out of favor.

The better educated the investor is, and the more demanding he or she becomes, the better the people delivering wrap fee programs will get. Utilize the services of someone who does investment management consulting on a full-time basis and has experience. In addition, refer to this book to give yourself a level of comfort, feeling assured that you are getting the job done properly.

Having this information doesn't mean that you should go out and do it yourself. You should understand how the process works even if somebody else is doing the work for you. This holds true if you are a fiduciary overseeing a $10 million pension account or an individual with a $100,000 individual account.

Finally, we need to give praise to those investment firms that are diligently providing information in an understandable way to their clients.

There are some marketers out there simply packaging a wrap account without doing any real investment analysis. Some firms even work solely off of mailed-in questionnaires. Ask the right questions and you will see through this.

You have a choice. The investment industry is a very competitive business. It doesn't take long to produce a slick brochure or put together an in-house wrap program. It is up to you, the investor, to recognize an unjustified high fee or an absence of responsible service. If you are paying for professional money management, and consulting to go with it, make sure you get a wrap manager that truly meets the tests. Use this book. Be discriminating about those who call themselves "consultants," and you should be very successful.

If you want to learn more about the consulting process, the Insititute for Investment Management Consultants makes a course available on the subject.

APPENDIX A

MAJOR BROKERAGE FIRMS
THAT OFFER
WRAP ACCOUNTS

The following information was obtained just prior to publication of this book. Given the rapid growth and change in the wrap fee industry, we cannot guarantee the accuracy of all the information. Since publication of the book, it's likely that some of the listed firms changed elements of their wrap fee programs. As we plan to revise the book in the future, we would ask the firms to please keep the authors updated on their wrap fee programs by contacting Mr. Chambers at P.O. Box 1810, Ojai, CA 93024-1810.

Appendix A

1. **NAME OF FIRM:** A.G. EDWARDS

2. **NAME OF PROGRAM:** Asset Performance Monitor (APM)

3. **MINIMUM ACCOUNT SIZE:** $100,000

4. **MANAGER SELECTION PROCESS:** Firm analyzes managers' performance record, transactions, characteristics of securities held, buy and sell disciplines, and adherence to the discipline, and their investment philosophy.

5. **NUMBER OF MANAGERS IN PROGRAM:** Provides on-going evaluations of 50 managers. Clients can choose from a total of 800 managers in data base.

6. **MANAGERS' STYLES:** Equity, Balanced, Fixed

7. **NUMBER OF MANAGERS IN FIRM'S DATA BASE:** 800+

8. **TOTAL NUMBER STAFF FOR PROGRAM:** 15

9. **MANAGER FEE:** variable

10. **FEE SCHEDULE:**
    First $500,000—2.00% (plus managers fee)
    Next $500,000—1.5% (plus managers fee)
    Next $1,500,000—1.0% (plus managers fee)
    Over $2,500,000—0.5% (plus managers fee)
    (has three different fee schedules to choose from:
    ALT I, ALT II, and ALT III)

11. **MINIMUM FEE:** $2,000 (ALT III: $1,500)

12. **IS FEE NEGOTIABLE?** Only over $5 million

13. **INSURANCE PER WRAP ACCOUNT:** $10 million

14. **ASSETS IN FIRMS PROGRAM:** Over $2 billion

15. **NUMBER OF ACCOUNTS:** 5,000

16. **DOES FIRM CONDUCT ON-GOING DUE DILIGENCE?** Yes

17. **NUMBER OF DUE DILIGENCE OFFICERS:** Four

18. **NUMBER OF MANAGER OFFICES VISITED PER YEAR:** N/A

19. **THE FIRM'S INVESTMENT MANAGER SELECTION PROCESS:** Client and financial consultant complete questionnaire planning form. Financial consultant with possible assistance of office and APM manager evaluate material and

manager information. Present three managers which appear to match client objectives. Client then makes selection.

20. **WHAT FIRM PRESENTS TO INVESTOR:** Investment philosophy, performance of proposed managers, how they compare to markets versus S&P 500 and other managers, the amount of assets an advisor manages and their number of accounts.

21. **CAN INVESTOR CONTACT MANAGER?** Yes

22. **DOES INDIVIDUAL BROKER HAVE A ROLE IN SELECTION PROCESS?** Yes

QUARTERLY REPORTING

23. **DOES FIRM OFFER A QUARTERLY REPORT (MONITOR)?** Yes

24. **DOES REPORT COMPARE INVESTMENT OBJECTIVES?** Yes

25. **DOES REPORT OFFER COMMENTS FROM MANAGERS?** No

26. **DOES REPORT GIVE MARKET OUTLOOK?** No

27. **DOES REPORT SHOW ASSET ALLOCATION?** Yes

28. **DOES REPORT SHOW (CPI) INFLATION?** Yes

29. **DOES REPORT COMPARE OTHER MANAGERS?** Yes

30. **DOES REPORT SHOW MARKET INDEXES?** Yes

31. **CAN REPORT SHOW CUSTOM INDEX?** Yes, within parameters

FIRM'S FINANCIAL INFORMATION

32. **YEAR FIRM WAS ESTABLISHED:** 1881

33. **FIRM'S REVENUES (est):** Year-end 1990 $675.9 Million

34. **TOTAL NUMBER OF FIRM'S EMPLOYEES:** 10,000+

Appendix A

1. **NAME OF FIRM**: DEAN WITTER

2. **NAME OF PROGRAM**: ACCESS

3. **MINIMUM ACCOUNT SIZE**:
   Equity $100,000
   Fixed $250,000

4. **MANAGER SELECTION PROCESS**: Performance over five-plus years, $100 million-and-under management, industry ranking, reviewed by Dean Witter selection committee

5. **NUMBER OF MANAGERS IN PROGRAM**: 25 managers

6. **MANAGERS' STYLES**: Core Equity, Balanced, Growth Equity, Fixed Income, International/Global

7. **NUMBER OF MANAGERS IN FIRM'S DATA BASE**: 100+

8. **TOTAL NUMBER OF STAFF FOR PROGRAM**: 40

9. **MANAGER FEE**: Included or unbundled

10. **FEE SCHEDULE**:
    First $500,000—3.00%
    Next $500,000—2.75%
    Next $1,000,000—2.25%
    Over $2,000,000—1.75%
    FIXED INCOME FEE SCHEDULE:
    First $500,000—1.50%
    Next $500,000—1.25%
    Next $1,000,000—1.00%
    Over $2,000,000—0.75%

11. **MINIMUM FEE**: $3,000

12. **IS FEE NEGOTIABLE?** Yes—30% maximum

13. **INSURANCE PER WRAP ACCOUNT**: $25 million

14. **ASSETS IN FIRM'S PROGRAM**: Over $1 billion

15. **NUMBER OF ACCOUNTS**: 5000

16. **DOES FIRM CONDUCT ON-GOING DUE DILIGENCE?** Yes

17. **NUMBER OF DUE DILIGENCE OFFICERS**: Three

18. **NUMBER OF MANAGER OFFICES VISITED PER YEAR**: N/A (Not a set program)

19. **THE FIRM'S INVESTMENT MANAGER SELECTION PROCESS:**
    A. Client completes questionnaire.
    B. Financial consultants meet to review risk tolerance, and investment objectives.
    C. Questionnaire sent to home office.
    D. Firm develops written policy statement.
    E. Firm recommends three managers.

20. **WHAT FIRM PRESENTS TO INVESTOR?** Performance of recommended managers, investment objectives, compares performance to markets indexes, investment philosophy

21. **CAN INVESTOR CONTACT MANAGER?** Discouraged

22. **DOES INDIVIDUAL BROKER HAVE A ROLE IN SELECTION PROCESS?**
    Financial consultant recommends manager without firm's input.

QUARTERLY REPORTING

23. **DOES FIRM OFFER A QUARTERLY REPORT (MONITOR)?** Yes

24. **DOES REPORT COMPARE INVESTMENT OBJECTIVES?** Yes

25. **DOES REPORT OFFER COMMENTS FROM MANAGERS?** Yes

26. **DOES REPORT GIVE MARKET OUTLOOK?**
    No (Managers issue report directly to client.)

27. **DOES REPORT SHOW ASSET ALLOCATION?** Yes

28. **DOES REPORT SHOW (CPI) INFLATION?** Yes

29. **DOES REPORT COMPARE OTHER MANAGERS?** Yes

30. **DOES REPORT SHOW MARKET INDEXES?** Yes

31. **CAN REPORT SHOW CUSTOM INDEX?** No

FIRM'S FINANCIAL INFORMATION

32. **YEAR FIRM WAS ESTABLISHED:** 1924

33. **FIRM'S REVENUES (est):** Year-end 1990, $2.5 billion

34. **TOTAL NUMBER OF FIRM'S EMPLOYEES:** 9,000

Appendix A

1. **NAME OF FIRM**: KIDDER-PEABODY

2. **NAME OF PROGRAM**: NOVA

3. **MINIMUM ACCOUNT SIZE**:
Equity $200,000
Fixed $750,000

4. **MANAGER SELECTION PROCESS**:
Risk-adjusted performance five-plus years experience,
$50 million-and-under management.

5. **NUMBER OF MANAGERS IN PROGRAM**: 10 managers

6. **MANAGERS' STYLES**: Equity, Fixed Income

7. **NUMBER OF MANAGERS IN FIRM'S DATA BASE**: 1000

8. **TOTAL NUMBER STAFF FOR PROGRAM**: 15

9. **MANAGER FEE**: Included

10. **FEE SCHEDULE**:
First $500,000—3.00%
Next $500,000—2.25%
Next $1,000,000—1.75%
Over $2,000,000—1.50%
FIXED INCOME FEE SCHEDULE:
First $100,000,000—1.50%
Next $500,000—1.25%
Next $1,000,000—1.00%
Over $2,000,000— 0.75%

11. **MINIMUM FEE**: $5,400

12. **IS FEE NEGOTIABLE?** Yes—offered 25%

13. **INSURANCE PER WRAP ACCOUNT**: $10 million

14. **ASSETS IN FIRM'S PROGRAM**: over $200 million

15. **NUMBER OF ACCOUNTS**: 500

16. **DOES FIRM CONDUCT ON-GOING DUE DILIGENCE?** Yes

17. **NUMBER OF DUE DILIGENCE OFFICERS**: Four

18. **NUMBER OF MANAGER OFFICES VISITED PER YEAR**:
N/A (not a set program)

19. **THE FIRM'S INVESTMENT MANAGER SELECTION PROCESS:**
    A. Client completes questionnaire.
    B. Financial consultants meet to review investment objectives.
    C. Makes preliminary choice.
    D. Questionnaire sent to home office.
    E. Firm develops written policy statement.
    F. Firm recommends three managers.

20. **WHAT FIRM PRESENTS TO INVESTOR:**
    Risk-adjusted performance, performance versus other managers, compares performance to markets indexes, investment philosophy, securities selection

21. **CAN INVESTOR CONTACT MANAGER?** Discouraged

22. **DOES INDIVIDUAL BROKER HAVE A ROLE IN SELECTION PROCESS?** No

QUARTERLY REPORTING

23. **DOES FIRM OFFER A QUARTERLY REPORT (MONITOR)?** Yes

24. **DOES REPORT COMPARE INVESTMENT OBJECTIVES?** Yes

25. **DOES REPORT OFFER COMMENTS FROM MANAGERS?** Yes

26. **DOES REPORT GIVE MARKET OUTLOOK?** Yes

27. **DOES REPORT SHOW ASSET ALLOCATION?** Yes

28. **DOES REPORT SHOW (CPI) INFLATION?** Yes

29. **DOES REPORT COMPARE OTHER MANAGERS?** Yes

30. **DOES REPORT SHOW MARKET INDEXES?** Yes

31. **CAN REPORT SHOW CUSTOM INDEX?** No

FIRM'S FINANCIAL INFORMATION

32. **YEAR FIRM WAS ESTABLISHED:** 1865

33. **FIRM'S REVENUES (est):** N/A

34. **TOTAL NUMBER OF FIRM'S EMPLOYEES:** 5,000

Appendix A

1. **NAME OF FIRM**: PRUDENTIAL-BACHE

2. **NAME OF PROGRAM**:
MANAGED ASSETS CONSULTING SERVICES (MACS)

3. **MINIMUM ACCOUNT SIZE**:
Equity $100,000
Balanced $250,000

4. **MANAGER SELECTION PROCESS**:
Long-range performance, investment philosophy, manager style, research capability, stability of organization, management quality and reputation, amount of risk, firm's reputation

5. **NUMBER OF MANAGERS IN PROGRAM**: 22 managers

6. **MANAGERS' STYLES**: Equity, Balanced, chosen in categories from conservative to aggressive.

7. **NUMBER OF MANAGERS IN FIRM'S DATA BASE**: 300

8. **TOTAL NUMBER STAFF FOR PROGRAM**: 20

9. **MANAGER FEE**: Included

10. **FEE SCHEDULE**:
First $500,000—3.00%
Next $500,000—2.50%
Next $1,500,000—1.75%
Over $2,000,000—1.50%

11. **MINIMUM FEE**: $3,000

12. **IS FEE NEGOTIABLE?** Yes—offer 25%

13. **INSURANCE PER WRAP ACCOUNT**: $10 million

14. **ASSETS IN FIRM'S PROGRAM**: $1 billion

15. **NUMBER OF ACCOUNTS**: 5,000

16. **DOES FIRM CONDUCT ON-GOING DUE DILIGENCE?**
Yes

17. **NUMBER OF DUE DILIGENCE OFFICERS**: Seven

18. **NUMBER OF MANAGER OFFICES VISITED PER YEAR**: 75

19. **THE FIRM'S INVESTMENT MANAGER SELECTION PROCESS:**
    A. Client/financial consultant establishes goals thru informal questionnaire.
    B. Financial consultant sends data to firm.
    C. Firm develops written investment policy statement.
    D. Firm recommends three managers.

20. **WHAT FIRM PRESENTS TO INVESTOR:**
    A. Performance versus markets indexes
    B. Firm profile, investment philosophy

21. **CAN INVESTOR CONTACT MANAGER?** Discouraged

22. **DOES INDIVIDUAL BROKER HAVE A ROLE IN SELECTION PROCESS?** No

QUARTERLY REPORTING

23. **DOES FIRM OFFER A QUARTERLY REPORT (MONITOR)?** Yes

24. **DOES REPORT COMPARE INVESTMENT OBJECTIVES?** Yes

25. **DOES REPORT OFFER COMMENTS FROM MANAGERS?** Yes

26. **DOES REPORT GIVE MARKET OUTLOOK?** Yes

27. **DOES REPORT SHOW ASSET ALLOCATION?** No

28. **DOES REPORT SHOW (CPI) INFLATION?** Yes

29. **DOES REPORT COMPARE OTHER MANAGERS?** No

30. **DOES REPORT SHOW MARKET INDEXES?** Yes

31. **CAN REPORT SHOW CUSTOM INDEX?** No

FIRM'S FINANCIAL INFORMATION

32. **YEAR FIRM WAS ESTABLISHED:** 1879

33. **FIRM'S REVENUES (est):** Year-end 1990, $3.6 billion

34. **TOTAL NUMBER OF FIRM'S EMPLOYEES:** 17,000

Appendix A

1. **NAME OF FIRM**: PAINE WEBBER

2. **NAME OF PROGRAM**: ACCESS

3. **MINIMUM ACCOUNT SIZE**: $100,000

4. **MANAGER SELECTION PROCESS**:
   Stability of staff, ability to outperform indices, consistent philosophy, experienced firm

5. **NUMBER OF MANAGERS IN PROGRAM**: 17 managers

6. **MANAGERS' STYLES**: Equity, Balanced, Fixed Income

7. **NUMBER OF MANAGERS IN FIRM'S DATA BASE**: 1,000

8. **TOTAL NUMBER STAFF FOR PROGRAM**: 32

9. **MANAGER FEE**: Included

10. **FEE SCHEDULE**:
    First $500,000—2.80%
    Next $500,000—2.20%
    Next $4,000,000—1.60%
    Over $5,000,000—1.40%
    FIXED INCOME FEE SCHEDULE:
    First $500,000—1.25%
    Next $500,000—1.10%
    Next $4,000,000—1.00%
    Over $5,000,000—0.80%

11. **MINIMUM FEE**:
    Equity/Balanced $2,800
    Fixed Income $1,250

12. **IS FEE NEGOTIABLE?** Yes—offer 25%, none for Fixed

13. **INSURANCE PER WRAP ACCOUNT**: $10 million

14. **ASSETS IN FIRM'S PROGRAM**: $750,000

15. **NUMBER OF ACCOUNTS**: 3,000

16. **DOES FIRM CONDUCT ON-GOING DUE DILIGENCE?** Yes

17. **NUMBER OF DUE DILIGENCE OFFICERS**: Nine

18. **NUMBER OF MANAGER OFFICES VISITED PER YEAR**: 150

19. **THE FIRM'S INVESTMENT MANAGER SELECTION PROCESS.**
    A. Client/financial consultant completes questionnaire.
    B. Financial consultant reviews client's investment objectives and determines investment category.
    C. Client/financial consultant selects appropriate manager.

20. **WHAT FIRM PRESENTS TO INVESTOR**:
    Risk-adjusted performance, investment philosophy, typical asset allocation, bios of key personnel, performance versus indices, market sector weightings

21. **CAN INVESTOR CONTACT MANAGER?** Discouraged (Yes on special situation)

22. **DOES INDIVIDUAL BROKER HAVE A ROLE IN SELECTION PROCESS?** No

QUARTERLY REPORTING

23. **DOES FIRM OFFER A QUARTERLY REPORT (MONITOR)?** Yes

24. **DOES REPORT COMPARE INVESTMENT OBJECTIVES?** Yes

25. **DOES REPORT OFFER COMMENTS FROM MANAGERS?** No

26. **DOES REPORT GIVE MARKET OUTLOOK?** No

27. **DOES REPORT SHOW ASSET ALLOCATION?** Yes

28. **DOES REPORT SHOW (CPI) INFLATION?** No

29. **DOES REPORT COMPARE OTHER MANAGERS?** Yes

30. **DOES REPORT SHOW MARKET INDEXES?** Yes

31. **CAN REPORT SHOW CUSTOM INDEX?** No

FIRM'S FINANCIAL INFORMATION

32. **YEAR FIRM WAS ESTABLISHED:** 1879

33. **FIRM'S REVENUES (est):** Year-end 1990, $2.98 million

34. **TOTAL NUMBER OF FIRM'S EMPLOYEES:** 12,700

Appendix A

1. **NAME OF FIRM**: MERRILL LYNCH

2. **NAME OF PROGRAM**: ML CONSULTS

3. **MINIMUM ACCOUNT SIZE**:
   $100,000: Individual
   $250,000: Institutional

4. **MANAGER SELECTION PROCESS**: Risk-adjusted perform-ance consistent philosophy, organizational stability, size of assets under management, and number of accounts

5. **NUMBER OF MANAGERS IN PROGRAM**: 27+ managers

6. **MANAGERS' STYLES**: Equity, Balanced, Fixed Income

7. **NUMBER OF MANAGERS IN FIRM'S DATA BASE**: 600

8. **TOTAL NUMBER STAFF FOR PROGRAM**: 47

9. **MANAGER FEE**: Included

10. **FEE SCHEDULE**:
    First $500,000—3.00%
    Next $500,000—2.25%
    Next $1,000,000—2.50%
    Over $2,000,000—2.25%
    Next $5,000,000—1.75%
    FIXED INCOME FEE SCHEDULE:
    First $500,000—1.75%
    Next $500,000—1.65%
    Next $1,500,000—1.55%
    Over $2,500,000—1.45%
    Next $5,000,000—1.35%
    $10,000,000—1.25%

11. **MINIMUM FEE**: None (But minimum account size required.)

12. **IS FEE NEGOTIABLE?** Yes—30% maximum

13. **INSURANCE PER WRAP ACCOUNT**: $25 million

14. **ASSETS IN FIRM'S PROGRAM**: $4.2 billion

15. **NUMBER OF ACCOUNTS**: 18,000

16. **DOES FIRM CONDUCT ON-GOING DUE DILIGENCE?** Yes

17. **NUMBER OF DUE DILIGENCE OFFICERS**: N/A

18. **NUMBER OF MANAGER OFFICES VISITED PER YEAR**: N/A

19. **THE FIRM'S INVESTMENT MANAGER SELECTION PROCESS**:
    A. Client/financial consultant completes questionnaire.
    B. Financial consultant meets to review investment objectives and determines client's risk category.
    C. Financial consultant assists client in selecting manager from managers at appropriate risk level.
    D. Review of questionnaire and manager selection by RVP/RM and consults administration.

20. **WHAT FIRM PRESENTS TO INVESTOR**: Risk-adjusted performance, compares performance to markets indexes, firm profile, investment philosophy, securities selection

21. **CAN INVESTOR CONTACT MANAGER?** Yes

22. **DOES INDIVIDUAL BROKER HAVE A ROLE IN SELECTION PROCESS?** No

QUARTERLY REPORTING

23. **DOES FIRM OFFER A QUARTERLY REPORT (MONITOR)?** Yes

24. **DOES REPORT COMPARE INVESTMENT OBJECTIVES?** Yes

25. **DOES REPORT OFFER COMMENTS FROM MANAGERS?** Yes

26. **DOES REPORT GIVE MARKET OUTLOOK?** Yes

27. **DOES REPORT SHOW ASSET ALLOCATION?** Yes

28. **DOES REPORT SHOW (CPI) INFLATION?** Yes

29. **DOES REPORT COMPARE OTHER MANAGERS?** Yes

30. **DOES REPORT SHOW MARKET INDEXES?** Yes

31. **CAN REPORT SHOW CUSTOM INDEX?** Yes

FIRM'S FINANCIAL INFORMATION

32. **YEAR FIRM WAS ESTABLISHED**: 1885

33. **FIRM'S REVENUES** (est): Year-end 1990, $11.2 billion

34. **TOTAL NUMBER OF FIRM'S EMPLOYEES**: 39,650

Appendix A

1. **NAME OF FIRM**: SMITH BARNEY SHEARSON

2. **NAME OF PROGRAM**: SELECT MANAGERS (SELECT) CHOICE ADVISORS

3. **MINIMUM ACCOUNT SIZE**:
   SELECT $100,000
   CHOICE $50,000

4. **MANAGER SELECTION PROCESS** Consistent performance and philosophy, reputation, size of assets under management and number of accounts research capability, investment style, and strategy

5. **NUMBER OF MANAGERS IN PROGRAM**: 27+ managers

6. **MANAGERS' STYLES**: Equity, Balanced, Growth, Fixed Income, Value, and Small-cap; 32 styles

7. **NUMBER OF MANAGERS IN FIRM'S DATA BASE**: 800+

8. **TOTAL NUMBER STAFF FOR PROGRAM**: 130

9. **MANAGER FEE**: Included

10. **FEE SCHEDULE**:
    First $500,000—3.00%
    Next $500,000—2.20%
    Next $1,000,000—1.90%
    Over $2,000,000—1.70%
    FIXED INCOME FEE SCHEDULE:
    First $500,000—1.25%
    Next $500,000—1.10%
    Next $1,000,000—0.95%
    Over $2,000,000—0.85%

11. **MINIMUM FEE**:
    Select and Choice:
    $2,500/Equity $1,250 Fixed
    $100,000 3% of assets

12. **IS FEE NEGOTIABLE?** Yes—40% maximum

13. **INSURANCE PER WRAP ACCOUNT**: $25 million

14. **ASSETS IN FIRM'S PROGRAM**:
    Select $4.6 billion
    Choice $1.3 billion

15. **NUMBER OF ACCOUNTS**:
Select 20,324
Choice 8,500

16. **DOES FIRM CONDUCT ON-GOING DUE DILIGENCE?** Yes

17. **NUMBER OF DUE DILIGENCE OFFICERS?** Five

18. **NUMBER OF MANAGER OFFICE VISITED PER YEAR:**
Approximately 350

19. **THE FIRM'S INVESTMENT MANAGER SELECTION PROCESS:**
    A. Client/Financial consultant completes questionnaire and asset summary form
    B. Financial consultants meet to review investment objectives
    C. Forms sent to firm
    D. Firm develops written policy statement
    E. Firm recommends one to three managers

20. **WHAT FIRM PRESENTS TO INVESTOR:** Risk-adjusted performance, performance versus market indexes, firm profile, investment philosophy

21. **CAN INVESTOR CONTACT MANAGER?** Discouraged

22. **DOES INDIVIDUAL BROKER HAVE A ROLE IN SELECTION PROCESS?** Financial consultant recommends managers without firms input.

QUARTERLY REPORTING

23. **DOES FIRM OFFER A QUARTERLY REPORT (MONITOR)?** Yes

24. **DOES REPORT COMPARE INVESTMENT OBJECTIVES?** Yes

25. **DOES REPORT OFFER COMMENTS FROM MANAGERS?** Yes

26. **DOES REPORT GIVE MARKET OUTLOOK?** Yes

27. **DOES REPORT SHOW ASSET ALLOCATION?** Yes

28. **DOES REPORT SHOW (CPI) INFLATION?** Yes

29. **DOES REPORT COMPARE OTHER MANAGERS?** No

30. **DOES REPORT SHOW MARKET INDEXES?** Yes

31. **CAN REPORT SHOW CUSTOM INDEX?** Yes

Appendix A

32. **YEAR FIRM WAS ESTABLISHED:** 1850

33. **FIRM'S REVENUES** (est): Year-end 1990, $10.2 billion

34. **TOTAL NUMBER OF FIRM'S EMPLOYEES:** 31,000

Note: Many smaller and regional firms also offer wrap accounts. Contact The Institution for Investment Management Consultants for further information (602) 265-6114.

A LISTING OF INVESTMENT MANAGERS OFFERING WRAP ACCOUNTS

Aegon USA Investment Management
4333 Edgewood Road, NE
Cedar Rapids, Iowa 52402-6601
Phone: (800) 535-1323

Investment style: Enhanced equity

Investment strategy:

Aegon USA Investment Management is an equity and balanced account investment manager, practicing asset allocation to lower volatility and enhance long term rates of return.

Affiliations:

AEGON USA, Inc.

Professional staff:

Portfolio mgr./analysts (perform both functions): 30
New business/client service: 1
   Total professionals: 31

Other investments:

Bonds Mortgages, Private placements
Equities, Mortgage back roll

Portfolio characteristics - equity portfolios:

Capitalization: Close to S&P 500
Earnings growth: Close to S&P 500
Dividend yield: Greater than S&P 500
P/E ratio: Less than S&P 500
Risk (beta): Less than S&P 500
Portfolio concentration: average

Average account turnover:

Stocks: relatively low
Bonds: relatively low

Equity investment approach:

Asset allocation

Decision making process:

Portfolio management totally integrated with research function

Total assets under management as of 1/93: $9,529 billion

Minimum account size: Stocks: $1 million

Assets in wrap programs: N/A

Ashland Management Inc.
26 Broadway
New York, NY 10004
Phone: 212-425-2803

Investment style: Growth stock

Investment strategy:

Ashland Management, Inc., founded in 1975, is a registered investment advisor. Ashland invests its clients' assets in equities only when the market offers a rate of return at least 50% over current short term interest rates. At all other times preservation of capital is sought by investing in high quality short term money market instruments.

All investment decisions are based only on reported financial information. Individual issues must have superior growth and profitability characteristics and sell at a discount to be considered for investment. Assets are reallocated to low risk investments when the equity markets become overloaded.

Professional staff:

Portfolio managers-equity: 4
Traders: 1
    Total professionals: 5

Investment specialties: Growth stocks

Portfolio characteristics - equity portfolios:

Earnings growth: Greater than S&P 500
P/E ratio: Less than S&P 500
Portfolio concentration: average

Average account turnover:

Stocks: relatively low

Equity investment approach: Bottom up

They only purchase those companies with above-average fundamentals which are selling at a substantial discount from rational value. When the market price of a stock previously selected for purchase reaches rational value the stock is sold unless this is prevented by tax considerations or other account restrictions.

Decision making process:

Their strategy utilizes six fundamental criteria: Return on Equity; Internal Growth Rate; Financial Rating; Current Earnings

Performance (recent quarter); Current Earnings Performance (12 month); and Price Rating.

Year founded: 1975

Fees:

Account size	Equities
$10 million	1.00%
$20 million	0.87%
$50 million	0.65%
$100 million	0.57%

Minimum account size:

Stocks: $1 million

Total assets under management as of 1/93: $1.3 billion

Assets in wrap programs: $80 million

Avatar Associates
900 Third Avenue
New York, NY 10022
Phone: 212-753-7710

Investment style: Asset allocation

Investment strategy:

Avatar Associates, an independent investment advisor has assets under management of $2.4 billion. The firm is 100% owned by seven key employees. The firm's only business activity is equity and balanced portfolio management.

They have practiced the same risk-averse asset allocation style with the same founding principals since inception. Their number one investment objective is to protect capital during declining markets and to produce healthy gains by participating in advancing markets.

Affiliations:

Zweig/Avatar Capital Management is a subsidiary of Avatar Assoc.

Professional staff:

Portfolio managers-equity: 4
Security analysts-equity: 4
Portfolio mgr./analysts (perform both functions): 1
Traders: 2
New business/client service: 4

Operations/administrative: 4
   Total professionals: 19

Investment specialties:
   Equities - U.S.:
      Large cap
      Growth stocks
      Market-timing
   Balanced accounts
   Tactical asset allocation

Portfolio characteristics - equity portfolios:
   Capitalization: Close to S&P 500
   Earnings growth: Greater than S&P 500
   Dividend yield: Close to S&P 500
   P/E ratio: Close to S&P 500
   Risk (beta): Greater than S&P 500
   Portfolio concentration: broad

Average account turnover:
   Stocks: moderate
   Bonds: moderate

Equity investment approach:
   Asset allocation
   Top down
   Bottom up

   The cornerstone of their equity strategies is flexible asset allocation. They devote the bulk of their research to being able to assess the overall positive/negative conditions for stocks. When participating in the market, they aim to generate solid gains with stocks combining value or growth characteristics. They strictly limit the impact of any investment error through the stop-loss discipline.

Decision making process: Centralized
   The analysts focus on broad monetary/fundamental stock market research. They generate the proprietary data used to make the critical asset allocation decisions. The portfolio managers conduct research on individual companies as well as manage the accounts, and have the discretion to construct their 50-60 stock portfolios from the predetermined 80 stock buy list. All portfolios are virtual mirrors of one another.

Year founded: 1970

Appendix B

Fees:

Account size	Equities
$1 million	1.00%
$5 million	1.00%
$10 million	1.00%
$20 million	1.00%

Total assets under management as of 1/93: $4.6 billion

Assets in wrap programs: $2 billion

Awad & Associates Asset Management
76 Beaver Street
New York, NY 10005
Phone: 212-809-7580

Investment style: Small cap value

Investment Strategy:

They are a small capitalization value investor. Using research from Raymond James they identify and invest in companies that consistently grow at above-average rates, which dominate their market and which have good balance sheets but sell at low P/E ratios and below strategic acquisition value.

Professional staff:

Portfolio managers-equity: 2
Portfolio mgr./analysts (perform both functions): N/A
Traders: 2
Operations/administrative: 2
    Total professionals: 6

Investment specialties:

Equities - U.S.:
    Large cap
    Growth stocks
    Low P/E, value stocks
    Diversified equities
Balanced accounts
Tactical asset allocation

Portfolio characteristics - equity portfolios:

Capitalization: Less than S&P 500
Earnings growth: Higher than S&P 500
Dividend yield: Close to S&P 500
P/E ratio: Less than S&P 500
Risk (beta): Equal to S&P 500

298

Portfolio concentration: N/A
Number of issues in average stock portfolio: 25
Number of companies followed regularly: 200

Fees:

Account size	Equities
$1 million	1.00%
$5 million	1.00%
$10 million	1.00%

Total assets under management as of 1/93: $125 million

Minimum account size: No minimum

Assets in wrap programs: Raymond James, $100 million

George D. Bjurman & Associates
10100 Santa Monica Boulevard, Suite 2300
Los Angeles, CA 90067
Phone: 310-553-6577

Investment style: Emerging growth

Investment strategy:
George D. Bjurman & Associates is a private corporation, established in 1970. Their firm manages three types of accounts: Balanced, Equity, and Fixed Income. Since inception, they have consistently applied the same investment philosophy emphasizing capital preservation, value, and growth of income and principal by investing in seasoned, high quality companies. All four of their portfolio managers have a CFA and/or CIC, and average over 25 years experience.

Professional staff:
Portfolio mgr./analysts (perform both functions): 4
    Total professionals: 4

Investment specialties:
Equities - U.S.:
    Large cap
    Growth stocks
Balanced accounts
Fixed income - U.S.:
    Actively managed: Governments

Portfolio characteristics - equity portfolios:
Capitalization: Close to S&P 500

Appendix B

Earnings growth: Greater than S&P 500
Dividend yield: Close to S&P 500
P/E ratio: Less than S&P 500
Risk (beta): Less than S&P 500
Portfolio concentration: average
Number of issues in average stock portfolio: 35
Number of issues in average bond portfolio: 25

Average account turnover:

Stocks: moderate
Bonds: moderate

Equity investment approach:

Fundamental analysis
Bottom up
Top down

Since inception, they have employed a value/growth oriented approach to investing. They emphasize high-quality companies and under-valued issues with superior growth in earnings and dividends. Preservation of capital, both absolutely and relative to inflation, is an important tenet of their investment philosophy. They also attempt to maximize total return within each client's acceptable risk tolerance.

Decision making process: Centralized

Portfolio management totally integrated with research function. They utilize the team approach to making all investment decisions. Investments are made within the appropriate guidelines.

Year founded: 1970

Fees:

Account size	Equities	Fixed Income
$1 million	0.85%	0.70%
$5 million	0.85%	0.70%
$10 million	0.85%	0.50%
$20 million	0.76%	0.47%

Minimum account size:

Stocks: $1 million
Bonds: $1 million

Total assets under management as of 1/93: $1.23 billion

Assets in wrap programs: $30 million

Brandes Investment Partners, Inc.
12760 High Bluff Drive, Suite 160
San Diego, CA 92130
Phone: 619-755-0239

Investment style: Value investing

Investment strategy:
They are a value oriented 'global' and cash and equity manager. They generally provide investment advice to trusts, estates, corporations, pension and profit sharing plans and individuals.

Professional staff:
Portfolio mgr./analysts (perform both functions): 5
Operations/administrative: 3
    Total professionals: 8

Investment specialties:
Cash/short-term equivalents
Equities - U.S.:
    Low P/E, value stocks
Equities - international:
    Actively managed

Portfolio characteristics - equity portfolios:
Capitalization: Less than S&P 500
Earnings growth: Greater than S&P 500
Dividend yield: Greater than S&P 500
P/E ratio: Less than S&P 500
Risk (beta): Less than S&P 500
Portfolio concentration: average
Number of issues in average stock portfolio: 20
Number of companies followed regularly: 75

Average account turnover:
Stocks: relatively low

Equity investment approach: Bottom up
Stocks are selected for purchase at a discount (66%) of intrinsic value. The discount equals their margin of safety. Stocks are sold at full value (100%) on a 'global' basis. Their holding period is typically 3 years.

Decision making process: Centralized
Charles Brandes makes all investment decisions. Portfolio managers carry out his instructions.

Year founded: 1974

Appendix B

Fees:

Account size	Equities
$1 million	1.25%
$5 million	1.00%
$10 million	1.00%
$20 million	1.00%

Total assets under management as of 1/93: $650 million

Assets in wrap programs: $205 million
For: Dean Witter, Raymond James, Rauscher-Pierce

Calamos Asset Management
2001 Spring Road, Suite 750
Oak Brook, IL 60521
Phone: 312-571-7115

Investment style: Convertible bonds

Investment strategy:

Calamos Asset Management is an investment firm specializing in convertible securities management and research. In addition to the basic program of convertibles, Calamos Asset Management offers option writing against convertible securities and other hedging programs. The firm's analysis of convertibles is based on a combination of statistical, fundamental, and mathematical factors.

Professional staff:

Portfolio mgr./analysts (perform both functions): 3
Traders: 2
New business/client service: 2
Operations/administrative: 2
   Total professionals: 9

Investment specialties:

Convertible bonds
Options

Portfolio characteristics - equity portfolios:

Capitalization: Close to S&P 500
Earnings growth: Close to S&P 500
Dividend yield: Greater than S&P 500
P/E ratio: Close to S&P 500
Risk (beta): Less than S&P 500
Portfolio concentration: average

302

Equity investment approach:
Risk/reward of convertibles
Top down
Fundamental analysis

Decision making process:
1. Multiple committee
2. Relative autonomy

Year founded: 1977

Fees:

Account size	Equities
$1 million	1.50%
$5 million	1.00%
$10 million	1.00%
$20 million	0.75%

Total assets under management as of 1/93: $590 million

Assets in wrap programs: N/A

Capstone Asset Management
P.O. Box 3167
Houston, TX 77253
Phone: 713-750-8000

Investment style: Growth

Professional staff:
Portfolio managers-equity: 5
Security analysts-equity: 4
Traders: 3
Marketing: 8
Administration: 15
Total professionals: 35

Investment specialties:
Equities - U.S.:
Growth stocks
Balanced accounts
Fixed income - U.S.:
Actively managed:
Governments
Industrials
Passive/indexed bonds

Appendix B

Other investments:
Financial futures
Options

Total assets under management as of 1/93: $1.3 billion

Minimum account size:
Stocks: $1 million

Assets in wrap programs: N/A

Compu-Val Investments Inc.
1702 Lovering Avenue
Wilmington, DE 19806
Phone: 302-652-6767

Investment style: Value

Investment strategy:
Compu-Val investments is an independent investment advisor registered with the SEC specializing in the management of investment portfolios consisting of common stocks and bonds. Compu-Val was founded on a conservative philosophy that investments should be made in undervalued companies which have strong financial positions, good management, liquidity and a promising long-term outlook.

Professional staff:
Portfolio mgr./analysts (perform both functions): 4
Traders: 2
New business/client service: 2
Operations/administrative: 1
Total professionals: 9

Investment specialties:
Large cap growth stocks
Balanced accounts
Fixed income - U.S.:
Actively managed:
Governments
Other investments:
Convertible bonds

Portfolio characteristics - equity portfolios:
Capitalization: Less than S&P 500
Earnings growth: Greater than S&P 500
Dividend yield: Less than S&P 500

P/E ratio: Close to S&P 500
Risk (beta): Greater than S&P 500
Portfolio concentration: average
Number of issues in average stock portfolio: 25
Number of issues in average bond portfolio: 5
Number of companies followed regularly: 2,200

Average account turnover:
Stocks: relatively low
Bonds: relatively low

Equity investment approach:
Undervalued, low price to book
Bottom up
Top down

They buy companies which sell in the lower 25% of the markets price to adjusted book value/share that are financially strong, have good management, a good long-term outlook and whose stock is liquid enough to buy/sell without greatly affecting the price. They remain full invested at all times. Wide diversification is practiced with approximately 5% invested in any one security and a 10% maximum investment in any one industry.

Decision making process:
Investment Committee
Centralized

Year founded: 1969

Fees:

Account size	Equities	Fixed Income
$1 million	1.00%	0.40%
$5 million	1.00%	0.40%
$10 million	0.87%	0.35%
$20 million	0.46%	0.31%

Total assets under management as of 1/93: $210 million

Assets in wrap programs: N/A

Connors Investor Services
1100 Berkshire Boulevard
Wyomissing, PA 19610
Phone: 215-376-7418

Investment style: Covered option

Appendix B

Equity investment approach:
Connors Investor Service specializes in equity hedging and invests in equities otherwise ignored by the professional investment community.

Investment specialties:
Equities - U.S.:
Small cap
Growth stocks
Low P/E, value stocks
Hedge Funds
Balanced accounts
Other investments:
Options

Total professional staff: 4

Portfolio characteristics - equity portfolios:
Capitalization: Equal to S&P 500
Earnings growth: Greater than S&P 500
Dividend yield: Close to S&P 500
P/E ratio: Greater than S&P 500
Risk (beta): Lower than S&P 500

Fees:

Account size	Equities
$1 million	1.00%
$5 million	0.9%

Total assets under management as of 1/93: $153 million

Assets in wrap programs: N/A

Dane, Falb, Stone & Company
33 Broad Street
P.O. Box 2155
Boston, MA 02106
Phone: 617-742-0666

Investment style: Balanced Value

Professional staff:
Portfolio managers-equity: 2
Total professionals: 2

306

Investment specialties:
> Equities - U.S.:
> > Low P/E, value stocks
> Balanced accounts
> Fixed income - U.S.:
> > Actively managed: Governments
> > High-yield
> Other investments:
> > Convertible bonds
> > Options
> > Convertible hedge

Year founded: 1977

Portfolio characteristics - equity portfolios:
> Capitalization: Close to S&P 500
> Earnings growth: Close to S&P 500
> Dividend yield: Greater than S&P 500
> P/E ratio: Less than S&P 500
> Risk (beta): Less than S&P 500
> Portfolio concentration: concentrated
> Number of issues in average stock portfolio: 15
> Number of companies followed regularly: 300

Average account turnover:
> Stocks: moderate
> Bonds: relatively low

Total assets under management: $130 million

Assets in wrap programs: $13 million

Davis, Hamilton Associates
909 Fannin, 2 Houston Center, Suite 550
Houston, TX 77010
Phone: 713-853-2322

Investment style: Growth equity

Investment strategy:
> Davis Hamilton Associates manages funds for institutional and high net worth individual clients. Balanced accounts emphasize a very active asset allocation decision-making process. Equities are growth oriented. Individual stock sell decisions are triggered by very structured fundamental and technical disciplines. Fixed income assets are generally high quality and maturities are generally in the intermediate range.

307

Appendix B

Professional staff:
Portfolio mgr./analysts (perform both functions): 2
Traders: 1
    Total professionals: 3

Investment specialties:
Cash/short-term equivalents
Equities - U.S.:
    Large cap
    Small cap
    Growth stocks
    Low P/E, value stocks
    Diversified equities
Balanced accounts
Fixed income - U.S.:
    Actively managed: Governments
Other investments:
    Convertible bonds

Portfolio characteristics - equity portfolios:
Capitalization: Less than S&P 500
Earnings growth: Greater than S&P 500
Dividend yield: Less than S&P 500
P/E ratio: Close to S&P 500
Risk (beta): Greater than S&P 500
Portfolio concentration: average
Number of issues in average stock portfolio: 35
Number of issues in average bond portfolio: 15
Number of companies followed regularly: 120

Average account turnover:
Stocks: moderate
Bonds: relatively low

Equity investment approach:
Bottom up
Fundamental analysis
Technical disciplines

Decision making process:
Portfolio management totally integrated with research function.

Year founded: 1988

Fees:

Account size	Equities	Fixed Income
$1 million	1.00%	0.50%
$5 million	0.50%	0.37%
$10 million	0.50%	0.37%

$20 million   0.50%   0.25%

Minimum account size:
Stocks: $1 million
Bonds: $1 million

Total assets managed as of 1/93: $472 million

Assets in wrap programs: $25 million
For: Kemper, Paine Webber, Shearson, Rauscher

Dawes Investment Service
900 South US Highway One, Suite 207
Jupiter, FL 33477-6493
Phone: 407-747-0896

Investment style: Value

Investment strategy:
Dawes Investment Service is a private investment advisory firm which provides discretionary equity-portfolio management to employee-benefit plans, endowments, foundations and individuals. Dedicated to the management of common stock portfolios, superior, long-term investment performance has been provided since the firm was founded in 1977.

Professional staff:
Portfolio managers-equity: 1
Portfolio managers-fixed income: 1
New business/client service: 1
    Total professionals: 3

Investment specialties:
Cash/short-term equivalents
Equities - U.S.:
    Large cap
    Growth stocks
    Low P/E, value stocks
Balanced accounts
Fixed income - U.S.:
    Actively managed: Governments

Portfolio characteristics - equity portfolios:
Capitalization: Less than S&P 500
Earnings growth: Greater than S&P 500
Dividend yield: Greater than S&P 500
P/E ratio: Less than S&P 500

Appendix B

Risk (beta): Less than S&P 500
Portfolio concentration: average
Number of issues in average stock portfolio: 20
Number of issues in average bond portfolio: 12
Number of companies followed regularly: 20

Average account turnover:

Stocks: relatively low
Bonds: relatively low

Equity investment approach:

Bottom up
Fundamental analysis
Sector rotation

In stock selection, they must first determine the true value of a company by examining long term earnings growth rate and stability and price to earnings ratios. They look for companies whose earnings are growing faster than general market averages, and favor companies with low price-to-earnings ratios relative to prevailing ratios in the general market. Using these standards, they locate well-managed companies which have unrecognized potential.

Decision making process:

1. Tailored to client objectives by the portfolio manager.
2. Portfolio management totally integrated with research function.

The timely sale of stocks, critical to the preservation of capital, is just as important as original selection. A specific objective for each stock forces rational decision-making and eliminates the subjective environment.

Client portfolios reflect substantial weightings in undervalued industry sectors. These weightings are monitored in a dynamic process to reposition portfolios into undervalued issues until utmost appreciation is reached.

Fees:

Account size	Equities	Fixed Income
$1 million	1.00%	0.50%
$5 million	0.75%	0.40%
$10 million	0.75%	
$20 million	0.50%	

Year founded: 1977

Total assets under management as of 1/93: $86 million

310

Assets in wrap programs: $6 million

Eagle Asset Management
880 Carillon Parkway
P.O. Box 10520
St. Petersburg, FL 33716
Phone: 800-237-3101

Investment style: Growth, large and small cap

Type of organization: Investment Bank/Broker
Eagle Asset Management offers equity, balanced and fixed income management. It is a wholly owned subsidiary of Raymond James Financial, a public corporation listed on the New York Stock Exchange. Eagle's basic goal is to deliver to their clients investment results superior to the market averages while maintaining portfolio risk characteristics below those of the S&P 500.

Affiliations:
Raymond James Financial is the parent company. Affiliated investment firms include Investment Management & Research, and Robert Thomas Securities.

Professional staff:
Portfolio managers-equity: 4
Portfolio managers-fixed income: 1
Security analysts-equity: 2
Security analysts-fixed income: 1
Traders: 4
New business/client service: 20
Operations/administrative: 45
    Total professionals: 72

Investment specialties:
Equities - U.S.:
    Large cap
    Small cap
    Growth stocks
    Low P/E, value stocks
Balanced accounts
Fixed income - U.S.:
    Actively managed: Governments and
    High-yield, Corporates
Other investments:
    Convertible bonds

311

Appendix B

Portfolio characteristics - equity portfolios:
    Capitalization: Less than S&P 500
    Earnings growth: Greater than S&P 500
    Dividend yield: Less than S&P 500
    P/E ratio: Close to S&P 500
    Risk (beta): Less than S&P 500
    Portfolio concentration: average
    Number of issues in average stock portfolio: 25
    Number of companies followed regularly: 100

Average account turnover:
    Stocks: relatively low
    bonds: relatively high

Equity investment approach:
    Bottom up
    Fundamental analysis

Decision making process
    Portfolio management totally integrated with research function

Year founded: 1976

Fees:

Account size	Equities
$1 million	1.00%
$5 million	1.00%

Minimum: $2 million

Total assets under management as of 1/93: $3 billion

Assets in wrap programs: N/A

Roger Engemann & Associates
600 N. Rosemead Boulevard
Pasadena, CA 91107-2101
Phone: 818-351-9686

Investment style: Long-term investor, large cap

Investment specialties:
    Equities - U.S.: Growth stocks

Equity investment approach: Fundamental analysis
    Stocks are selected by analyzing the fundamental or business
    value of a company to find candidates believed to have strong

managements, sound business plans and potential for above average earnings growth. Quantitative indicators are also used.

Investment Strategy

Engemann's growth-oriented portfolio management philosophy emphasizes long-term price appreciation rather than current income. This philosophy is consistently applied over suitable time frames. In seeking to achieve their investment objectives, Engemann is willing to accept the higher volatility associated with growth stock investing in an effort to provide investors with superior long-term results.

Although Engemann normally prefers that a portfolio be fully invested, during 1974, 1979, and more recently 1987, the cash position has been as much as 50% when market conditions have warranted it. Typically portfolios are concentrated in 20 to 25 holdings at any one time.

Affiliations:

Pasadena National Trust Company (in organization)

Professional staff:

Portfolio managers-equity: 1
Security analysts-equity: 2
Portfolio mgr./analysts (perform both functions): 1
Traders: 2
New business/client service: 3
Operations/administrative: 1
     Total professionals: 15

Portfolio characteristics - equity portfolios:

Capitalization: Close to S&P 500
Earnings growth: Greater than S&P 500
Dividend yield: Less than S&P 500
P/E ratio: Greater than S&P 500
Risk (beta): Greater than S&P 500
Portfolio concentration: average
Number of issues in average stock portfolio: 20
Number of companies followed regularly: 150

Average account turnover:

Stocks: moderate

Decision making process:

Centralized / Portfolio management totally integrated with research function.

Fees:

Account size	Equities
$1 million	2.00%
$5 million	1.00%

Total assets under management as of 1/93: $5 billion

Year founded: 1969

Assets in wrap programs: $3 billion

Frontier Capital Management
286 Congress Street
Boston, MA 02210
Phone: 617-261-0681

Investment style: Growth

Investment Strategy:

Frontier Capital Management has had one business goal—to build a strong, medium-size, independent investment management firm serving a variety of institutional clients. Distinguishing characteristics of the firm are; 1) independent: employee owned, 2) Specializing in institutional equity portfolios, 3) Blending the best of top-down and bottom-up approaches, 4) Discovering value among rapidly growing companies, 5) Focusing on maximization of capital gains, 6) Leveraging their experience, special skills and disciplines to produce the best possible equity products.

Professional staff:

Portfolio managers-equity: 5
Security analysts-equity: 4
Traders: 1
New business/client service: 2
Operations/administrative: 1
    Total professionals: 14

Investment specialties:

Equities - U.S.:
    Growth stocks
    Small cap equity
Balanced accounts

Portfolio characteristics - equity portfolios:

Capitalization: Close to S&P 500
Earnings growth: Greater than S&P 500

Dividend yield: Less than S&P 500
P/E ratio: Greater than S&P 500
Risk (beta): Greater than S&P 500
Portfolio concentration: average
Number of issues in average stock portfolio: 35

Average account turnover:
Stocks: moderate

Equity investment approach:
Top down
Bottom up
Fundamental analysis

Their philosophy is based on the belief that security prices ultimately follow company fundamentals such as earnings growth, dividend growth and growth inequity. Equally important is the ability to fairly assess value when initiating purchases or considering sales.

Decision making process:
Portfolio management totally integrated with research function combining a top-down thematic approach with a bottom-up stock ranking system to establish their universe.

Year founded: 1980

Fees:

Account size	Equities
$5 million	0.75%
$10 million	0.75%
$20 million	0.65%

Total assets under management as of: $1.3 billion

Minimum account size:
Stocks: $10 million

Assets in wrap programs: N/A

Godsey & Gibb Associates
7814 Carousel Lane, Ste. 300
Richmond, VA 23229
Phone: 804-285-7333

Investment style: Equities: Large cap, growth stocks;
Balanced accounts

Appendix B

Investment Strategy:

Godsey & Gibb Associates, an investment advisor registered with the Securities and Exchange Commission, was formed to provide individuals, corporations and foundations with professional investment management services. They recognize that each client relationship is unique; and with a thorough understanding of each client's needs and objectives, portfolio programs are designed, implemented and continuously monitored. By keeping the number of clients limited, they can assure that each receives the attention it deserves and requires.

Professional staff:

Portfolio mgr./analysts (perform both functions): 2
Traders: 1
Operations/administrative: 1
    Total professionals: 4

Portfolio characteristics - equity portfolios:

Capitalization: Close to S&P 500
Earnings growth: Greater than S&P 500
Dividend yield: Close to S&P 500
P/E ratio: Less than S&P 500
Risk (beta): Less than S&P 500
Portfolio concentration: average
Number of issues in average stock portfolio: 30
Number of issues in average bond portfolio: 20
Number of companies followed regularly: 100

Average account turnover:

Stocks: relatively low
Bonds: relatively low

Equity investment approach:

Top down
Asset allocation
Fundamental analysis

They have two steps to their equity investment approach:

1. Asset Allocation - While a broad array of data is analyzed quantitatively, the final decisions are subjective.
2. Investment Selection (two criteria) - Quality Issues and Qualitative Analysis to determine value employing five screening models: Dividend growth/Yield, Earnings Growth/PE, Technical Model, Earnings Momentum/Surprise Model and Composite Value Model.

Decision making process:

Portfolio management totally integrated with research function

Year founded: 1985

Fees:

Account size	Equities	Fixed Income
$1 million	0.75%	0.75%
$5 million	0.50%	0.50%
$10 million	0.40%	0.40%
$20 million	0.40%	0.40%

Total assets under management as of 1/93: $295 million

Minimum account size:
Stocks: $1 million
Bonds: $1 million

Assets in wrap programs: N/A

Gulf Investment Management
820 Gessner, Suite 720
Houston, TX 77024-4258
Phone: 713-461-0660

Investment style: Equities: Growth stocks; Balanced accounts

Investment Strategy:
Gulf takes a "value" approach to the management of equity portfolios. They use "bottom-up" analysis to identify individual securities out of favor in the stock market and thus selling below Gulf's calculation of their intrinsic or "fair value."

Investment Process:
Gulf's equity selection process begins with a screen that narrows a universe of some 7,500 common stocks to approximately 250 candidates, using such quantitative criteria as low price to book value and low percentage of debt to capital. This screen also includes a review of the company's cash flow and the stock's two-year history of market lows as compared to its current price.

Gulf then calculates an intrinsic or "fair value" for each of the 250 common stocks, based on an analysis of the underlying company's assets, earnings growth and dividend payout. Gulf's valuation is then compared to the stock's current market price, as the basis for their evaluation of the stock's potential for substantial price appreciation over the next several years.

Gulf will on occasion buy a company's convertible bonds if they are offering a higher income stream than the underlying common stock and if the common stock meets their selection criteria. In line with their buy discipline, Gulf may also sell a stock if it has reached a premium relative to its projected price objective, or if Gulf believes the stock has experienced a fundamental deterioration that has permanently lowered its intrinsic value.

Gulf prefers to be fully invested in equities. However, cash equivalents have occasionally accounted for over 30% of a portfolio's assets, if Gulf cannot identify individual issues that meet their selection criteria or if they believe that stock market conditions warrant lowering the portfolio's sensitivity to the market. Typically a portfolio contains from 25 to 35 individual issues.

Professional Staff:
Portfolio Managers and Analysts: 4
   Total Professionals: 7

Investment Approach: Bottom-Up
Style: Value/Out of Favor
Asset Allocation Strategy Ranges:
   Equity: 70-100%
   Cash and Equivalents: 0-30%
Historical Composite Asset Allocation:
   Equity: 86%
   Cash and Equivalents: 14%
Approximate Number of Holdings: 26-35
Characteristics versus S&P 500:
   Average Company Size: Lower
   Price/Earnings Ratio: Lower
   Price/Book Value Ratio: Lower
   Growth Rate of Company:
      Earnings: Higher
      Dividend Yield: Higher

Year founded: 1980

Assets Under Management (306 Accounts): $365 million

Heartland Capital Management
36 South Pennsylvania, Suite 610
Indianapolis, IN 46204-3634
Phone: 317-633-4080

Investment style: Growth

Investment strategy:

Heartland Capital Management is an employee-owned investment advisor that offers U.S. equity and fixed income management to retirement plans, foundations and endowments, and individuals. The firm was founded in February, 1984 by the professionals at Merchants Investment Counseling Service. Since the inception of the group, they have never had any negative equity returns and have not lost any investment professionals.

Professional staff:

Portfolio managers-equity: 2
Portfolio managers-fixed income: 1
Traders: 1
New business/client service: 1
Operations/administrative: 3
Other professionals: 1
Total professionals: 9

Portfolio characteristics - equity portfolios:

Capitalization: Less than S&P 500
Earnings growth: Greater than S&P 500
Dividend yield: Less than S&P 500
P/E ratio: Close to S&P 500
Risk (beta): Close to S&P 500
Portfolio concentration: average
Number of issues in average stock portfolio: 30
Number of issues in average bond portfolio: 15
Number of companies followed regularly: 250

Average account turnover:

Stocks: moderate
Bonds: relatively low

Equity investment approach:

Bottom up
Fundamental analysis
Asset allocation

Their equity investment style emphasizes growth issues. In selecting stocks, we look for stability of past growth and acceleration of current growth as measured by an increase in analyst earnings estimates. Issues are deleted from portfolios when these characteristics are lost.

Decision making process:

1. Portfolio management totally integrated with research function
2. Centralized

Appendix B

Year founded: 1984

Fees:

Account size	Equities	Fixed Income
$1 million	1.00%	0.50%
$5 million	0.70%	0.42%
$10 million	0.60%	0.41%
$20 million	0.55%	Neg.

Total assets under management as of 1/93: $1.1 billion

Minimum account size:
Stocks: $1 million

Assets in wrap programs: $225 million

Investment Counsel Company
56 East Pine Street, Suite 22
Orlando, FL 32801
Phone: 800-848-4120

Investment style: Value

Investment strategy:
Investment Counsel Company was founded in 1971 and manages assets of over $625 million. The firm manages stock, bond and balanced portfolios for institutional and individual clients. The company is owned by its four principal officers, and has an overall investment philosophy which emphasizes risk control, accountable portfolio management, and the use of proven disciplines.

Affiliations:
ICC Realty Advisors is wholly-owned subsidiary that manages the real estate portion of the business.

Professional staff:
Portfolio managers-equity: 1
Portfolio managers-fixed income: 2
Traders: 2
New business/client service: 4
Operations/administrative: 7
    Total professionals: 17

Portfolio characteristics - equity portfolios:
Capitalization: Less than S&P 500
Earnings growth: Greater than S&P 500

320

Dividend yield: Greater than S&P 500
P/E ratio: Less than S&P 500
Risk (beta): Close to S&P 500
Portfolio concentration: broad
Number of issues in average stock portfolio: 50
Number of issues in average bond portfolio: 10
Number of companies followed regularly: 200

Average account turnover:

Stocks: moderate
Bonds: moderate

Equity investment approach:

Bottom up
Broad diversification
Sector rotation

Decision making process:

Portfolio management totally integrated with research function

Year founded: 1971

Fees:

Account size	Equities	Fixed Income
$1 million	1.00%	0.50%
$5 million	0.78%	0.48%
$10 million	0.64%	0.44%
$20 million	0.57%	0.42%

Total assets under management as of 1/93: $625 million

Assets in wrap programs: N/A

Tom Johnson Investment Management
211 N. Robinson, Suite 1510
Oklahoma City, OK 73102-7101
Phone: 405-236-2111

Investment style: Value, sector rotational

Investment Strategy:

Tom Johnson Investment Management is an independent investment advisor wholly-owned by individuals active within the firm. The firm offers money management services to both non-taxable and taxable clients throughout the U.S. The investment approach is a conservative one which emphasizes low volatility and minimal risk.

Appendix B

Professional staff:
Portfolio mgr./analysts (perform both functions): 4
Traders: 1
Operations/administrative: 2
　　Total professionals: 8

Portfolio characteristics - equity portfolios:
Capitalization: Greater than S&P 500
Earnings growth: Greater than S&P 500
Dividend yield: Close to S&P 500
P/E ratio: Less than S&P 500
Risk (beta): Close to S&P 500
Portfolio concentration: average
Number of issues in average stock portfolio: 30
Number of issues in average bond portfolio: 8
Number of companies followed regularly: 100

Average account turnover:
Stocks: relatively high
Bonds: moderate

Equity investment approach:
Top down
Fundamental analysis
Sector rotation

Decision making process:
1. Centralized
2. Multiple committee
3. Portfolio management totally integrated with research function

Year founded: 1983

Fees:

Account size	Equities	Fixed Income
$1 million	1.00%	1.00%
$5 million	0.70%	0.70%

Total assets under management as of 1/93: $1.6 billion

Assets in wrap programs: $300 million

NewSouth Capital Management, Inc.
755 Crossover Lane, Suite 233
Memphis, TN 38117-4907
Phone: 901-761-5561

Investment style: Value

Introduction:

NewSouth Capital Management, Inc. is a privately owned investment advisory firm engaged exclusively in the management of portfolios for individuals and institutions. Clients include individuals, endowments, retirement plans, trusts, corporations, banks and insurance companies.

Their staff is comprised of experienced portfolio managers and investment analysts who place great emphasis on client needs and objectives. Each portfolio manager works with a limited clientele and brings to each client an appreciation for individual circumstances, a sound fundamental investment approach and a demonstrated record of success.

Affiliations:

The principals of NewSouth own a minority interest in First Coast Capital Management located in Jacksonville, Florida.

Professional staff:

Portfolio managers-equity: 5
Portfolio managers-fixed income: 2
Security analysts-equity: 4
Security analysts-fixed income: 2
Portfolio mgr./analysts (perform both functions): 6
Traders: 1
New business/client service: 5
   Total professionals: 25

Investment specialties:

Equities - U.S.:
   Low P/E, value stocks
Balanced accounts
Fixed income - U.S.:
   Actively managed:
   Governments
   Finance/banking
   Industrials
   Transportation
   Utilities
Other investments:
   Options

323

Appendix B

Portfolio characteristics - equity portfolios:
Capitalization: Less than S & P 500
Earnings growth: Close to S&P 500
Dividend yield: Greater than S&P 500
P/E ratio: Less than S&P 500
Risk (beta): Less than S&P 500
Portfolio concentration: average
Number of issues in average stock portfolio: 25
Number of issues in average bond portfolio: 10

Average account turnover:
Stocks: relatively low
Bonds: relatively low

Equity investment approach:
Bottom up

They look for financially strong companies with significantly understated assets and/or important off-balance sheet assets. The shares must be reasonably priced in relation to current earnings, book value and dividends.

Decision making process:
Centralized
Portfolio management totally integrated with research function

Fees:

Account size	Equities	Fixed Income
$1 million	1.00%	0.505
$5 million	0.75%	Neg.
$10 million	0.75%	Neg.
$20 million	0.75%	Neg.

Total assets under management: $1 billion

Assets in wrap accounts: $10 million

Nicholas-Applegate Capital Management
701 B Street, Suite 2040
San Diego, CA 92101
Phone: 619-234-4472

Investment style: Bottom Up Growth

Introduction:
Nicholas-Applegate Capital Management is a registered investment advisor with over $1 billion under management. The firm

uses a bottom-up approach which emphasizes individual stock research and selection, and services a client base that includes corporate pension and profit sharing plans, foundations, endowments, Taft-Hartley funds and individuals.

Professional staff:

Portfolio mgr./analysts (perform both functions): 7
Traders: 2
New business/client service: 5
Operations/administrative: 2
Other professionals: 2
    Total professionals: 16

Investment specialties:

Equities - U.S.:
    Large cap
    Small cap
    Growth stocks
Balanced accounts
Other investments:
    Convertible bonds
    Other

Portfolio characteristics - equity portfolios:

Capitalization: Less than S&P 500
Earnings growth: Greater than S&P 500
Dividend yield: Less than S&P 500
P/E ratio: Greater than S&P 500
Risk (beta): Greater than S&P 500
Portfolio concentration: average
Number of issues in average stock portfolio: 30
Number of companies followed regularly: 2500

Average account turnover:

Stocks: relatively high

Equity investment approach:

Bottom up
Fundamental analysis
Relative price strength

They have one equity philosophy and approach, which they implement in two segments of the market:
    a. Emerging Growth Equity invests in growth companies with market capitalizations below $500 million, and
    b. Growth Equity invests in growth companies with market capitalizations above $500 million.

Year founded: 1984

Appendix B

Decision making process:
Portfolio management totally integrated with research function
Team approach

Minimum account size:
Stocks: $10 million

Total assets under management as of 1/93: $7.8 billion

Assets in wrap accounts: $2 billion

NMCM
NM Capital Management
7510 Montgomery, N.E., Suite 201
Albuquerque, NM 87109
Phone: 505-888-9500

Investment style: Value

Introduction:
NMCM's investment philosophy is primarily guided by a concern for preservation of capital. A portfolio is designed to meet client objectives and incorporate their fundamental value approach to produce consistent returns over economic and financial market cycles.

Professional staff:
Portfolio mgr./analysts (perform both functions): 3
Traders: 2
New business/client service: 3
Operations/administrative: 2
    Total professionals: 10

Investment specialties:
Equities - U.S.:
    Large cap
    Low P/E, value stocks
    Diversified equities
Balanced accounts
Fixed income - U.S.:
    Actively managed
    Governments
    Mortgages
    Industrials
    Utilities
    Municipals
    Passive/indexed bonds

326

Other investments:
   Convertible bonds

Portfolio characteristics - equity portfolios:
   Capitalization: Close to S&P 500
   Earnings growth: Greater than S&P 500
   Dividend yield: Greater than S&P 500
   P/E ratio: Less than S&P 500
   Risk (beta): Close to S&P 500
   Portfolio concentration: average
   Number of issues in average stock portfolio: 15
   Number of issues in average bond portfolio: 10
   Number of companies followed regularly: 50

Average account turnover:
   Stocks: relatively low

Equity investment approach:
   Bottom up
   Top down
   Asset allocation

   NMCM's philosophy is characterized by an emphasis on value from a'"top down" approach with regard to macro-economic considerations and the impact of such on anticipated market sector performances. Within sectors, a "bottom-up" approach typifies the value selection process. Equity investments will generally have the following: large capitalization, earnings and dividends; low P/E multiples; low volatility; low debt to total capitalization.

Decision making process:
   Portfolio management totally integrated with research function. Principals and portfolio managers are responsible for new investment opportunities presented and discussed at weekly strategy meetings. When agreement is reached, the new target investment is included on the firm's accepted equity list. This precludes individuals from deviating from the general NMCM value orientation. A re-evaluation occurs when short-term performance significantly exceeds the market or when prices drop 10% to 15%.

Year founded: 1977

Total assets under management as of 1/93: $380 million

Total assets in wrap accounts: N/A

Appendix B

NorthWest Quadrant, Inc.
450 Newport Center Drive, Suite 420
Newport Beach, CA 92660
Phone: 714-720-9232

Investment style: Conservative, protected equity

Introduction:
NorthWest Quadrant is a hedge equity manager using convertible bonds and preferreds, covered options, long stock/long put and closed end funds. They offer U.S. Equity, International, Bond Substitution, and Natural Resources Management. Asset allocation is also offered.

Professional staff:
Portfolio managers-equity: 3
Traders: 1
New business/client service: 1
Operations/administrative: 1
    Total professionals: 6

Investment specialties:
Equities - U.S.:
    Large cap
Equities - International:
    Actively managed
Other investments:
    Options
    Portfolio insurance

Portfolio characteristics - equity portfolios:
Capitalization: Close to S&P 500
Earnings growth: Close to S&P 500
Dividend yield: Close to S&P 500
P/E yield: Close to S&P 500
Risk (beta): Less than S&P 500
Portfolio concentration: average
Number of issues in average stock portfolio: 25
Number of companies followed regularly: 700

Average account turnover:
Stocks: relatively low

Equity investment approach:
Quantitative
Broad diversification
Asset allocation

Decision making process:
Computer model

Year founded: 1981

Fees:

Account size	Equities	Fixed Income
$1 million	1.50%	1.50%
$5 million	1.00%	1.00%
$10 million	0.75%	0.75%
$20 million	0.50%	0.50%

Total assets under management as of 1/93: $54 million

Palley-Needelman Asset Management
1501 Quail, Suite 110
Newport Beach, CA 92660
Phone: 714-752-2233

Investment style: Mid large cap, value

Introduction:
Palley-Needelman Asset Management, Inc. is an independent investment counseling firm specializing in the professional management of security portfolios. All investment decisions are made by its owners.

The company was formed with the specific intent of providing a high quality, personalized investment management service to meet the standards they have set for research, client services and results.

Professional staff:
Portfolio managers-equity: 4
Security analysts-equity: 5
Traders: 2
New business/client service: 2
Operations/administrative: 6
    Total professionals: 15

Investment specialties:
Equities - U.S.:
    Large cap
Balanced accounts

Appendix B

Portfolio characteristics - equity portfolios:
   Capitalization: Greater than S&P 500
   Earnings growth: Greater than S&P 500
   Dividend yield: Greater than S&P 500
   P/E ratio: Less than S&P 500
   Risk (beta): Less than S&P 500
   Portfolio concentration: average
   Number of issues in average stock portfolio: 25
   Number of issues in average bond portfolio: 10
   Number of companies followed regularly: 300

Average account turnover:
   Stocks: relatively low
   Bonds: relatively low

Equity investment approach:
   Bottom up
   Fundamental analysis
   Technical disciplines

   Palley-Needelman's equity approach is to purchase low P/E, high yield, low beta, strong balance sheet issues with positive free cash flow and stable industry characteristics. They use a bottom-up security selection as well as a top-down asset allocation process.

Decision making process:
   Portfolio management totally integrated with research function Palley-Needelman utilizes the value approach to equity investing. Computer screens and fundamental analysis are directed toward buying quality stocks at prices below their estimated intrinsic worth. Sources of research are the firm's internal and proprietary approach to asset valuation and security selection. Wall Street research is used for informational purposes only and not for its recommendations.

Minimum account size:
   Stocks: $1 million

Total assets under management as of 1/93: $1.9 billion

Assets in wrap accounts: $170 million

330

Provident Investment Counsel
225 South Lake Avenue, Suite 1001
Pasadena, CA 91101
Phone: 818-449-8500

Investment style: Growth

Introduction:

Provident Investment Counsel evolved from a predecessor firm founded in 1951. For the first 20 years of its history, the firm managed primarily taxable accounts. Since the early 70's it has managed tax-exempt assets and today approximately 90% of assets under management are non-taxable. Provident Investment Counsel is independent and wholly owned by its employees.

Professional staff:

Portfolio managers-fixed income: 1
Security analysts-equity: 4
Security analysts fixed income: 1
Portfolio mgr./analysts (perform both functions): 6
Traders: 2
New business/client service: 2
Operations/administrative: 1
    Total professionals: 17

Investment specialties:

Equities - U.S.:
    Small cap
    Growth stocks
Balanced accounts
Fixed income - U.S.:
    Actively managed:
    Governments
    Mortgages
    Finance/banking
    Industrials
    Transportation
    Utilities

Portfolio characteristics - equity portfolios:

Capitalization: Less than S&P 500
Earnings growth: Greater than S&P 500
Dividend yield: Less than S&P 500
P/E ratio: Greater than S&P 500
Risk (beta): Greater than S&P 500
Portfolio concentration: average
Number of issues in average stock portfolio: 35

Appendix B

Number of issues in average bond portfolio: 10
Number of companies followed regularly: 60

Average account turnover:
Stocks: relatively high
Bonds: relatively high

Equity investment approach:
Bottom up
Fundamental analysis
Technical disciplines

Decision making process:
Portfolio management totally integrated with research function
Relative autonomy
Multiple committee

Year founded: 1951

Fees:

Account size	Equities	Fixed Income
$1 million	1.00%	0.50%
$5 million	1.00%	0.50%
$10 million	1.00%	0.50%
$20 million	0.87%	0.43%

Minimum account size:
Stocks: $1 million
Bonds: $1 million

Total assets under management as of 1/93: $11 billion

Assets in wrap accounts: $1 billion

Savoy Capital Management
3700 S. Tamiami Trail, Suite B
Sarasota, FL 34239
Phone: 813-951-6550

Investment style: Asset allocation

Professional staff:
Portfolio managers-equity: 1
Traders: 1
New business/client service: 2
Total professionals: 4

Investment specialties:
Equities-U.S.:
Diversified equities
Fixed income-U.S.:
Actively managed:
Governments

Portfolio characteristics - equity portfolios:
Capitalization: Close to S&P 500
Earnings growth: Greater than S&P 500
Dividend yield: Close to S&P 500
P/E ratio: Less than S&P 500
Risk (beta): Less than S&P 500
Portfolio concentration: average
Number of issues in average stock portfolio: 20
Number of issues in average bond portfolio: 8

Average account turnover:
Stocks: relatively high
Bonds: relatively low

Equity investment approach:
Bottom up
Asset allocation
Fundamental analysis

The firm uses Quantitative Analysis in re (a) value, and (b) earnings momentum and Asset Allocation usually in one of three positions: (a) 90-100% invested, (b) 40-60% invested, (c) 0-10% invested.

Decision making process:
Portfolio management totally integrated with research function

Year founded: 1987

Fees:

Account size	Equities	Fixed Income
$1 million	1.00%	0.50%
$5 million	Neg.	Neg.
$10 million	Neg.	Neg.
$20 million	Neg.	Neg.

Minimum account size:
Bonds: $1 million

Total assets under management: $112 million

Assets in wrap accounts: $80 million

Appendix B

Seaboard Investment Advisors
150 Boush Street, Suite 800
Norfolk, VA 23510
Phone: 804-640-7300

Investment style: Large cap value

Investment strategies:

Seaboard Investment Advisors is a highly disciplined, person-alized investment firm specializing in "niche" management for a limited number of clients, with strengths in options/income and convertible bond sectors. Seaboard blends proprietary technical management tools with a strong fundamental ap-proach to securities management.

Professional staff:

Portfolio managers-equity: 2
Traders: 1
New business/client service: 1
   Total professionals: 4

Investment specialties:

Equities - U.S.:
   Large cap
   Growth stocks
Balanced accounts
Other investments:
   Options

Portfolio characteristics - equity portfolios:

Capitalization: Close to S&P 500
Earnings growth: Greater than S&P 500
Dividend yield: Less than S&P 500
P/E ratio: Close to S&P 500
Risk (beta): Close to S&P 500
Portfolio concentration: concentrated
Number of issues in average stock portfolio: 14
Number of issues in average bond portfolio: 15
Number of companies followed regularly: 65

Average account turnover:

Stocks: moderate
Bonds: moderate

Equity investment approach:

Asset allocation
Fundamental analysis
Top down

334

The firm emphasizes fundamental analysis followed by a heavy reliance upon the market and specific technical tactics. They stress listed, highly rated, and optimal securities in stock selection.

Decision making process:
Portfolio management totally integrated with research function

Fees:

Account size	Equities	Fixed Income
$1 million	0.75%	0.75%
$5 million	0.50%	0.50%
$10 million	0.50%	0.50%
$20 million	0.50%	0.50%

Total assets under management: $1.3 billion

Assets in wrap accounts: $300 million

Spears, Benzak, Salomon & Farrell
45 Rockefeller Plaza
New York, NY 10111
Phone: 212-903-1200

Investment style: Value

Introduction:
The firm provides portfolio management services to individuals, non-profit organizations and pension funds in the U.S. and overseas.

The firm was founded in 1972 by William Spears. In 1978 he was joined by Louis Benzak, who had worked with him for several years at Loeb Rhoades & Co. In 1982, Richard Salomon and Vincent Farrell joined the firm and ownership was distributed equally among the four principals.

Initially, the firm's business was exclusively high net worth individuals. Over the years, the client base has grown to include non-profit and retirement fund assets.

They manage equity, fixed income and balanced accounts. In addition, they invest their own capital and client capital in public and private small capitalization special situations.

Finally, they manage the SBSF family of mutual funds.

Appendix B

Affiliations:

In early 1988, the principals sold 20% of the firm to an affiliate of one of its investment advisory clients.

Professional staff:

Portfolio managers-equity: 5
Security analysts-equity: 2
Traders: 2
Other professionals: 4
    Total professionals: 12

Investment specialties:

Equities - U.S.:
    Growth stocks
    Low P/E, value stocks
    Diversified equities
Fixed income - U.S.:
    Actively managed:
    Governments
    High-yield
    Finance/banking
    Industrials
    Utilities
Other investments:
    Convertible bonds
    Mutual funds
    Venture capital

Portfolio characteristics - equity portfolios:

Capitalization: Less than S&P 500
Earnings growth: Close to S&P 500
Dividend yield: Close to S&P 500
P/E ratio: Less than S&P 500
Risk (beta): Less than S&P 500
Portfolio concentration: average
Number of issues in average stock portfolio: 30
Number of companies followed regularly: 600

Average account turnover:

Stocks: relatively low
Bonds: relatively low

Equity investment approach:

Bottom up
Fundamental analysis
Top down

The firm's guiding principle is value. They endeavor to identify equities that have the following characteristics: positive cash flow, high quality earnings, the prospect of earnings growth, underpriced assets, strong management, and a price that does not expose their clients to excessive risk.

This does not necessarily imply low earnings multiples.

Their approach does imply constant attention to acceptable risk levels for each client.

Decision making process:
1. Portfolio management totally integrated with research function
2. Centralized
3. Relative autonomy

When the firm makes investment decisions their objective is to build and carefully monitor focused portfolios, to make certain they are not exposing clients to undue risk. They confer daily to discuss portfolio strategy and exchange information. They work closely on all strategic decisions. They administer accounts in a uniform and systematic manner. They monitor each portfolio separately on a continuing basis.

Year founded: 1972

Fees:

Account size	Equities
$1 million	1.00%
$5 million	1.00%
$10 million	1.00%
$20 million	0.50%

Total assets under management: $2 billion

Assets in wrap accounts: $100 million

Starbuck, Tisdale & Associates
301 East Carrillo
Santa Barbara, CA 93101
Phone: 805-963-5963

Investment style: Growth

Introduction:
Starbuck, Tisdale's predecessor firm was formed in 1933 in Santa Barbara, California and has been providing investment management services since that time.

Their investment style would be categorized as fundamentalist, using asset allocation amongst financial investments to meet in-

Appendix B

dividual client objectives. They are most effective with individual trusts, foundations and smaller (less than $10 million) pension funds.

Professional staff:

Portfolio managers-equity: 2
Portfolio managers-fixed income: 2
Security analysts-equity: 2
Traders: 1
Total professionals: 7

Investment specialties:

Equities - U.S.:
Large cap
Growth stocks
Balanced accounts
Fixed income - U.S.:
Actively managed:
Governments

Portfolio characteristics - equity portfolios:

Capitalization: Less than S&P 500
Earnings growth: Greater than S&P 500
Dividend yield: Greater than S&P 500
P/E ratio: Less than S&P 500
Risk (beta): Close to S&P 500
Portfolio concentration: average
Number of issues in average stock portfolio: 15
Number of issues in average bond portfolio: 10
Number of companies followed regularly: 100

Average account turnover:

Stocks: relatively low
Bonds: relatively low

Equity investment approach:

Bottom up
Fundamental analysis
Asset allocation

The firm's approach is fundamental. Emphasis is placed on earnings history of the company and prospects for continued growth. Companies are broken down by size and yield characteristics rather than industries. Their strategy is to make investments in quality companies and hold until such time as the fundamental characteristics of that company changes, or the market environment becomes unfavorable. Turnover is minimal.

Decision making process:
1. Centralized
2. Portfolio management totally integrated with research function
3. Approximately 100 companies are reviewed and analyzed for client portfolios

Year founded: 1933

Fees:

Account size	Equities
$1 million	1.00%
$5 million	0.60%
$10 million	0.55%
$20 million	0.52%

Minimum account size:
Stocks: $1 million

Total assets under management: $267 million

Assets in wrap accounts: $5.7 million

Thompson Siegel Walmsley Inc.
5000 Monument Avenue
P.O. Box 6883
Richmond, VA 23230
Phone: 804-353-4500

Investment style: Value, large cap

Introduction:
Thompson, Siegel & Walmsley is a registered investment advisor offering equity and balanced account investment management services. The firm manages approximately $2.5 billion.

Affiliations:
The firm is a wholly-owned subsidiary of United Asset Management, an investment management holding company.

Professional staff:
Marketing: 3
Portfolio mgr./analysts (perform both functions): 10
Traders: 2
    Total professionals: 15

Appendix B

Investment specialties:
  Equities - U.S.:
    Large cap
    Growth stocks
  Balanced accounts

Equity investment approach:
  Top down
  Sector rotation
  Technical disciplines

  The firm's approach is risk-averse, value oriented with a highly-structured decision-making process.

Decision making process:
  Portfolio management totally integrated with research function

Year founded: 1969

Fees:

Account size	Equities	Fixed Income
$5 million	0.85%	0.85%
$10 million	0.65%	0.65%
$20 million	0.55%	0.55%
$50 million	0.45%	0.45%
$100 million	0.35%	0.35%

Total assets under management: $3 million

Assets in wrap accounts: N/A

Vantage Global Advisor
630 Fifth Avenue
New York, NY 10111
Phone: 212-247-5858

Investment style: Growth, large cap, small cap

Investment Strategy:

Vantage Global Advisor is a wholly owned subsidiary of Lincoln National Corporation. MPT clients use them for a variety of different management styles including core equity, balanced, restricted (South African free and others) aggressive equity and fixed income. They are a disciplined, bottom-up manager capable of structuring portfolios fitting a variety of risk and return objectives. Clients include corporations, endowments, foundations and unions.

340

Affiliations:

The parent company is Lincoln National Corporation of Ft. Wayne, IN.

Professional staff:

Portfolio managers-equity: 3
Portfolio managers-fixed income: 1
Security analysts-equity: 2
New business/client service: 1
Operations/administrative: 5
    Total professionals: 12

Other investments: Portfolio insurance

Portfolio characteristics - equity portfolios:

Capitalization: Close to S&P 500
Earnings growth: Greater than S&P 500
Dividend yield: Close to S&P 500
P/E ratio: Close to S&P 500
Risk (beta): Close to S&P 500
Portfolio concentration: broad
Number of issues in average stock portfolio: 50
Number of issues in average bond portfolio: 20
Number of companies followed regularly: 1,300

Average account turnover:

Stocks: moderate
Bonds: relatively low

Equity investment approach:

Bottom up
Fundamental analysis
Broad diversification

To create a risk level for portfolios about equal to the S&P 500. Portfolios hold sector weights similar to the market in four main areas; growth, cyclical, energy, stable, similar to the stock market.

Their 1,500 stock universe is screened through four contrasting valuation methods. "Alpha" rankings are developed for each stock, reflecting composite expected returns relative to the market. Portfolios are built form the top 25% ranked stocks.

Decision making process: Centralized

Year founded: 1979

Appendix B

Fees:

Account size	Equities	Fixed Income
$1 million	1.00%	
$5 million	1.00%	0.60%
$10 million	0.75%	0.50%
$20 million	0.67%	0.40%

Assets managed: N/A

Assets in wrap programs: N/A

Winrich Capital Management
23702 Birtcher Drive
Lake Forest, CA 92630
Phone: 714-380-0200

Investment style: Balanced, mid to large cap, relative value, plus growth

Introduction:

Winrich Capital Management is a conservative, diversified, equity-oriented balanced manager of financial assets. The primary goal is to achieve an above-average total rate of return over time with very low volatility or risk. This implies good participation in strong market environments and excellent protection of capital during poor times. Stocks, bond and cash equivalents are combined to be consistent with the objectives and risk levels of each portfolio.

Affiliations:

Winrich Investment Group is a wholly-owned subsidiary.

Professional staff:

Portfolio managers-equity: 4
Portfolio managers-fixed income: 1
Traders: 1
New business/client service: 2
Operations/administrative: 2
Total professionals: 12

Investment specialties:

Equities - U.S.:
Large cap
Balanced accounts

Portfolio characteristics - equity portfolios:
Capitalization: Close to S&P 500
Earnings growth: Close to S&P 500
Dividend yield: Greater than S&P 500
P/E ratio: Less than S&P 500
Risk (beta): Less than S&P 500
Portfolio concentration: average
Number of issues in average stock portfolio: 40
Number of issues in average bond portfolio: 15
Number of companies followed regularly: 100

Average account turnover:
Stocks: relatively low
Bonds: relatively low

Equity investment approach:
Bottom up
Fundamental analysis
Broad diversification

Decision making process:
1. Centralized
2. Multiple committee

Year founded: 1976

Fees:

Account size	Equities	Fixed Income
$1 million	1.00%	0.50%
$5 million	1.00%	0.50%
$10 million	0.87%	0.42%
$20 million	0.75%	0.37%

Total assets under management: $300 million

Assets in wrap accounts: $60 million

Minimum account size:
Stocks: $1 million
Bonds: $2 million

A SAMPLING OF QUALIFIED CONSULTANTS

Dennis Ardis, CIMC
SMITH BARNEY SHEARSON
Dallas, Texas
800/933-3936

Stephen Baumgarten, CIMC
DEAN WITTER REYNOLDS,
INC.
Beachwood, Ohio
216/292-9040

Mark Billeadeau, AIMC
CRAIG-HALLUM, INC.
Minneapolis, Minnesota
612/342-0639

Gerald F. Bott, CIMC
MERRILL LYNCH
Jacksonville, Florida
800/937-0268

Michael Walden Brinton, CIMC
PRUDENTIAL SECURITIES,
INC.
Nashville, Tennessee
601/742-0511

Jerry W. Caswell, AIMC
INVESTMENT ADVISORY
SERVICES
St. Petersburg, Florida
800/248-8863

Brian P. Cunningham, CIMC
RAUSHCER PIERCE REFSNES
Englewood, Colorado
800/695-2503

Derick L. Driemeyer, AIMC
A.G. EDWARDS & SONS, INC.
St. Louis, Missouri
314/289-3472

Charles L. Fahy, CIMC
OPPENHEIMER & CO., INC.
Houston, Texas
800/231-7509

Irene Feeley, CIMC
COMPLETE INVESTMENT
MANAGEMENT, INC.
Horsham, Pennsylvania
215/672-6200

345

Appendix C

Robert Foersterling, CIMC
KEMPER SECURITIES, INC.
Barrington, Illinois
800/544-4507

Robert M. Foretich, CIMC
FIRST WALL STREET CORP.
Seattle, Washington
206/621-8638

Gary F. Forte, CIMC
SMITH BARNEY SHEARSON
Greenville, South Carolina
803/242-1691

Craig A. Hammond, CIMC
DEAN WITTER REYNOLDS
Bellevue, Washington
206/451-2600

Leigh A. Hodgdon, CIMC
PRUDENTIAL SECURITIES
Palo Alto, California
415/858-3582

Marty Jensen, CIMC
THE JENSEN GROUP
Manhattan Beach, California
213/546-2751

Jim Johnston, AIMC
DAIN BOSWORTH
Cedar Rapids, Iowa
800/728-3246

Richard L. Kesner, CIMC
THE COMMONWEALTH
GROUP, INC.
Boca Raton, Florida
305/781-1129

William T. Leakas, CIMC
SMITH BARNEY SHEARSON
Dayton, Ohio
800/223-0644

David B. Loeper, CIMC
WHEAT FIRST SECURITIES
Richmond, Virginia
804/782-3283

Anthony F. Lotruglio, CIMC
QUAN-VEST CONSULTANTS, INC.
Manhasset, New York
516/365-4619

Pervaiz P. Massey, CIMC
SMITH BARNEY SHEARSON
Syracuse, New York
800/234-8133

Tom McDonald, CIMC
BATEMAN EICHLER HILL
RICHARDS
Anchorage, Alaska
907/258-6565

Bert Meem, CIMC
DEAN WITTER REYNOLDS
New York, New York
800/227-1512

346

George A. Minor, CIMC
PAINE WEBBER,INC.
Santa Barbara, California
805/963-3771

James A. Pupillo, CIMC
SMITH BARNEY SHEARSON
Scottsdale, Arizona
602/990-4525

Charles L. Raymond, Jr., CIMC
PAINE WEBBER, INC.
Chesterfield, Missouri
314/537-3500

Myrna Rivera, CIMC
SMITH BARNEY SHEARSON
Puerto Rico
809/759-8333

Jay H. Schmallen, AIMC
PIPER JAFFRAY, INC.
Fargo, North Dakota
701/237-5220

James D. Suellentrop, CIMC
PORTFOLIO CONSULTING
SERVICES
Richardson, Texas
214/644-7800

J. Speed Thomas, CIMC
DEAN WITTER REYNOLDS,
INC.
Nashville, Tennessee
615/321-3974

John D. Vance, CIMC
DEAN WITTER REYNOLDS
Tacoma, Washington
800/755-5720

Charles J. Zondorak, CIMC
DEAN WITTER REYNOLDS
Virginia Beach, Virginia
800/736-3108

FOR INFORMATION ABOUT QUALIFIED CONSULTANTS IN YOUR AREA, PLEASE CONTACT:

William G. Mullen, CAE
Executive Director
INSTITUTE FOR INVESTMENT MANAGEMENT CONSULTANTS
3101 N. Central Avenue, Suite 560
Phoenix, Arizona 85012
602/265-6114

■ **Alpha** is a measurement of the amount of reward earned for the risk taken. An alpha of 0.00 indicates that the risk versus reward relationship is that of the market itself. A positive alpha shows the portfolio achieved higher returns for the risk level assumed. A negative alpha means lower returns for the additional risk taken.

■ **Asset Allocation** is the mix of various investment vehicles in an investment pool (i.e., how much of the portfolio is invested in stocks, bonds, cash equivalents, etc.)

■ **Balanced Index** is a market index that serves as a basis of comparison for balanced portfolios. The balanced index used in the Monitor is comprised of a 60% weighting of the S&P 500 Index and a 40% weighting of the SLH Government/Corporate Bond Index. The balanced index relates unmanaged market returns to a balanced portfolio more precisely than either a stock or a bond index would alone.

■ **Beginning Value** is the market value of a portfolio at the inception of the period being measured by the Monitor.

■ **Beta** shows the level of volatility of a portfolio's return relative to the market's return. Each index (balanced 60/40, S&P 500) is set at a value of 1.00. For the portfolio as a whole and its component sectors, a beta greater than 1.00 means that the portfolio sector had higher volatility relative to its corresponding index. A beta of 1.00 means that the portfolio segment's volatility was the same as its respective index. A beta less than 1.00 means that the portfolio sector had less volatility than its corresponding index.

■ **Comparative Universe** consists of a relevant group of professionally managed funds which are managed with an investment philosophy or objectives similar to those of the manager of a fund being measured by the Monitor.

■ **CPI**. Consumer Price Index, maintained by the Bureau of Labor Statistics, measures the changes in the cost of a specified group of consumer products relative to a base period. Because it represents the rate of inflation, the CPI can be used as a general benchmark for gauging the maintenance of purchasing power.

■ **Market Value** is the market or liquidation value of a given security or of an entire pool of assets.

■ **Net Contributions** refers to funds placed in the portfolio by the client. "Net" refers to the excess of such placements over disbursements and withdrawals during the period measured by the Monitor.

■ **Quartile** is a ranking of comparative portfolio performance. The top 25% of portfolio managers are in the 1st Quartile, those ranking from the 26% to 50% are in the 2nd Quartile, from 51% to 75% in the 3rd and the lowest 25% in the 4th Quartile.

■ **Rank** refers to a ranking of performance in percentiles, with the 1st percentile being the highest and 99th being the lowest. The ranking evaluates a manager's performance in relation to other managers: a 10th percentile ranking means that this manager has performed better than 90% of managers in the comparative universe for similar funds.

Return is the time-weighted rate of return which was achieved over the indicated time period.

Risk is the level of variability among the quarterly returns of a portfolio, portfolio segment, or index. Within the Monitor, it is represented by Standard Deviation over a period of time.

RSQR. R-Squared, also called the coefficient of determination, indicates the percentage of risk for an investment pool that is market-related and so cannot be reduced through diversification.

S&P 500. The Standard and Poor's 500 Composite Stock Index is a capitalization-weighted index of 400 industrial, 40 public utility, 40 financial, and 20 transportation equities (including dividend reinvestment). It is a widely accepted proxy for the domestic stock market. The S&P 500 can be used as a benchmark for evaluating the performance of equity portfolios.

SLH Government/Corporation. The Shearson Lehman Hutton Government/Corporate Bond Index is a market index that represents the fixed income market. It includes U.S. Treasury and investment grade corporate instruments.

Standard Deviation measures the level of variability or volatility in the return shown by the portfolio or the market index. The higher the value, the greater the variability (or risk) of the portfolio or indexes.

T-Bills are promissory notes issued by the U.S. Treasury and sold through competitive bidding, with a short term maturity date, usually 13 to 26 weeks. The return on T-bills has almost no variation, so it serves as a proxy for a "riskless" investment.

Time-Weighted Rate of Return is the rate at which a dollar invested at the beginning of a period would grow if no additional capital were invested and no cash withdrawals were made. It provides an indication of value added by the investment manager, and allows comparisons to the performance of other investment managers and market indexes.

■ **Total Return** refers to the complete return earned by the portfolio being measured and encompasses income earned plus capital appreciation.

■ **Wrap Account Fee** is a single, all-encompassing fee based on a percentage of assets under management. It is a management fee that covers all charges, including advisor fees, commissions, and other transaction charges, and reporting.

■ **Wrap Fee** is a fee that bundles the services of the broker/consultant which includes consulting services, custodianship of assets, and brokerage transactions. This fee is sometimes known as an all-inclusive fee.

Glossary of Various Investment Styles

■ **Value**—In this instance, the manager uses various tests to determine an intrinsic value for a given security, and tries to purchase the security substantially below that value. The goal and hope is that the stock price will ultimately rise to the stock's fair value or above. Price to earnings, price to sales, price to cash flow, price to book value, and price to break-up value (or true net asset value) are some of the ratios examined in such an approach.

■ **Emerging Growth**—Here a manager is looking for industries and companies whose growth rates are likely to be both rapid and independent of the overall stock market. *Emerging* of course, means *new*. This implies such companies may be relatively small in size, with the potential to grow much larger. Such stocks are generally much more volatile than the stock market in general and require constant close attention to developments.

- **Quality Growth**—This term implies long-term investment in high-quality growth stocks, some of which might be larger emerging companies, while others might be long-established household names. Such a portfolio might have volatility equal to or above that of the overall market, but less than that of an "emerging growth" portfolio.

- **Balanced**—This term can be applied to any kind of portfolio which uses fixed income (bonds) as well as equity securities to reach goals. Many "boutique" investment managers are balanced managers, because it permits them to tailor the securities in a portfolio to the specific client's cash flow needs and objectives. Balanced portfolios are often used by major funds and charitable endowments, as well as by individuals. They provide great flexibility.

- **Income Growth**—The primary purpose in security selection here is to achieve a current yield significantly higher than the S&P 500. The stability of the dividend and the rate of growth of the dividends is also of concern to the income buyer. These portfolios may own more utilities, less high-tech and may own convertible preferreds and convertible bonds.

- **Fixed Income**—This term largely speaks for itself. Fixed income managers invest in bonds, notes and other debt instruments. They have a broad range of styles, involving market timing, swapping to gain quality or yield, setting up maturity ladders, etc. A typical division of the fixed income market is between short (up to 3 years), intermediate (3-15 years), and long (15-30 years). Managers that specialize in each can be found.

- **Sector or Industry Rotators**—These managers attempt to be invested in specific industries or specific economic

353

sectors they believe will out-perform the general stock market during specific periods. An example would be the recognized switch on behalf of many managers, from "growth" to "cyclical" stocks, since they believe the cyclicals should benefit from an economic pickup, whereas growth stocks have moved up sharply over the past period.

■ **Cash Management**—Cash managers invest in short-term fixed instruments and cash equivalents. These instruments make up the portfolio, and their objective is to maximize principal protection. Even though these accounts have short-term (1-day) liquidity, they typically pay more like 90-180-day CDs versus passbook or one-week CDs.

INDEX

Index

Index

Index

Index

Q

Qualified
  investment manager, 263
  retirement plan, 245
Quality
  control, 26
  growth managers, 107
  standards, 255

R

Rate of return, *see* Return, Time-weighted
Real estate, 68, 70, 256
  limited partnership, 29
Recordkeeping, 12, 16, 17
Redemption, *see* Net
Registered
  investment advisor, 141
  investment manager, 137
Reinvestment risk, 60
Relative value manager, 105
Replacement costs, 104
Report monitoring, 5
Retail
  brokerage, 46
  stockbroker, 7
Retirement, 62
  fund, 244, 245
  income, 60, 61
  plan, *see* Qualified
  assets, 269
Retroactive compliance, 192, 193
Returns, 78, 102, 189, 191, 197, 201,
    244, 256, 257
  see Bond, Composite, Investment,
    Long-term, Portfolio, Risk, Risk-
    adjusted
  calculations, 186
  distribution, 88
  rate, 47, 83, 89, 91, 186, 188, 254
  tradeoffs, 33
Revenues, 5, 114
Review
  see Investment manager
  procedures, 135-136
Reward-to-risk ratio, 169
Risk, 48, 98, 200, 202, 256, 257
  see Default, Emotional, Financial,
    Inflation, Investment, Liquidity,
    Market, Reinvestment, Reward
  control, 111
  evaluation, 244
  level, 47, 247

measures, 191
reduction process, 62-65
return evaluation, 256-257
tolerance, 32, 33, 35, 45, 129, 254
  levels, 8, 33
tradeoff, 33
understanding, 59-81
Risk-adjusted
  analysis, 268
  returns, 30, 98
Risk-and-return statistics, 186
Risk/return environment, 79
Rotator, *see* Industry

S

Salary Reduction/SEP (SAR/SEP), 270
SAR/SEP, *see* Salary
SEC, *see* Securities and Exchange
    Commission
Securities, 59, 65, 104, 130, 172, 199
  see Convertible, Debt, Fixed-income,
    Fixed-principal, Foreign, Publicly,
    U.S. government
  custodianship, 3
  market, 63
Securities and Exchange Commission,
    24, 123, 247
  SEC, 24, 26, 116, 123, 124, 127, 141,
    142, 197, 266
Security
  see Employee
  selection
    criteria, 171
    process, 172
  sell disciplines, 172
Selectivity, 189, 201
SEP, *see* Simplified
Service(s), 3, 175
  see Value-added
  areas, 239, 241
Shearson Consulting Group, 15
Shearson-Lehman Brothers, 14, 15
Short selling, 267
Short-term horizon, 110
Simplified employee pension (SEP),
    269-271
  see Salary
  SEP/IRA, 271
Single assets, diversification comparison,
    64-65
Single-asset
  composites, 190

362

Index